Breaking **B**ad and **P**hilosophy

Popular Culture and Philosophy® Series Editor: George A. Reisch

For full details of all Popular Culture and Philosophy® books, visit www.opencourtbooks.com.

Popular Culture and Philosophy®

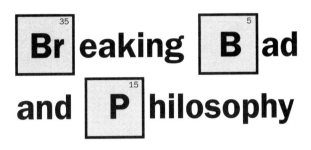

Breaking Bad and Philosophy

Badder Living through Chemistry

Edited by

DAVID R. KOEPSELL

and

ROBERT ARP

OPEN COURT
Chicago and LaSalle, Illinois

Volume 67 in the series, Popular Culture and Philosophy ®, edited by George A. Reisch

To order books from Open Court, call toll-free 1-800-815-2280, or visit our website at www.opencourtbooks.com.

Open Court Publishing Company is a division of Carus Publishing Company.

Copyright © 2012 by Carus Publishing Company

First printing 2012
Second printing 2013

Printed and bound in the United States of America.

Library of Congress Cataloging-in-Publication Data

Breaking bad and philosophy : badder living through chemistry / edited by David R. Koepsell and Robert Arp

    p. cm. — (Popular culture and philosophy ; v. 67)
    Includes bibliographical references and index.
    ISBN 978-0-8126-9764-3 (pbk.)
    1. Breaking bad (Television program : 2008-) I. Koepsell, David R. (David Richard) II. Arp, Robert.
    PN1992.77.B74B74 2012
    791.45'72—dc23

                           2012013078

Contents

Nothing Here But Chemistry

Now You're Cooking

Free Radicals

Pink, White, and Blue

A Fine Meth We've Gotten Into

DAVID R. KOEPSELL AND ROBERT ARP

Breaking Bad emerged on the airwaves at a critical time in American history. Deep in a never-ended recession, losing confidence with our technical and innovative prowess worldwide, outpaced by competitors, and nervous about the future and what we leave for the next generation, we are all Walter White. Our dreams and hopes for ourselves and our futures seem crushed by the everyday. Middle-aged, over-educated, and struggling to make ends meet, the bright, shiny futures we had been promised if only we lived right were never more elusive.

Then Walter White came along and gave us all hope. He's a twenty-first century *geek* hero. Chemistry teacher turned meth manufacturer, dealer, and eventually king pin, he skirts his failures in the straight world by delving deep into a dark underworld, both physical and psychic. Walter White shows us that the nebishy, flabby, middle-aged nerd can *be someone*, despite being marginalized by a society and economy that have moved on without him.

It's the someone he becomes that makes the show so interesting. It's a modern morality play, showing us the shame, degradation, and moral decline that come from pursuing a life of crime. But it's a morality play without the moralizing. Walter White remains our hero, and we root for his success, and the defeat of his foils. What this says about us, our society, and the meaning and roots of success are all great mysteries behind the success of the series, and the appeal of Walt.

Walt's path in *Breaking Bad* is clear from the start. Once he has begun down the road he chooses, we know his fate. We've seen this story before. He is Macbeth, he is Faust, he is Milton's Lucifer, and he's all of these while being just typical enough to be Everyman. The fallen anti-hero can be sympathetic, but he must fail. That's why we so desperately want him to succeed. But what does his success mean? What are the repercussions for his friends, family, and society at large if Walt's pure blue meth conquers the Southwest? How do we grapple with these implications even while cheering for his success against the odds?

In these chapters, our authors consider the philosophical, psychological, and sociological issues behind this critically acclaimed drama. What motivates Walt, really? Is Walt in conflict with science itself? Is there something wrong with the American psyche that makes a Walter White into a hero? What are the ethical issues behind drugs? What lessons does *Breaking Bad* have about existentialism? Can Walt be redeemed? Who is Gus Fring? These questions are just the tip of the iceberg (if you'll pardon the expression). There are so many philosophical issues in the complexly unfolding characters and plots we've been treated to as we follow Walt and company's descent into badness.

While *Breaking Bad* clearly focuses upon a single (anti) hero, there are many important relationships with supporting characters that are worth exploring. Jesse Pinkman, for instance, serves as a sort of surrogate child even while Walter Jr. seems to diminish into the background of Walt's everyday existence the further he delves into the meth business. Skyler—who at some time came across as a one-dimensional, harping, nagging middle-class wife—emerges in Seasons Three and Four as a partner in crime for her husband. Male-female relationships in the show, the archetypes each embodies, and the evolution of each serve as a backdrop for discussing feminism on TV. Finally, Gus Fring's complex character and relationship with Walt provide us with an opportunity to explore evil, to consider Walt's path, and reflect upon the values we seem to admire in this cold-blooded villain.

The show is rich with complexity and poetry of a sort. Race, class, good, and evil are all confronted for thirteen episodes per year in the guise of a show about drugs, violence, and money set in the deserts around Albuquerque, New Mexico. The shame is that the show will someday end. The contract has been signed, and the final season is in the works. By the time you read this book, you'll know more than we did in writing it about the philosophical implications of *Breaking Bad*. Did the ends finally justify the extremes?

Walter White goes from geek hero to Greek Tragedy, and as we said above, we know how it ends. But we desperately want him to succeed, even as he goes from bad to evil. As in Greek tragedy, his failure is inevitable, but his situation and motivations make him sympathetic. We feel his pain, and are empowered by his successes. Lucifer too was sympathetic in Milton's *Paradise Lost* if only because he had the guts to rebel, however hopelessly, against a tyranny he didn't create, and against whose dictates he would no longer stand.

Walt rebels too. He confronts a system that cheated him out of his just reward, and against a society that outlaws acts of self-destruction. He convinces himself that it is family, and not ego, that drives him. He's the hero of his own drama, and a suitable anti-hero for the long, dark recessionary times we live in. The American dream lives on in Walt, and we cling to it with fading hope. But as Milton shows us, it is hope we must abandon at the gates of Hell, just as we know that Walt must fail, or meet a nasty death, and likely both.

An **Al** yze
Thi **S**

1

Walt's Rap Sheet

DAVID R. KOEPSELL AND VANESSA GONZALEZ

Walter White's body count grows at an impressive rate over the course of the first four seasons, but more significant than the sheer number of those killed is the manners of their killings and Walt's changing attitude to each new killing.

We can easily score Walt's body count in the hundreds, if we include the deaths he causes indirectly. What of the innocent passengers of Wayfarer 515 (167 dead) in the final episode of Season Two ("ABQ")? Is Walt the *cause* of their deaths? His actions are certainly part of a causal chain of events that leads to the crash of the flight, and morally we might hold Walt *somehow* responsible, though he would not legally be to blame. Other indirect deaths result from Walt's actions, but we'll focus on the easy cases.

Walt seems directly responsible for *at least* nine deaths by the end of Season Four:

Emilio

Krazy-8

Jane

the two guys he killed with his car to save Jesse

Gale

Gus

Tyrus

Hector "Tio" Salamanca

The nature and blame of Walt's involvement or guilt in these deaths is complicated enough without us having to fret over Walt's potential responsibility for hundreds of lives lost, so let's concentrate on these deaths and evaluate Walt's role in each, his moral and legal culpability, and theories of moral responsibility as applied to Walt's guilt.

Emilio

Walt's first *bona fide* kill is Emilio. In the series pilot, Walt breaks bad in the worst way imaginable. His effort to raise money for his family in the wake of a diagnosis of likely fatal cancer goes horribly wrong. In deep over his head, he's set upon by street-level drug thugs who intend on holding Jesse and Walt captive to force a demonstration (and presumably, to make a quantity of meth they can peddle) of Walt's meth-making skills. Walt, in a panic, cooks up (sorry!) a scheme to win his and Jesse's liberty from the thugs (Emilio and Krazy-8) by, basically, using a chemical weapon. It works, to the extent that Emilio is killed by inhaling the phosphine gas, but Krazy-8 survives the attack. Emilio is Walt's first victim. The question is, of what?

Walt is directly responsible for Emilio's death. He's both the legal and actual agent of his demise. But is Walt's killing justifiable in some moral way, or in some legal way, so that it isn't a murder? In other words, for what is Walt morally responsible?

Dating as far back as Aristotle (384–322 B.C.E.), philosophers have considered under what conditions an agent might be praised or blamed for an action. Among the criteria he considered relevant, and still argued by many to be relevant today, are:

> **the person's *capacity* for choosing an action.** In a sophisticated bank robbery, for example, we'd never think to look for the culprit at a nursery school, because those kids could never pull off the job!

> **the person's *motivations* for an action.** We wouldn't hold Johnny morally responsible for kicking the ball into Sally's face on the playground if it was an accident. On the other hand, if Johnny's *motive or intention* was in fact to hurt Sally, then we would see this as immoral in some way, and punish him accordingly.

the *consequences* of the action. Justice still needs to be served and someone has to pay for damages that result from an automobile accident (a true accident, not due to a drunk driver, but an honest mistake), even though we know it was an accident. Also, if someone commits a crime that has multiple bad consequences—like *many* people died in the explosion you caused with your bomb, or a *whole lot of* money was stolen from a whole lot of people in your credit card scam—then we punish that person more severely.

the *justification* for an action. What's meant here is really the moral theory or rule that one uses to justify an action, complete with rational argument and explanation. For example, you might use the moral rule that says, "You should never lie" as your justification when you actually tell the truth, or an interrogator might use, "A great, good *end* justifies a little, evil *means* to attain that end" when torturing someone who knows where a bomb is located that will soon go off, killing hundreds of people.

More recently, debates about **the truth of *determinism*** (according to which the universe unfolds as it does regardless of our supposed choices) have complicated issues of moral responsibility, but a dominant theme has emerged with ***compatibilism,*** which holds that assigning guilt is still compatible with a deterministic universe. Even though it may be true that you were determined by your nature (genes and brain) and your nurture (your daddy beat you regularly and put you down constantly) to act immorally and break the law, we can still hold you morally responsible, and put you in prison, give you therapy, and give you drugs so as to change your motivations so that you'll be *determined* to act morally and lawfully, instead!

A final factor to consider, both in moral and legal responsibility, is **the degree to which the actor is the *proximate cause* of a wrong or harm.** Walt is a scientist, and probably also a determinist, but he clearly feels guilt about his choices, expressing horror at his role in Emilio's demise, and later both horror and regret, as we shall see.

Walt's moral culpability for Emilio's death is arguably reduced given that he was attempting to, and did save, Jesse and himself from almost certain death. Emilio and Krazy-8 were cold-blooded killers who weren't going to show Walt or Jesse any mercy. Moreover, the stress and duress of the situation in which he and Jesse found themselves further acts to relieve Walt of moral culpability for murder. Killing in self-defense is a well-known and widely recognized legal and moral justification or excuse. But this justification clearly dissolves (sorry again!) with the killing of Krazy-8.

Krazy-8

Walt had intended to kill Krazy-8 and Emilio with the phosphine gas in the RV. His and Jesse's safe escape and future safety could only have been guaranteed by successfully eliminating both on the spot. Unfortunately, Walt failed to kill both immediately, and the job of finishing Krazy-8 was left for later. The immediacy of self-defense no longer existed, as Krazy-8 was bound in Jesse's basement, slowly recovering from the phosphine poisoning. Imprisoned, immobile, and slowly regaining consciousness and strength, Krazy-8's fate is clearly to die, and the killer is determined by a coin toss, which Walt loses. At this point, the nature of any excuse is considerably different than in the case of Emilio.

Walt is agonized by his duty to kill Krazy-8, so much so that he resorts to making a list of pros and cons either to help make or to justify his decision. The final, overpowering rationale that convinces him is the single *pro*, that Krazy-8 will kill Walt and his family if Walt doesn't kill him. This outweighs the immorality of killing in itself.

Ultimately, Walt remains unable to kill Krazy-8, striking up conversations with him, getting to know him a bit, and sympathizing with him. The process apparently makes it harder for him to follow through with the killing, and he's on the verge finally of letting Krazy-8 go. Walt finally realizes he must follow through when a knife-shaped shard of a plate Walter breaks accidentally while feeding Krazy-8 a sandwich goes missing. Krazy-8 intends to kill Walt once freed. Walt has nearly been tricked, and he brutally chokes Krazy-8 in a final confrontation, sustaining a stab would in the process. Arguably, Walt's actions now amount to valid self-defense, but his moral blameworthiness for killing Krazy-8 seems greater than for Emilio. What accounts for this distinction?

Krazy-8's captivity seems to alter Walt's moral responsibility for his killing. While Walt tried to kill them both under a clear situation of self-defense, it's harder to claim self-defense against a captive. Walt's choice is clearly different in Krazy-8's death. He's had time to deliberate, and has options. He could contact the authorities and confess. His crimes at this stage are significantly more minimal than the murder of Krazy-8. Killing Emilio would have likely been seen as justified or excusable legally.

By choosing to kill an imprisoned and immobilized victim, Walt has taken on an extra degree of moral guilt. He's the direct cause of Krazy-8's demise, he has other options, he intends the death, and lacks any immediate excuse or justification. While not cold-blooded murder given Krazy-8's intent and attempt to kill Walt, Walt's killing of Krazy-8 is certainly more morally blameworthy than that of Emilio. He had less morally problematic alternatives available and chose to not pursue them. He took the path less taken, and descended further into the depths of his ultimate moral degradation, starkly illustrated in the deeply troubling circumstances surrounding the death of Jane in Season Two.

Jane

Jesse's girlfriend, Jane, was a recovering junkie, building an honest new life as manager of her father's apartment complex, and pursuing a job as a tattoo designer. Unfortunately, she met Jesse, an active drug dealer and addict. The net result is predictable, as she slips back into drug addiction and introduces Jesse to heroin. Addicted to heroin and in love with Jesse, Jane convinces him to turn against his partner and blackmail Walt to give Jesse his share of their drug profits. Walt knows full well that Jane and Jesse will inject the money straight into their veins, likely dying of overdoses, but at least wasting their lives. Nonetheless, he relents, realizing he must let Jesse make his own choices, and tries to deliver Jesse's money. In the process, he accidentally knocks a heroin-addled Jane onto her back in bed next to Jesse, and Jane vomits, chokes and dies in front of Walt while Jesse remains deeply drugged and asleep ("Phoenix"). So, to what degree is Walt responsible for Jane's death?

Jane's death presents a complicated set of problems for Walt's moral culpability. She died, technically, due to her own choice to use heroin and the deadly consequences that come with its use. She knew full well that, when under the influence, a user can vomit, choke, and die. This is why she warns Jesse to lie on his side, and she does so herself. She had reduced the risks, but not eliminated them, as users can change position once under. But it was Walt's actions in trying to waken Jesse, and accidentally turning Jane on her back, that was the direct reason for her becoming vulnerable. Jane's vomiting wasn't a necessary consequence of her lying prone, but was potentially fatal once she did. Walt was in a position to save her life, but consciously chose not to. His guilt over that choice and its result was obvious. He cries at her death.

But is he morally responsible, and to what degree? Part of this judgment hinges upon the distinction between active and passive responsibility. Ordinarily, we don't view anyone as having a moral duty to save anyone unless they have some special knowledge or relationship with the victim. There's no active responsibility to save a drowning stranger unless you're a lifeguard and have thus placed yourself in a special relationship with swimmers. Strangers who fail to save drowning children aren't murderers, nor are they morally blameworthy in any but a *passive* manner. They have some moral guilt, but they aren't the cause nor did they have an active *duty* to save. They may be passively responsible, especially if they had the clear capacity to save, but they're neither legally nor morally *culpable* for the death unless they have somehow created the situation from which the victim requires saving, having taken some *active* responsibility.

Walt plays some active role, by breaking into Jesse's home and disturbing the sleeping Jesse and Jane. His physical attempts to wake Jesse have the unintended side-effect of jostling Jane who flops onto her back, prone, and vulnerable to choking in case she vomits . . . which she then does. Walt has therefore contributed to the danger that Jane is in, and then consciously withholds his ability to save her. His reasons are clear: he fears Jane's knowledge of his activities in the drug trade, and his influence on Jesse, his one-time partner who now, with his junkie girlfriend, will flee and work with Walt no more. Walt's motives in failing to aid are clearly to save his relationship with Jesse, and possibly to save Jesse, but they're nonetheless motives to see to her demise. He isn't a guiltless, innocent bystander in the death of a stranger, he's actively responsible for her vulnerability, and consciously aware of the repercussions for his failure to aid, *choosing* to allow her to die for mixed motives, including the beneficial effects her death will have for his own future.

Walt's moral responsibility or blame for Jane's death is reduced, but present, as well as a mixed form of both active and passive responsibility. The next two deaths are less complicated, both factually and morally.

Aztec Speed Bumps 1 and 2

Walt saves Jesse once again in the episode, "Half Measures," near the end of Season Three. Jesse has discovered that Gus Fring was behind the use of his new girlfriend's young brother's employment to kill Jesse's friend, Combo, and Jesse plans to use the chemical ricin to kill Gus Fring. A dose of ricin as small as a few grains of salt can kill someone. Jesse's subtlety and sneakiness being what they are—nonexistent— Jesse's threat to Gus becomes clear, and Gus orders Jesse's death. But Walt saves Jesse once again (if we assume that Walt saved Jesse's life by allowing Jane to die), ramming Jesse's would-be killers with his Aztec, and shooting the one who survived the collision, point-blank.

Walt's murders of Aztec Speed Bumps 1 and 2 are straightforward killings for which Walt is actively responsible. Unlike Emilio and Krazy-8, which were killings in self-defense (obviously self-defense with Emilio, arguably self-defense with Krazy-8), Walt wasn't threatened by the men he killed. Jesse was. The question is: is Walt's killing of those who threatened his friend justifiable—or even morally praiseworthy?

The *duty* to save might arise in the case of some sort of special relationship. Jesse and Walt have such a relationship, and in many ways Walt is a surrogate father to Jesse, seemingly more attached and interested in Jesse's life than in that of his own son, Walt, Jr. As a guide, teacher, sometime friend, and partner to Jesse, Walt gives him direction, confidence, and skills he never would have acquired otherwise. True, Walt was involved in the death of Jesse's great love, Jane, but he has also helped him kick heroin, provided him training in cooking his famous blue meth, and watched his money and saved his life when it was threatened. Because of this special relationship and all it entails, Walt has taken on a special duty to protect Jesse, and his involvement first in preventing Jesse from trying to kill Gus, and then in saving Jesse when Gus's thugs were going to kill him, may have been morally justifiable due to this special relationship.

Unlike the lack of active responsibility to intervene in saving strangers, we have heightened duties we owe to our friends, family, and others with whom we have certain special relationships like Walt and Jesse's. While Jesse is certainly not an innocent, he was more so than was Gus or his hired henchmen bent on killing Jesse. At this point, Jesse has killed no one, and his intent to kill was perhaps somewhat morally justifiable as vengeance for his friend's death, and to punish Gus for using an innocent child to do it.

Weighing Walt's moral guilt in this instance involves a complex calculus. Is his killing of two non-innocents to prevent the death of another non-innocent justifiable? Jesse surely wouldn't have been in the position of weighing whether to murder Gus but for Walt, so Walt's own actions and intentions are partly responsible for Jesse's intent to murder, and thus his targeting for murder. In a utilitarian calculus, if the total happiness is increased so that it outweighs the total amount of unhappiness from an action, the happiest result must be preferred, ethically speaking. Weighing Jesse's life against the lives of Gus's thugs, Walt's actions would be justifiable. Moreover, because Walt himself has helped create the situation Jesse is in, his saving Jesse is perhaps morally justifiable based on Walt's active responsibility, and given their special relationship and Walt's *relatively* honorable intentions.

Gale

Walt's moral guilt falls to a new low with the death of Gale. Although Jesse is the direct, proximate cause of Gale's death, Walt is clearly morally responsible. Weighing the degrees of moral blame for Gale's death becomes complicated due to the critical role of *choice* in assigning moral responsibility, and deciphering who has what choices in the final actions undertaken.

Gale is nearly innocent in the scheme of all of the characters in *Breaking Bad*. He's a gentle geek, with ideological justifications for making quality meth. He has a pure and simple love for chemistry, appears not to be driven by greed or pride, and has genuine reverence and affection for Walt. He knows that what he's doing is illegal, but justifies it based upon his libertarian ideals, the fact that meth addicts will find meth anyway, and at least he can provide them with chemically pure meth. He seems driven to do his job merely for the creativity it allows, his love of chemistry, and his need for a job. He also respects Walt and strives for his approval.

But Gale is being used by Gus to glean Walt's knowledge, so that Walt can be eliminated. Walt realizes that Gale's education in his methods means that Walt will become disposable, and knows full well that it's either him or Gale. But Walt doesn't pull the trigger. Instead, he sends Jesse to do so, although Walt himself has prevented Jesse from killing Gus, which would have also (presumably, had Jesse had even a chance of success) prevented the necessity to kill. Jesse is put in the position of either killing Gale, or allowing Walt's death. Walt has, of course, put Jesse in this and every other horrible position requiring equally horrid decisions, but Gale's death will be Jesse's first murder. It's a turning point, both for Walt and for Jesse. A nearly complete innocent is shot point-blank in cold blood to save the life of a cancer-stricken, significantly-less-than-innocent Walt ("Full Measure"). Moreover, Walt doesn't commit the murder but uses Jesse, who until then has no blood on his hands. Is Jesse a murderer? Is Walt, despite his lack of direct involvement in Gale's killing?

Jesse is now guilty of murder, both morally and legally. He pulled the trigger that killed Gale, and moreover, he had a choice. Although he acted under the knowledge that failing to kill Walt would result in Walt's murder, he had no legal justification to kill Gale, as Gale wasn't the threat. He may have had passive moral responsibility for Walt's death had he failed to kill Gale, but he had no active responsibility to kill an innocent Gale in order to save Walt's life. Killing Mike would have been more justifiable, certainly. Killing Gus—absolutely.

But Walt's ordering Jesse to kill Gale under the threat of Walt's own demise, due to Walt's own actions, makes Walt complicit, and morally guilty for Gale's death perhaps as much as if he had himself pulled the trigger. Mitigating this a bit is the fact that Walt's survival helped ensure Jesse's survival, and was after all a better plan with greater chance of success than Jesse's. But Walt was the driving force, who gave the order, and upon whose fate Jesse's decision hinged—a fate that was entirely avoidable had Walt only helped Jesse carry out his act of—perhaps justifiable—vengeance against Gus, or heaven forbid, had Walt not decided to enter the meth business in the first place.

Gus, Tyrus, and Hector Salamanca

Walt saves the best for last. Well, last of Season Four, anyway . . . maybe he'll nuke Albuquerque for the series finale. The trifecta of deaths at the end of the Season Four seems to accomplish a number of things: eliminating Walt's biggest threats, settling a couple of outstanding grudges, and paving the way for Walt's dominating the local meth market once and for all. But it's the complex web of moral guilt that makes this explosive finale best for the purposes of this book.

Gus and Tyrus were direct threats to Walt, and his and Jesse's attempts to poison and then blow up Gus failed, as many of their plans do. But in Hector Salamanca, Walt sees his salvation. Salamanca and Gus have a history of hatred. Salamanca was the triggerman who gunned down Gus's partner, the chemist other-half of the original Pollos Hermanos. Salamanca's nephew was Tuco, and "Tio" (uncle) as they call Hector, has a grudge against Walt as well, given Walt's role in Tuco's death. But Salamanca's hatred of Gus goes deeper, as Gus has taken great joy recently to visit and quietly torment Hector as he convalesces in his nursing home. So Hector serves as the perfect bait, and Hector detonates the bomb that Walt could not, sacrificing his own life to kill Gus, and Tyrus who stood by ("Face Off"). What, we should ask, is Walt's moral responsibility for this suicide bombing, if any?

Walt is certainly responsible for supplying Tio with the means to kill himself, Gus, and Tyrus. Without Walt's bomb, built for the express purpose of killing Gus in the first place, it's clear that Tio would have remained a helpless victim of Gus's ongoing taunts. None of the dead were innocent. Salamanca, Gus, and Tyrus are all killers, wrapped up in the drug trade. But then so is Walt. Walt has used Tio as the instrument for ridding himself of Gus. Getting rid also of Salamanca, who remains a threat to Walt due to what he knows, and Tyrus, who would no doubt go after Walt in case of Gus's coming to harm, are both bonuses.

Walt is morally responsible to the extent he supplied the instrumentality (the bomb) and had choices that led him to the murder/suicide bombing. Tio had the ultimate choice, however, and was the immediate cause of the deaths of Gus and Tyrus. He bears the brunt of both moral and legal responsibility, and Walt shares it. Legally, he was involved in a conspiracy, and is complicit in a murder. Morally, he acted with alternatives, not under duress, and with the intent to take lives. Unlike Jesse, who had not yet murdered when Walt ordered him to shoot, Tio was a practiced killer, with a grudge to settle. Tio had his own set of reasons to off Gus. Walt was, arguably, doing Tio a favor by giving him an honorable way to cash out and to settle his score. The triple deaths serve as Walt's greatest triumph, and a much more morally acceptable season ending than the death of poor, innocent Gale by poor frightened, non-killer Jesse.

Collateral Damage

We've delved a bit into Walt's moral guilt in the deaths of nine people who are most clearly directly killed due to Walt's actions, inactions, or orders. But there are others who die, arguably because of Walter White, though less directly. Notably, the deaths of the 167 aboard Wayfarer 515, and Donald Margolis, who kills himself thereafter, in response no doubt to the plane crash and his daughter's death ("ABQ"). His daughter was Jane, and as we saw, Walter is morally guilty in part for her death. Her death leads to her father's error causing the crash of the plane, and the deaths of the 167. Is Walter at all morally responsible for the Wayfarer 515 deaths and Donald's suicide?

Looking again at the elements of moral responsibility—including causation, capacity, motivation, and consequences, and justification—it's a stretch to hold Walt morally responsible for these deaths. Although his actions are complexly implicated in the two related events of the Wayfarer crash and Donald's suicide, and some of Walt's decisions helped lead to them, they seem far too remote to *blame* upon Walt. He's a cause, but not the *proximate* or immediate cause of these deaths. His actions and decisions created their *possibility*, but did not make them inevitable. Rather, Donald Margolis held the capacity to avoid both the crash of Wayfarer 515 (perhaps reduced a bit due to his emotional state, but it was his choice to return to work) and his own death.

Yes, Walt bears moral blame for Jane's death, but her addiction, her choices, and her actions seem also to be a family trait. Donald is wrestling with recovery from his addiction as well. Walt did not make Jane take heroin, nor did he fail to ensure that she remain clean. Donald's failures were implicated in her death. Sometimes just loving your child isn't enough. Walt actively intervenes to save Jesse, after all. Donald trusts his daughter too much, and fails to intervene when he could have to save her life. Donald's guilt is real, and deserved, though Walt is surely not blameless. Donald also had the final responsibility to not return to his job, directing air traffic (one of the most stressful jobs on the planet), and taking the lives of thousands of people every day into his hands while still mourning the loss of his daughter.

Ultimately, however, we should hold Walt accountable for a lot of harm. His excuse is flimsy: lots of people die leaving their families with no money or legacy. Perhaps his earlier decisions have led him to this point (we don't know why he left Grey Matter, nor whether pride, ego, jealousy, or some other factor caused his split with Elliot), but his family love him and respect him for who he is, or who he *was* before he breaks bad.

By the end of Season Four, he has broken *evil*, just as evil as Gus—though apparently bent on becoming just as successful in his new life of crime. He has taken his wife down this path too, corrupting her, involving her in a conspiracy, and endangering his family and friends. Walt's moral responsibility is complex in numerous cases, as we have seen, but broad as well—applicable to a whole range, a community of parties whose lives have changed for the worse because of Walt's decisions and actions.

Like the fate of any Greek anti-hero, Walt's end in this *geek* tragedy can only be doom. We'll see how many more he takes down with him in the process.

2

Heisenberg's Uncertain Confession

DARRYL J. MURPHY

I had prayed to you for chastity and said "Give me chastity and continence, but not yet."

—St. Augustine's *Confessions*, Book 8, Chapter 7

His respirator keeps him safe from the toxic mists of hydrofluoric acid that saturate the air around him, but it doesn't block the acrid tang of iron and salt from percolating into his nose. It's the smell of blood, and he can taste it in the very back of his throat. The taste triggers a thought he can't bury: this is what Emilio tastes like. This is what murder tastes like. Walter White, high-school chemistry teacher turned methamphetamine chef extraordinaire, killed Emilio days before, but it's only now that he's wrist deep in the chemical soup of his victim that Walt is seized by the guilt of his actions.

As he shovels another scoop of Emilio slurry into a bucket, Walt remembers a moment poetically relevant to his present. In his memory, Walt and Gretchen (a former girlfriend) are studying the chemical composition of the human body:

Hydrogen	63 %
Oxygen	26 %
Carbon	9 %
Nitrogen	1.25 %
Calcium	0.25 %
Iron	0.00004 %
Sodium	0.04 %
Phosphorus	0.19 %
TOTAL	99.888042%

Apparently, that's everything. What about the rest? Gretchen has a suggestion: "What about the soul?" she asks. But for Walt, a man of science, the soul is something completely foreign to his way of thinking. "There's nothing but chemistry here," Walt whispers to Gretchen dismissing her suggestion. Walt's flat dismissal, however, doesn't explain the 0.111958 percent discrepancy the couple has uncovered. It's this 0.111958 percent missing from the Emilio slurry that will prove to be of the greatest philosophical significance.

Soul, Choice, and Responsibility

Walt's dismissal of the idea of the soul is consistent with what philosophy calls a *materialist* point of view, and Walt is a materialist. In the pilot episode, he expresses materialism quite clearly in his classroom: "Chemistry is the study of matter . . . electrons, they change their energy levels; molecules, molecules change their bonds; elements, they combine and change into compounds," and that, "that's all of life!"

For a materialist like Walt, chemistry and matter is "all of life." There's nothing more to understand when it comes to life and the world because everything that does or could ever happen, including your choice to read this book, can be explained according to the rules that govern the behavior of the chemicals things are made of. Strict materialists believe that no one chooses to break bad. Rather, a series of chemical reactions in your body combined with chemical interactions between the body and the environment dictate your actions. These same chemical interactions trigger the feeling you might have that you chose to break bad.

This might be the sort of perspective you would want to have if you were ever shoveling the soupy mess of your murder victim into a toilet. If you think about the world and your behavior strictly in terms of the rules that govern the behavior of your chemical components, you might be able to convince yourself that you didn't decide to kill anyone, that it wasn't your will, but the laws of nature that took the life recently ended. This point of view allows you to believe that you do not *choose* to break bad; rather, bad and evil just happen.

If, however, chemistry is only able to account for 99.888042 percent of the human body, then this 0.111958 percent discrepancy represents a tiny, but important, hole in the materialist point of view. Gretchen's suggestion that this hole is filled by the soul expresses the sort of idea that's cancerous to materialism. It leaves open the possibility that there's something in the world that can't be account for by, or doesn't obey, the laws of chemistry. And, if each person is partially composed of something that doesn't obey the laws of chemistry, then maybe each person is responsible for his or her own actions.

Not only does the soul bring with it the notion of responsibility or culpability for one's actions, it brings with it all the other notions that go along with it: guilt, pride, and the one drive that Walt seems to wrestle with in his new career as a meth manufacturer—that is, the desire for a clean conscience, relief from the guilt he feels for his actions. In a word: redemption.

Ri-demp-shuhn

Redemption isn't a hot-button issue. It's not commanding a lot of blog time, tweet time, pod time, or airtime. It's not even a particularly popular word among contemporary philosophers. It is, however, a serious philosophical issue that's relevant to everyone with a moral compass. According to the *Oxford English Dictionary*, redemption is "the action of saving or being saved from sin, error, or evil." At its most basic level, redemption involves some sort of release from the feelings of guilt that he or she might feel for their wrong actions.

One of the classic philosophical discussions of redemption can be found in St. Augustine's *Confessions*. The *Confessions* was written approximately four hundred years after the time of Christ when the Catholic Church was rapidly becoming entrenched as one of the world's dominant political and ideological forces. *Confessions* is Augustine's autobiography and portrays his experience of redemption during his passage from layperson, to priest, to Bishop.

Being a creature of his time, Augustine's redemption is grounded in his religion and his understanding of God. Religion and God don't usually find a place in the materialist point of view, but what's common to both Augustine and Walt's struggle for redemption is the question of whether our actions are guided by genuine choices or whether our dispositions, choices, and actions are dictated by certain higher rules. In

Walt's case, the higher rules are those that govern our chemical make-up; for Augustine the rules are those laid down by God.

Walt seems to believe that our actions are governed by the indifferent laws of chemistry, but his feelings of guilt contradict this commitment because chemistry (and the materialist point of view) suggests that breaking bad isn't something that we choose; rather, we are chemically driven a certain way.

Breaking Bad or Born That Way

Many of history's greatest philosophers broke bad at some point in their lives: Heidegger was a Nazi; Kierkegaard was excommunicated; Abelard was an infamous playa before his lover's father and brother castrated and dishonored him (cut-off his junk and sent him packin'); Boethius, Anaximander, and, of course, Socrates were all executed for heresy, among other things. Even Plato was accused of "profaning the mysteries" (revealing the secrets of his crew to an outsider). This was punishable by death in most creative ways. Fortunately for Plato, he was merely ostracized from Athens (forced to 'bounce from his crib') until the heat died down.

Before he earned the name, Saint Augustine, Aurelius Augustinus was a confessed adulterer (had a rep for hooking up with the MILFs of Carthage) and fornicator (had mad relations with the females). Aurelius too was a man of science; he was deeply committed to the mother of all sciences—namely, philosophy. Like Walt, Aurelius made his living as a teacher (before becoming a priest); he taught rhetoric and argumentation in Rome. Like Walt, Aurelius expressed a nagging concern for redemption. And like Walt, this concern led Aurelius to be deeply troubled by the origins and nature of evil; whether evil is part of nature and, as such, just a thing that happens, or whether evil comes about through people's choices and actions.

The Problem of Evil

The context of Augustine's life was considerably different from Walt's. For Augustine, God's existence is the one truth that science must bring into agreement with our experiences of evil. As he explains in Book Seven of the *Confessions*, if God is all the things that the Judeo-Christian traditions says that God is—namely, all knowing, all powerful, and all good—then God must have knowledge of evil and possess the power to prevent it. Yet, apparently, God doesn't prevent it. What's even more problematic is the Judeo-Christian claim that God is present in all things and at all times. If this is so, then one must conclude that God himself is in some way corrupt; that evil is part of, or mixed with, God. This is inconsistent with the notion that God is all-good. Throughout the history of philosophy, this set of problems has been collectively referred to as *the problem of evil*.

Walt's own problem of evil is effectively the same, even though it stems from an assumption essentially opposite to that of Augustine. Walt never says that there's no God, but it's implied in the claim that chemistry is "all of life." From Walt's materialist point of view, no thing is more or less evil than anything else. Evil, fear, guilt, and the like are no more than chemically induced feelings that serve the human organism in its drive towards self-preservation. From this point of view there's no such thing as free will because, like fear and guilt, will is nothing more than a chemically induced feeling that isn't free at all. Evil is only problematic from this perspective if there is some part of the human organism that functions independently from the laws of chemistry and, being free from those laws, can genuinely choose evil actions over good ones.

St. Augustine answers the problem of evil by arguing that evil and corruption aren't created at all. In fact, evil occurs in destruction—that is, in the undoing of creation. And so, Augustine is able to say without contradiction or heresy that God is present in all of existence because evil exists only where existence is falling apart. What causes this to happen? Corruption of the will. In other words, evil occurs when one chooses or takes actions that lead him away from God, away from goodness, that is, towards destruction.

Augustine's analysis of evil is the same as that of the materialists. Both identify goodness with continued existence and self-preservation. Both identify evil, in one way or another, with self-destruction. And so it would seem that with or without God in the picture, breaking bad involves some action leading towards self-destruction. This thought troubles Walt as he considers what to do about Krazy-8.

Requiem for Krazy-8

His heart was racing. His thoughts were racing, "He knows my name, he knows everything about me." The pot he smoked slowed down his heart, but nothing could keep Walt's head from spinning. Pacing didn't help either. Wandering back and forth between a strange kitchen and a strange living room burned up the hours, but it didn't make the problem go away. Krazy-8 was still chained by the neck to the beam in the basement and, according to the sacred coin toss, it was Walt's job to "take care" of him.

The situation was all the more troubling when the boy coughed. From time to time, Krazy-8 would let out a wheezing cough. It sounded so much like Walt's own that it brought tears to his eyes. Sympathy is a bitch! Walt knew that sympathy could only make this already complicated situation all the more complicated. At least from where he sits now, on the throne in the upstairs bathroom, Walt can't hear the coughing, the wheezing, or any of Krazy-8's barely vital signs. In this little sanctuary, with this little bit of peace, Walt decides to approach the problem rationally:

Let him live

—It's the moral thing to do
—Judeo-Christian
 principles
—You are not a murderer
—He may listen to reason
—Post-traumatic stress
—Won't be able to live
 with yourself
—Murder is wrong!

Kill him

—He'll kill your entire family if
 you let him go.

Walt's deliberations amount to this: In favor of letting Krazy-8 live Walt offers three claims grounded in commonly held moral principles, one inculcation of two of the world's most widespread religions, one fervent claim concerning his own identity, and three very practical considerations. Still, when considered in light of Walt's one very compelling reason to kill Krazy-8, the rational path is far from clear. What's clear is Walt's struggle to be a good person while doing bad things.

Here too, Walt's life and sentiments parallel those of Augustine. Contrary to what you might expect from what I told you about Augustine's *Confessions*, it's not a story in which Augustine, the lascivious protagonist, has a great epiphany and suddenly goes straight. Quite the contrary, according to his own confession, Augustine desired from an early age to be a moral person, to understand the origins of evil while, at the same time, indulging in excess. What changes and matures over the course of Augustine's life are his arguments and beliefs with respect to these issues and the questions that these concerns raise.

Augustine expresses with frank honesty the pleasure he took in the fulfillment of his carnal desires. Despite his mother's warning not to have sex outside of marriage, Augustine admits that he had lots of sex. Even after Augustine broke-up with his girlfriend (and baby momma) in anticipation of marrying a woman of his mother's choosing, Augustine confesses, "because I was more a slave of lust than a true lover of marriage, I took another mistress" (Book Six, Chapter 15). In all this Augustine is saying the same thing: he wanted to be badass, he enjoyed being badass, and you can't be badass without being bad.

All the while, and despite his great indulgences, Augustine asked God for redemption, but what he wanted was redemption of a particular kind: redemption without sacrificing the fun, the debauchery, and the gratification of the bodily desires he was enjoying at the time. He wanted redemption, but not yet.

This is precisely what Walt wants: a clean conscience without sacrificing the adrenaline rush, the freedom, and the fat stacks that he believes will secure his family's future. Walt too wants redemption, but not yet. Walt's desire for redemption as he continues to break bad is epitomized when, after making a deal with Tuco and witnessing the man beat his associate to death, Walt says to Jesse, "$737,000; that is what I need . . . eleven more drug deals, and always in a public place from now on. It's doable, definitely doable." (Season Two, "Seven Thirty-Seven"). Despite all he's seen, Walt still believes that a "no-rough-stuff-type deal" is possible. This, of course, isn't what a man of reason anticipates. It's not what Walt anticipates either. It's what Walt wants, and he wants it because it's the only way to remain a good person while doing bad things. Before this plan is played-out, however, Walt will kill Krazy-8, blow-up a car, blow-up a building, and adopt the name, Heisenberg.

La Vita Heisenberg

Werner Heisenberg (1901–1976), German physicist and mathematician, revolutionized science by devising what is commonly referred to as the *Heisenberg Uncertainty Principle*. The principle operates at the sub-atomic level of the universe and governs the behavior of chemical molecules. The practical import of Heisenberg's Uncertainty Principle is this: given that the measurement of a particle's location and velocity is a necessary part of the determination of the laws that govern them, Heisenberg's uncertainty principle requires that those laws themselves involve a certain degree of uncertainty. This uncertainty may be slight scientifically speaking, but its philosophical import is immense! Heisenberg's uncertainty principle makes room for a wide array of hitherto unexplained phenomena within the materialist point of view. This uncertainty might, for example, account for the 0.111958 percent discrepancy in Walt's accounting of the chemical composition of the human body. It answers Gretchen's question, "What about the soul?" by suggesting that 0.111958 percent of the body's volume is uncertain by scientific necessity.

Heisenberg's uncertainty principle makes room for free will in the otherwise-deterministic materialist paradigm by turning rigid laws of particle behavior into *tendencies*. This is the case because the principle requires that we soften the claims arrived at by means of science in recognition of the inherent uncertainty in the recording and prediction of sub-atomic behavior. We might, for example, say that, "pseudoephedrine *tends to* trigger an alpha-adrenergic response" rather than saying "pseudoephedrine *causes* alpha-adrenergic responses." The difference is subtle but important. Tendencies are like laws because they govern behavior, but they're unlike laws in that they allow for deviation. It's possible, given Heisenberg's uncertainty principle, that in some cases—that is, some highly improbable, but possible cases—pseudoephedrine will not trigger an alpha-adrenergic response. Laws, in the scientific sense, are meant to be iron clad, and if thing which go against the law do happen, then the law must be either modified or abandoned.

Tendencies are flexible and can be deviated from without necessarily changing the anticipated outcome of a similar future event.

By this reckoning, Walt hasn't taken the name Heisenberg as a way of giving props to a man he idolizes, Walt has taken the name of the principle he seeks to exemplify. He's taken the name of the metaphysical truth he now embraces and embodies because Heisenberg's Uncertainty Principle opens to him the possibility that he wasn't destined to be bad. Heisenberg allows Walt to believe that he *chose* to break bad and that he can *choose* to be good again. In the absence of a soul, Heisenberg's Uncertainty Principle opens up to Walt the possibility for redemption. What that redemption will look like is another question.

Remission Is Not Redemption

Echoing calls for "Speech!" rang across the White family living room, now full of Walt's friends and family. The call drew his thoughts back to the grey office and the moment he heard the news they had all gathered to celebrate. "You're showing signs of remission," said Dr. Delcavoli before launching into a stream of warnings and qualifications concerning just what the term "remission" really means. According to Dr. Delcavoli, remission usually refers to shrinkage of a malignant tumor; but he cautions, one is also technically in remission when the tumor simply stops growing. Walt's remission is a little more promising: "Walt, your tumor has shrunk by eighty percent" ("4 Days Out").

Remission fulfills the dictionary definition of "redemption" mentioned above. In a metaphorical sense, remission saves the body from evil—namely, the evil that threatens the survival of the living organism. This metaphor is often used in relation to cancer; the word malignant, after all, is derived from the Latin word *malum* meaning "evil." A malignant or cancerous cell is one that replicates very rapidly and invades other cells causing tumors and tumor growth. If remission is, as Dr. Delcavoli says, the cessation of tumor growth or shrinkage of the tumor, then remission is tantamount to being saved from evil of the cancerous sort.

Dr. Delcavoli's news was greeted with laughter, hugs, and more than a few tears. Now, however, standing in front of the friends from whom he has sought desperately to keep his life as Heisenberg a secret, his words repeated the very first thought that greeted it.

"When I got my diagnosis, cancer, I said to myself . . . you know . . . 'Why me?'"

Walt continues: "And then . . . the other day, when I got the good news . . . I said the same thing" (Season Two, "Over").

Walt's question can be read many ways, but for those of us who're aware of his life as Heisenberg the question represents a direct attack upon the idea that remission is tantamount to redemption. From the audience's point of view, Walt is asking why he was spared despite the horrible things he's done. From the audience's point of view, remission doesn't bring Walt redemption because remission undermines the very reason Walt had for committing such horrible acts in the first place. Sure he iced a few guys while feeding poison to junkies, but he made a fortune doing it and that fortune will secure his family's future long after his untimely death. On the other hand, if Walt lives, there's no reason to think that he couldn't continue to support his family without manufacturing poison and without killing anyone. Walt's speech expresses his recognition of this truth.

In the light of Heisenberg's Uncertainty Principle we can understand Walt's remission as a very strong change in the tendencies of his physical organism. Its behavior is no longer threatening its own physical survival, at least, not to such an extreme degree (twenty percent of the tumor remains). This does, perhaps, suggest an excellent general definition of health—that being, the body's tendency towards behavior that does not threaten its prolonged survival. These tendencies, however, belong to the 99.888042 percent of Walt that's subject to the laws of chemistry. They are governed by chemistry and, as such, their relevance to Walt's moral disposition (his redemption) is questionable.

When Walt shares the news of his remission with Jesse, we're given a glimpse of the tendencies for which Walt is most concerned: Walt vows to leave the meth business (presumably for good), and in this decision Walt hopes to achieve his redemption. Simply put, when Walt stops cooking he'll no longer be a bad person because he'll no longer be doing bad things ("Over"). Like in the case of remission, this behavior will tend to promote Walt's physical survival; but unlike in remission this behavior seems to originate in that 0.111958 percent that falls beyond the governance of his chemical make-up. Walt's vow to Jesse seems to suggest that his decision to stop cooking necessarily follows from his remission but, as the remainder of this part of Walt's story suggests, the connection is tenuous.

Delayed Redemption

"We've got rot." Walt calls up to Walter Jr. through a hole in the floor of their family home. "Rot?" Walter Jr. Responds. "Ya . . . here . . . I'll show ya . . . here . . . take a look at that." Walt says passing his son a piece of wood that he's excised from the bowels of their home.

Walter Jr. continues to look puzzled as his dad explains to him how the rot is caused by fungus that ultimately threatens the integrity of the physical structure of the home. "Is the whole house gonna' collapse or something?" Walter Jr. asks. "Not if I can help it!" Walt replies ("Over").

In the meantime Skyler, another integral part of Walt's home, is engaging in behavior that threatens to undermine its integrity. Walt's efforts to eliminate fungus from his home while Skyler engages in an affair with Ted Beneke, her boss, poetically mirrors Walt's personal struggle for redemption. As Walt irradiates the cancer causing rot to his physical self, another part of him is engaging in behavior resulting in rot of a different sort. The rot caused by Skyler and Walt's free choices persists no matter how fresh, strong, and new is the physical structure of Walt's home or body.

It's the rotting tendencies that linger. Walt's vain mission to secure the physical integrity of his home seems to come to an end when, in the parking lot of Raks Building Supply, he warns a would-be meth cook, "stay out of my territory!" ("Over"). We see that Walt's physical condition doesn't dictate the tendencies that guide his choices. These tendencies are strong and they persist, despite Walt's remission.

Are these tendencies determined by Walt's chemistry? Are they choices Walt is predetermined to make? The Heisenberg Uncertainty Principle suggests that these questions may be fundamentally unanswerable. Yet the tendencies and choices to which these questions refer remain morally relevant. The tendencies and choices referred to in these questions are the tendencies and choices that will determine Walt's redemption. They are morally relevant precisely because the answers to these questions are fundamentally uncertain. If we can't with certainty say that they are governed by chemistry and therefore predetermined, then, in the absence of any certain cause, we must conclude that our free choice is the only thing that can change them.

But Not Yet

The character of Walter White offers us this truly philosophical insight: it's the tendencies of Walt's free choices, and not those that govern Walt's physical organism, that are relevant to his redemption. It's Walt's tendency to choose his Heisenberg persona over that of the humble family man that prevents him from achieving the redemption he seeks. It's these tendencies that cause Walt to question whether he's deserving of his remission.

For those of us who believe with Walt that chemistry is "all of life," these tendencies hold the possibility, if not the necessity, for redemption: redemption for the man of science, it turns out, is a matter concerning those behaviors that seem to fall within the realm of uncertainty with respect to their cause. These are the behaviors that we believe to be the effect of our choices because Heisenberg's Uncertainty Principle dictates that they have no other certain cause. Redemption for Walt as well as for those that share his materialist paradigm can be achieved when their choices (rather then their chemistry) consistently tend towards the preservation and longevity of their organism.

For the time being, Walt seems to be praying for chastity and continence, "but not yet." What Walt shows us is that he'll have his redemption when he chooses to no longer be breaking bad.

3

Was Skyler's Intervention Ethical? Hell, It Shouldn't Even Be Legal!

DAN MIORI

Well-written and well-acted, *Breaking Bad* is highly watchable television. Despite its somewhat outrageous premise (like Walt could bag the Skyler level of hotness; right?), it accurately portrays many of the complexities of life that confront each of us every day.

In the Season One episode, "Gray Matter," for example, an aspect of medical decision making was shown in a way that was possibly well beyond anything the writers, actors, and director had ever intended. In it, there was a scene involving an event that Skyler called a "family meeting," structured more like an intervention minus the professional counselor, but in the end was neither. This event is a critical part of establishing Walt's character. His relationships, his tendency to intellectualize, his ill-ease with Hank's hulking manliness, they're all folded in.

The scene sets the stage for Walt's transformation from a hapless, passive-aggressive chemistry teacher to a hapless passive-aggressive meth cook. As we watch, we're troubled by how things play out at this meeting. Not only is Skyler's intervention unethical, it shouldn't even be legal. But why? What makes it so wrong? In a word: coercion. Walt's autonomy—his freedom to make his own decision about his cancer treatment—is limited by Skyler at a point when he most needs the open loving support of his entire family. In effect, Walt is coerced into aggressive treatment.

Family Meeting . . . Quote, Unquote

Most people have some understanding of what an intervention is, a group of concerned people, usually family and friends, come together to intervene in the life of a loved one to make a positive change in that person's life. The person may be some kind of addict or somehow socially maladapted, and the event is used to urge that person to make positive changes. There's usually a professional counselor or therapist at the intervention, lthough not always.

Handling interventions ethically as well as professionally is important; and ethics, or more accurately *bioethics*, in case you haven't figured it out yet, is important to *me*. Bioethics is a branch of ethics (itself a branch of Western philosophy) where philosophical positions are actually put into practice when making decisions concerning matters like physician-assisted suicide, abortion, contraception, use of animals for research, and other issues in the realms of biology, medicine, and clinical practice.

Hey, Come Watch This

In the interest of full disclosure, I should tell you that I'm a physician assistant in palliative care (the specialized area of medicine that focuses on how to alleviate pain and suffering) in Buffalo, New York. I routinely sit in on family meetings where the risks and benefits of life-sustaining treatment are discussed. Since most of what I deal with has a strong ethical component, I'm involved in the bioethics system where I work and in my community. I also like to write about the things I do and get my writings published.

Since, like most of us, I think everyone understands the stuff I understand, whenever I do take on project like writing this chapter, I try and make sure I'm addressing real gaps in understanding; or at the very least not sounding like a pompous dick. To limit the already dangerously high risk of sounding dickish for this discussion of Walt and Skyler, I did some research to make sure the issues I saw at the family meeting were also issues to other people and that I was addressing them appropriately.

Research Methods

A scientist at heart, I began gathering data by carrying a portable DVD player around with me and showing the intervention scene to as many people as I could. I also did this so that I could include a bunch of research-y sounding terms in this chapter. Most of the people I showed it to are aware of what I do for a living, and I worried that this would cause a thing called *expectation bias*. In other words, I worried that they might give me answers they thought I would want to hear, not their honest opinion. My *inclusion* criterion for this study was as follows: I say "Hey, come watch this" and anyone who didn't run away was included. My *exclusion* criteria were people who could run faster than me, and the vascular surgeon who calls me "Doctor Death."

Analysis

It turned out that my estimation of how much people care about what I think was seriously flawed (a common failing of us academic types) and consequently my database was varied and incredible insightful. Almost everyone recognized that Skyler's actions didn't seem to be right. Even the bold iconoclasts who said they would have done the exact same thing also said that, although her heart was in the right place, Skyler wasn't fighting fair. I believe the reason people feel that way is that while Skyler's actions toward Walt may have been appropriate given his tendency to behave like a pouty child, they weren't ethical. She coerced him into accepting treatment he didn't want, and no matter how far ahead you can read in the script, that's wrong.

Walt's Medical Situation

To take the scene apart and point out the dirty bits, it would be helpful to review Walt's medical options. When Walt says he just has a couple years to live, he's right on target. He questions his diagnosis and prognosis in the same way any of us would. One question that he asks himself, however, is fundamental: are the side effects and potential additional problems, like life-threatening infections, worth the theoretical time I will receive in trade?

We actually know a fair amount about the type of lung cancer Walt has. In the pilot episode, at his visit with the eminent (and out of plan) Dr. Del Cavoli, Walt is told he has Stage IIIA adenocarcinoma of the lung. By giving him one to two years to live, the writers put him just about in the middle of the expected prognosis for this type of cancer. In fact, depending on factors like the size and location of the tumor, his chance of still being alive five years after diagnosis ranges as low as ten percent. This survival presumes he receives treatment, but there's something worth knowing about the treatment of Stage IIIA adenocarcinoma of the lung: it's not all that effective.

Surgery can't help, even Dr. Mustard Stain got that one right; radiation, which may be helpful in limiting symptoms like shortness of breath or pain, won't have a great impact on survival; and chemotherapy, which, while on average may increase survival by one to two months, won't dramatically alter the course of the disease.

There's even a study, published in the *New England Journal of Medicine*, which suggests that when using very aggressive cancer treatment—particularly adding second and third line chemotherapy agents once the first line fails—we can actually shorten people's lives by one to two months. These B squad treatments are often second line because they haven't shown any clear benefit over first line, in fact they often don't work as well, they just work differently or have fewer side effects. They don't result in better survival and often reduce the quality of life. These fall-back treatments would only function to do the one thing Walt wants to avoid, medicalize his final months. What he would get in trade for all of this treatment is the *possibility* of time; maybe a year or two, maybe none at all, no guarantees. The chance that the treatment will shorten the amount of time he has is actually greater than the chance it will help him be alive five years after his initial diagnosis.

Autonomy and Coercion

What's autonomy, then? A basic definition of *autonomy* is "the ability to act, free from coercion, provided it does not harm others." In Western philosophy autonomy is discussed along with the concept of *coercion*; autonomy and coercion being the absolute opposite endpoints in the spectrum of decision making.

Immanuel Kant (1724–1804) believed in a thing called the categorical imperative, which he described as "Act only on that maxim which you can at the same time will to be a universal law"—vaguely similar to the golden rule, "Do unto others as you would have them do unto you." In the first season I'm pretty sure Walt still believed this too, he looked like he felt awful for *days* about those two guys he killed. Kant felt we have the ability to choose the rules we live by freely and autonomously, provided we do it independent of emotion and circumstance which act as coercive elements.

John Stuart Mill (1806–1873) also discussed autonomy and coercion. According to Mill, by virtue of the fact that an individual person is a conscious being, he or she has the right to act in ways which aren't smart, ways which may generally be considered wrong, or even in ways which might be self-destructive. You could yell at that stupid person, you could beg or reason with that stupid person, but neither you, nor anyone else—including the government—can prevent that person from acting in a self-destructive way, as long as that person isn't hurting anyone else. According to Mill, we're autonomous enough to be able to maim or even kill ourselves without anyone stopping us—because the stopping part is a form of coercion.

Coercion Due to Chickenshit

The struggles of the non-medically trained layperson to come to grips with this understanding of autonomy are not helped by us medically trained laypeople. In fact, in many ways we're part of the problem. The one aspect of the "Gray Matter" family meeting that I was disappointed in was that it underplayed the responsibility we medical professionals have in establishing a better understanding of the limits of what we actually can do, as opposed to the things we can't do but we want to try anyway.

You see, the people offering the treatment have their own agendas and ways of coercing decisions. If we imagine the conversation between Dr. Del Cavoli and Walt which would have taken place if the nausea and weakness of his treatment had gotten worse, we would most likely have heard Del offering second or third line chemotherapy agents as a substitute. Treatment that he would have been certain would not help, and in fact might even shorten Walt's already poor survival, but he would offer it anyway.

He would do this for any number of reasons; because he understands the importance of hope; because he truly would like to believe it will work; because his eminent ego wouldn't allow him to admit defeat; possibly because he shares ownership of the out-of-system center where Walt is getting all that lucrative treatment; but most likely because he is just as big a chickenshit bastard as the rest of us who don't want to deal with Walt's, and therefore our own, mortality.

When I say *we*, by the way, unfortunately I do mean we. I'm ashamed to say that there have been times when I lacked the insight or the courage to tell my patients exactly what I thought was going on. I did so for almost all the reasons stated above except the one where I get lots of money, that one still evades me. So why am I telling you this dirty little secret while I'm trying to tell you about coercion? Because when we don't want to deal with your (our) mortality we'll suggest, hint at, cajole, and otherwise manipulate you into taking treatment that you might not ordinarily take. We try and coerce you into accepting this treatment by how we present it. We make the things we want to choose sound highly probable and the things we don't want you to choose sound inhumane.

It also affects how we answer your questions, "Doctor, will he survive the surgery?" "Sure, he could survive," we say. If we told you the truth—"If he lives through the surgery there is a nearly one hundred percent chance that he will live in an ICU for the rest of his life with tubes coming out of every orifice"— you wouldn't let us do the surgery.

On the surface, the idea of buying a little time doesn't seem so bad. This makes the coercion fairly easy; we're selling people something they really want. Unfortunately the result of that coercion is that what little time we gain with all those intrusive things comes at a cost. They aren't guaranteed effective, they are rarely comfortable, and some of the supportive measures like ventilators and kidney dialysis, could be considered outrightly inhumane. Sometimes the only thing that technology buys us is very little time, measured in hours or even minutes. We slow the process of dying but we don't stop it. We're usually left with situations where we must decide on a least bad outcome; and when the best thing we have to offer is a long shot gamble, choices based on the patient's values become just as important as decisions based on incomplete or non-existent medical understanding.

Because of this, the idea of autonomy is now applied in far more subtle and personal ways than ever before. As the idea of autonomy has become more important, the understanding of coercion has changed, which brings us back to Walt and Skyler. In an unfortunate, even ironic, twist, as the stress of decision-making increases along with the stakes, many of us may become less able to courageously and independently assert our autonomy. We fall back on our family, who also just happen to be under a fair amount of stress and may even have their own agenda as well. In some situations, the people we need most can be the people upon whom we can least depend. Not fun, kinda scary, but it happens; and God bless them, *Breaking Bad*'s writers found a way to allow us to view that conundrum.

The Ambush

Armed with a few ideas about autonomy and coercion, we can now tease apart the ethics of the "family meeting." At Skyler's behest, Hank, Marie, and Walt Jr. sit in ambush in the family room, waiting for Walt to bring his tired self home from work. Skyler leads off armed with the sacred talking pillow, announcing her intention with a candor that, as a witness to many such meetings, I was ready to dismiss as floridly untruthful. Being the lazy consumer of television I am though, I continued to watch and, as the dialog played out, was thrilled with just how well the truth of such meetings was captured. Issues that would have taken hours to unmask even with the help of the most skilled counselor (which, for the record, I am not) were laid bare in moments with the artistic medium of drama.

Skyler speaks first, but we already know this is a meeting in name only; her intent is to make Walt act in the way she wants, to embrace the idea of treatment, to fight the good fight, to embrace the illusion that a cure is possible and paying with the ugly reality of aggressive treatment is not too much. When Walt attempts to express his thoughts, he is admonished for speaking without the talking pillow, reinforcing the contrast between the family meeting Skyler would have us believe we're witnessing, the tough-love intervention she believes she's running, and the blatant attempt at coercion that is taking place. She hands off to Hank who, having received his assignment, tries to coach Walt through this test of manhood in the way Skyler intended.

Uncomfortable with the subject matter, speaking in a way everyone senses as ineffective, after a few sports metaphors obscured by the pre-cut domestic cheddar in his mouth, he hands off to the first completely honest voice so far, Walt Jr. Skyler points him at Walt like a gun, not once but twice, in order to maximize the effect of his raw expression of emotion, and her manipulation works. Walt absorbs the pain of being called "a pussy" by the son who has overcome so many physical challenges, but is unaware of just how wrong he is about "a little chemotherapy."

Skyler's willing ally Marie is next, but she floors everyone with her unexpected acceptance of Walt's decision. Having listened, precisely what people ought to do in meetings, she speaks her feelings honestly. Slightly overwrought, a bit lame, but her sincerity strikes a chord with Hank. Now able to reframe Walt's decision in a way that he finds understandable and honorable—to die like a man—Hank also jumps to Walt's defense. Their defection does not sit well with Skyler, and she announces her true purpose; her belief that Walt "doesn't have to die at all." In one brief, angry moment her motivation for bringing them together is made plain: to make Walt take medical the treatment that she believes will cure him. The verbal mêlée which ensues is only ended with Walt's whistle. It's then that we hear the empirical medical truth of Walt's situation. True in the real world and true (as far as we can tell without sitting in on the writer's meeting) in Albuquerque, too.

Skyler's Coercion

The simplest, most straightforward example of coercion in the meeting is, of course, Skyler's. Walt is seeking to take an action that she doesn't want. For the record, although the writers suggest this as an intervention, it's not even close. Interventions are intended to make people aware of the damage that has arisen as a result of actions they've taken; for example, the destruction alcoholism has caused to a marriage. They are not intended to change lawful behaviors that aren't, in themselves, destructive; and Walt's decisions don't exceed any standard for autonomy and don't even remotely approach John Stuart Mill's generous allowance for autonomous decisions.

This meeting is not to reflect on the damage that Walt's choice has caused but as Skyler's fatal attempt to manipulate his decision, and her strategy is to imply a threat of emotional isolation if he chooses to withhold treatment. We can presume emotional isolation is the threat given from what we see of their relationship in the four prior episodes but we will also see the evidence of this in Skyler's transformation, from her icy cold response to her husband's embrace at the sink the morning after the meeting to her loving and attentive presence at the treatment center while Walt's veins are filled with what he likely considers to be poison. She does all of this in a clear and premeditated way (the cheese and crackers were covered with plastic wrap, for Christ's sake!) with the purpose of making Walt take aggressive treatment.

Hank

Hank was used by Skyler, he was manipulated into providing exactly what he was programmed from birth to provide, manly manliness; she simply misjudged her tool. While Hank is the concrete foil to Walt's aestheticism for the plot line, and presumably existing in Skyler's mind as the prototypic protector male, she didn't give him credit for the brain and loving concern suggested before, and shown after this episode in abundance. Hank didn't coerce anyone; he just ate up the scenery . . . and the cheese.

Walt Jr.

Walt Jr. doesn't plan on making his father change his decision; he simply states his feelings in response to his father's choice. This certainly decreases Walt's freedom to act on his choice, but that decrease in freedom to act is simply a consequence of his love for his son, not a result of being coerced by him. Walt Jr. is the only person to have conducted himself in a way that I would hope to find at an intervention. His statement to his father is "I'm pissed off!"—a true emotional response, not a threat. He didn't say he *would be* pissed off, and he didn't suggest that being pissed off would cause him to act in ways Walt would find unacceptable. Most importantly, he didn't suggest that his emotional response would alter his basic relationship with his father in any way. These important details make Walt Jr.'s response non-coercive. Walt would, and most likely already has, given over control of his life for his namesake. He would even comply with Skyler's coercion and magical thinking in order to regain his son's love.

But Why Walt—Why?

Given Walt's values, his decision to accept aggressive treatment is a poor one, but was made autonomously and therefore one that he has the right to make. It's a decision that may cost Walt the cancer patient dearly, but for Walt the dad, it's worth the price for the moment. The difference in the source of motivation for Walt's decision is probably best expressed in how Walt would act during treatment. If flatly coerced by Skyler's threat of emotional isolation Walt would go slouching and pouting, passively making Skyler pay for every episode of chemobarf. He doesn't though, at least not at first. Convinced of the utility of accepting this sham of treatment and its consequences, he puts on his bravest face and takes his medicine, but why does he?

Autonomous Beneficence

As a parent and grandparent, I'm subject to a certain amount of beneficent decision-making. Not just handing out twenty-dollar bills in the same way my grandfather did, but sacrificing time and money, that I may not have to spare, in assisting with the care of my family. In the same way we see casual beneficence from the people around us, we also see them take actions which may not be in their best interest, but benefits their loved ones.

In my lifetime I have watched my parents put themselves financially in a deep hole to support their children, particularly the one writing this chapter. I find this behavior highly justifiable, my parents aren't fond of going into debt after their retirement, and my siblings will most likely be completely pissed off if they ever find out. I call this behavior autonomous beneficence and have come to anticipate a certain level of this in the decision making of my patients.

It's autonomous because it is a choice freely made; it's beneficence because it involves doing good things we aren't otherwise compelled to do. It deserves discussion because sometimes it's difficult to accept by outsiders like friends, my siblings, and medical staff. An individual on a ventilator may prefer death over continuing to be shackled to medical devices, but will delay a planned withdrawal of treatment in order to get past a birthday, a graduation, or other seemingly insignificant family events. For someone trapped in a hospital bed who has lost control of every aspect of their lives including taking in nutrition and eliminating waste, it may be the only way they have to help out; I consider it a positive quality and seek to support it when able.

An example can be found in a family meeting I made up. A pretend wife, who was alive only because of spending hours at a time attached to a dialysis machine three times a week, found out that her husband's pretend heart was failing and that he was advised to have surgery. His response, very consistent with the response I would expect even from an actual person, was to postpone his surgery. When she found out she said: "if I don't make him get that cardiac bypass he never will, and then I'll be forced to haunt him." Although camouflaged with humor, her act was autonomous, it was supremely beneficent, and it was not consistent with any good plan she might have come up with herself. Clearly her own pretend medical condition was far more urgent than her husband's pretend medical condition. The problem—and it's not a small one—is where we draw the line between an act as autonomously beneficent and as coerced. On a day-to-day basis this degree of coercion is virtually impossible to identify, and even if you could it would be impossible to call shenanigans on.

In "Gray Matter" however, we have a case where the relationship issues are out in the open (complements of episodes one through four), where the medical reality has been positioned like an Acme anvil over a pile of birdseed, and where we have the luxury of dissecting the dynamics of the meeting-in-name-only holding everyone accountable for their actions. My opinion, for what it's worth, is that Walt decided to take treatment because of Walt Jr., not because Skyler had him by the emotional short hairs.

Accepting Autonomy

the real world of medicine, we have to deal with the specific details of each situation. We hope that we can guide each person, whether patient or family, to some level of understanding and acceptance. We hope that decisions made by the patient will be made with the complete self interest that each of us deserves to be given at the end of life. We hope that patients withholding treatment will have the full loving support of their family and friends and that it will allow them to be comfortable. Comfortable, not as a euphemism for assisted suicide, but in the same way we mean when we invite a guest into our home; to be free from onerous discomfort. We work hard to make sure that decisions are not coerced, but in the end we must accept the decision a patient makes and hope that we can give treatment in as humane a way as possible. Although it's difficult to watch harmful treatment we know to be futile, it can happen that an individual can accept that treatment autonomously, from a genuine desire to provide their loved one with whatever comfort they can.

Now, Wait Just a Damn Minute . . .

For those readers who have been paying close attention and who foolishly thought I was actually going to suggest that there's a way to make coercion like Skyler's illegal, sorry, it just doesn't work like that. I only made the claim that it *shouldn't* be legal, remember? One of the ways we're coerced is by rule of law. Not everyone can be trusted to act honestly, that's why we have locks; to keep out the curious. Any thief worth his salt can bust into a house faster than the time it took to write this sentence (which, for the record, took the better part of twenty minutes. I'm a really slow writer.) Laws are necessary to prevent chaos, but we can't completely dictate all action. We still have to have autonomy in decisions with regard to our own lives and most particularly with regard to our own bodies. A Kantian might argue that Walt had made his decision to withhold treatment exactly the way Kant would want, free from emotion. A Millian might suggest that Skyler butt the hell out because Walt gets to make this decision for himself.

The bottom line is that whether at the end of life or in the middle, we should have the freedom to make the same dumb-assed decisions we make for the same indecipherable reasons we always make them. Our job—and I do mean all of us—is to help our loved ones make sound decisions and to give them the freedom to make those decisions and support them, whether we like the decision or not.

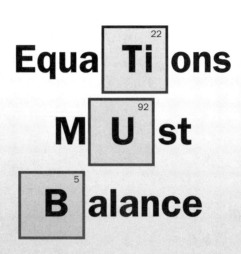

4

Finding Happiness in a Black Hat

KIMBERLY BALTZER-JARAY

> But though I have wept and fasted, wept and prayed,
> Though I have seen my head (grown slightly bald) brought in upon a
>   platter,
> I am no prophet—and here's no great matter;
> I have seen the moment of my greatness flicker,
> And I have seen the eternal Footman hold my coat, and snicker,
> And in short, I was afraid.
>
> *—The Love Song of J. Alfred Prufrock*

At the beginning of the *Breaking Bad* story, Walter White has a lot in common with J. Alfred Prufrock. Prufrock is filled with regret about his life because he has been indecisive, inarticulate, anxious, and overly concerned about how his actions will be judged by others to the point of being almost paralyzed. Prufrock's been living a very inauthentic life, one where he's failed to define himself as a free individual.

Walt too has a lot of regrets about his life, and appears to be a victim of circumstance: he's an underpaid, over-educated chemistry teacher, whose promising career was cut short by greedy, fair-weather friends; he works part time at a car wash to make ends meet; he lives with an overbearing wife, a disabled teenage son, and a new baby on the way; and he's been told he'll die soon from cancer.

Existentialists like Albert Camus and Jean-Paul Sartre would say that Walt, like Prufrock, is living deeply in something called *bad faith*, which is a bad thing (which you probably gathered, given the *bad* part) whereby someone adopts false values and doesn't live a rational and truly free life. Walt fails to see the absurdity of it all, that the universe is silent, purposeless, and ultimately meaningless.

According to the existentialists, Walt's life lacks authenticity. He fails to take hold of his freedom and responsibility because he sees himself as defined completely by others. However, there's one major difference between Walter White and J. Alfred Prufrock: Walt takes his cancer diagnosis as a wake-up call to become a free individual and define what remains of his life, whereas with Prufrock we're left at the end of the poem with the impression that he's fated to live and die in the same inauthentic frame of mind.

Believe it or not, when Walt becomes Heisenberg, the meth cooker and dealer, he becomes an authentic individual—the ideal person Camus and Sartre speak of—finding the balance between defining himself and the role others play in shaping him. He acknowledges the absurdity of the universe and his inevitable death, and he takes hold of his freedom and responsibility for his choices.

Heisenberg isn't an alter ego, but is Walt becoming true to himself and living in *good* faith! Walt as Heisenberg is like the mythical character, Sisyphus, endlessly pushing his rock up the mountain, filled with rebellion and a silent joy, since his fate and his essence belong to him and no one else. And, like Sisyphus, we must imagine Walt is happy. Who'd have thought the choice to become a drug dealer could bring about such benefits?

Born without a God

Existentialism is a philosophy of the ground rather than the sky—a philosophy of the streets of man, born without a god, without the necessity of an objective truth, and without an overriding moral code. It pertains to the daily lives of everyone, not just professional philosophers, and in fact many of us practice ideas central to existentialism without even being aware we're doing it. It can best be described as a twentieth-century philosophy that focuses on existence and how people find themselves existing in the world.

The slogan of existentialism is "existence comes before essence." A person comes into existence, and only after that, through free will, choice, and responsibility, defines their self, creates meaning in their life, and continues the search and discovery of who they are until death comes. Not an easy task at all, since decisions often come with consequences and stress, and people are entirely responsible for their actions. This is precisely why *anguish* is another key concept existentialists speak of: I feel anguish because nothing other than my free will makes me choose how to act, I am ultimately responsible for myself, and these free actions have consequences for myself and the others around me.

Since my personal responsibility extends to others and I recognize this fact, however, this is not a philosophy of "Do whatever I want, whenever I feel like it." In fact, because there's no god out there who has given humans moral rules to live by, we're all the more responsible for making moral laws that people can live by so as to interact with one another in peace and good faith. That there's nothing out there in the universe but the harshness of a purposeless and meaningless reality *doesn't mean* that we don't try to make meaning, purpose, and morality in our lives.

A Social Movement

Existentialism isn't purely philosophical business because many of its contributors wrote plays, fictional novels, and short stories, and so it is also a literary, social, and cultural movement. Famously though, it was part of a political movement. Existentialism was born a rebel, the "James Dean" of philosophy or the "bad boy in the black beret," and the themes of subversion and rebellion are key characteristics of its philosophy, whether political, social, moral, or religious in nature.

It started in the underground resistance movement of Paris during World War II, with a group called Socialism and Freedom, whose members included Jean-Paul Sartre, Simone de Beauvoir, and Albert Camus. Picture the Mole and La Resistance from the *South Park: Bigger, Longer, and Uncut* movie, and you've got this French group of philosophers and Existentialism in a cartoon nutshell.

Existentialism offered people a defense of individual freedom during the time of, and later the recovery from, Nazism and Fascism. It also heavily criticized authoritarian dictated social norms and religion, and was a voice for men and women alike. Existentialism would later play a key role in the feminist movement of the 1960s, with Simone de Beauvoir's infamous work, *The Second Sex*. Existentialists believed that when an individual, or a society, or a religion, imposed its arbitrary beliefs, values or rules onto others, to be followed obediently and blindly, it was the end of the individual: being imposed upon in this way turns people into objects, into unfree things.

Bad Boy in a Black Pork Pie Hat

In the Season One episode titled "Crazy Handful of Nothin'," Walt calls himself Heisenberg for the first time when meeting with Tuco, while in the episode "A No-Rough-Stuff-Type Deal" from the same season Walt wears a black pork pie hat and sunglasses to the scrapyard drug deal with Tuco. Heisenberg as we know him is born.

As Heisenberg, Walt is a meth cooker and businessman, with little patience for error and drugged-out associates—a man who isn't afraid to injure or kill someone to get a point across. However, this scheme of two different identities doesn't work for long, and Heisenberg slowly seeps into Walt's life and takes over. We see Walt standing up to his wife and being more sexually aggressive with her, we see him communicating more directly with his family and friends about his wants and feelings, he confronts students and strangers who try to disregard him, and he even occasionally wears the black hat at home. Heisenberg isn't an alter ego or by-night personality—he's Walt transformed existentially.

King Sisyphus

In Greek mythology, Sisyphus was a king who was punished by the gods for trickery and hubris; he thought he was smarter than Zeus. His punishment was to roll a large boulder up a steep hill for eternity: every day would begin the same with him rolling it uphill, but before he could reach the top of this steep hill the boulder would always roll back down, and he was forced to start again. This task was meant to be an eternity of frustration for Sisyphus, a punishment of hopeless, meaningless, futile labor.

Camus, however, sees Sisyphus as an absurd hero and not a defeated man. Sisyphus was rebellious during his life; he scorned the gods and defied their will. He had a passion and love for life, and he hated death. Sisyphus knows at every moment rolling the giant boulder that this fate was his own doing since he knew when he defied the gods he would be punished, and so he owns his punishment. Sisyphus also wouldn't give the gods the pleasure of seeing him suffer or be defeated, so he scorns them by owning the rock and making it meaningful. Camus imagines Sisyphus happy, smiling as he rolls the boulder uphill over and over, further scorning the gods who sought to make him obedient.

When Walt becomes Heisenberg, he also becomes like Sisyphus. Walt has a silent joy in his rebellion: he rebels against death, societal laws and norms, and his demanding wife, and he owns his fate. Walt, like Sisyphus, is an absurd hero.

Happiness and the Absurd—Two Sons of the Same Earth

I know what you're thinking: how can happiness and absurdity go together? For an existentialist like Camus—who made the above claim—it makes perfect sense. Absurdity lies in the chaos and irrationality of the universe, a universe that is not oriented toward our concerns but is rather indifferent to our aspirations and endeavors. Twists of fate, strange patterns of behavior, and unpredictable events are all glimpses of the absurd. These also serve as evidence that there is no God or higher destiny present in the universe. For Sartre, too, the absurd lies in the fact that there is no divine design or ultimate purpose in the universe that dictates how humans ought to exist: everything exists for no reason at all, an existence without necessity and without definition. To exist is simply *to be there*.

The biggest source of absurdity for Camus is death since it negates any aspirations and achievements. It destroys any meaning we have created and any importance we give to things, and this means that all human desires, goals, and achievements are irrational. Every single person on this earth knows that they will die at some point, and in the face of this fact they continue to spend every day creating meaning, aspiring, and desiring, and for Camus that is absurdity in its clearest form.

Death is the great equalizer; everyone from Charles Manson, to the Pope, to Bono, to Walter White will come to the same end—nothingness. Living each day to the fullest and creating meaning for yourself is a revolt against death and the extinction it brings. Camus sounds a bit like Dylan Thomas in his famous poem, *Do Not Go Gentle into That Good Night*, because one must always "Rage, rage against the dying of the light."

So, how does this recognition of my being condemned to death relate in any way to happiness? For Camus, once you acknowledge the absurdity of the universe you must also accept that your fate is your own matter to handle and belongs solely to you. Knowing the universe is without a god, without an ultimate meaning and purpose, means that you're free to create your own for yourself, and you can stop searching for something that isn't there. Having no master in the universe means you are master of yourself. The person who acknowledges and accepts the absurdity of the universe becomes like Sisyphus, a happy rebel with his own rock, owning his fate.

A Happy Upward Battle

When Walt becomes Heisenberg, he accepts all the absurdity in and around his life, the biggest of which is his impending death: he accepts his cancer diagnosis and the reality of how treatment cannot help him long-term, and he knows that everything he does leading up to his last breath will be extinguished once he dies. Even the choice of *Heisenberg* as his drug-world moniker reflects Walt's knowledge of absurdity in the world: Werner Heisenberg, a German theoretical physicist, is credited with conception and publication of the Uncertainty Principle, which states that "the more precisely the position is determined, the less precisely the momentum is known." In other words, the more you know about one physical property, the less you know about, can determine, or control another. This is both absurd and unsettling since it flies in the face of our understanding causality and seems to render any future scientific investigation pointless.

Walt originally became a meth cooker to be able to leave his family money to survive after his death, but it quickly became much more than that. Walt found great strength, pride, and satisfaction in cooking meth: he had a position of power and control over his lab and product; he was appreciated for his skills and high-quality product; and he was rewarded with large sums of cash and demand for more. Cooking meth wasn't the thankless job teaching high school chemistry was, and it was always exciting and intense. Being Heisenberg became less about making money and more about feeling an ownership over his shortening life, a sense of control over what he does and what direction the end of his life will take.

Walt's turn to meth cooking is also a revolt against the life he has led so far. Before his cancer diagnosis, Walt was a guy who followed the rules and did everything he was supposed to, and yet he ended up broke, unhappy, bored, and stepped on by others. Heisenberg is the complete opposite of the old Walt in every way: he lives by his own rules, he engages in illegal activity with dangerous individuals, and he isn't afraid to threaten, hurt, or kill others to get what he wants.

Being a meth cooker and businessman in the drug world has been an "uphill battle" all the way, whether it's Jesse's incompetence and drug abuse, or psychotic drug dealers like Tuco and Gus, or constantly being hunted down by the police and his DEA agent brother-in-law, Hank. But with every obstacle and setback that has occurred, Walt has learned, adapted, and fought on. Walt's meth cooking is a rebellion in every sense of the word, and we must imagine him happy as he struggles onward, creating more meaning in the end of his life than he did during the rest.

About Authenticity

In addition to creating more meaning in the end of his life than he did during the first part, Walt is being authentic. Authenticity is being true to your self as a free individual. For Camus and Sartre, to be authentic involves acknowledging and exercising the freedom you have to direct your own life through choices. When you resolve to be what you freely choose to be, you are being authentic.

Existentialism isn't a philosophy that advocates doing whatever you want, and we see this precisely in the fact that with freedom comes responsibility. Yes, Existentialism sounds very much like Spider-Man here: with great power comes great responsibility, and freedom is a great power. Inasmuch as you're free to choose your own course of action, free to define yourself, you're also entirely responsible for the consequences of those choices and actions. You're entirely responsible for yourself in every way. Being free entails that no other person or thing determined your choice or action. If something did 'force' you, still, you freely allowed it. Responsibility is about owning your actions and your character since both are part of creating your own essence.

In the Season Two episode, "Breakage," Walt asks Hank this question about Tuco and other drug lords: "What do you think it is that makes them who they are?" This is an existential question about authenticity. Walt also asks Hank for his opinion about where someone like Tuco comes from. Walt is asking these questions to find out what makes a successful drug dealer, since he and Jesse are trying to survive and be successful meth dealers. If Tuco's like the rest of the drug lords out there, then this knowledge helps Walt know his competition, his enemies. Hank has met many drug dealers like Tuco, and this experience is valuable. But Walt also seems to be asking because he envies Tuco in some way, that sense of power he radiates, the fear he creates. Walt as Heisenberg seeks to embody certain characteristics he sees in guys like Tuco, so he can have more effective control over his meth operations and personal life in order to be authentic in the sense Camus and Sartre talk about.

Gustavo Fring, the meth distributor Walt comes to work for after Tuco, is also another great authentic character, and a man Walt has a great amount of respect for. Gus is the polar opposite of Tuco: he is restrained, methodical, authoritative, appearing almost apathetic, and is a successful, legitimate businessman in addition to his drug enterprise. As a businessman, Gus doesn't use the product he sells, he simply distributes it, and this is a position Walt can relate to and respect.

When Gus is disappointed or angry, he's a man of quick action and few words, as when he discovered Jesse killed Gale Boetticher in the Season Four episode, "Box Cutter." Gus slits his faithful associate Victor's throat with a box cutter in front of Jesse and Walt, and says absolutely nothing; to make his point, Gus relies on his body language, the action itself, and the force he uses to pull back Victor's head, keeping the wound open so it spurts blood everywhere. The only words he says to Jesse and Walt are, "Well, get back to work" before leaving the room, and he says them in a matter of fact tone. Gus freely chose this course of action, knowing it would convey in the most direct and powerful way that he is a free individual, willing to exercise his freedom in whatever way he deems necessary.

Bad Faith

Being authentic is no easy task, and as Sartre points out we are often living in something he calls *bad faith*. Bad faith is a form of self-deception, and Sartre uses this concept to characterize those who are unwilling to acknowledge the freedom they possess or those who fail to be responsible for their actions. Bad faith occurs when we're never really sure of who we are, failing to see the truth that we are beings in a constant state of becoming. To deny you're free is to deny you can change yourself, that your character can be modified. To deny you're responsible for past actions is to deny that your existence creates an essence, to think that your freedom to act in the future excuses you from what was previously done.

There are two forms of bad faith that come about in our relationships with other people: giving other people the full responsibility and credit for defining our essence, and completely ignoring the impact other people have on our essence. In other words, if I care too much about what others think, I fall into bad faith, and if I don't care at all what others think, I fall into bad faith. To escape bad faith is to walk the tiniest of tightropes, and in stilettos, too!

When we first meet Walt, he's living a very inauthentic life and deeply in bad faith. His life appears dictated by his overbearing wife, Skyler, and their family financial situation, he's unhappy and unfulfilled working as a high school chemistry teacher and car wash attendant, and when he is told he has inoperable lung cancer his initial reaction is to decline any treatment and die. Walt comes across as trapped, doomed to keep living the same unsatisfying life, and so death seems to him his only way out.

Authenticity Again

Once he becomes Heisenberg, all this changes. Walt begins to act freely and define himself, as when he blows up Tuco's establishment with fulminated mercury and demands that Tuco pay for the meth he stole, pay for Jesse's injuries, and that he buy two pounds of meth with the money upfront weekly in the episode, "Crazy Handful of Nothin'." Walt also accepts the consequences for each decision and action he makes as Heisenberg, such as when he runs over the two low-level drug dealers working for Gus to save Jesse from being shot in the episode, "Half Measure." Walt knew running over these two men could very well cost him his life. When he later talked to Gus, he accepted responsibility for killing the two men and attempted to negotiate a future course of action that would benefit everyone.

And we see Walt's authenticity again in the episode, "No Mas," when he tells Skyler the truth about his meth cooking, knowing that she could turn him in to the DEA or keep his children from him. When he told her, he took responsibility for his behavior, his previous lies and deceptions, and he didn't allow her reactions to override his own feelings. And in the episode, "Full Measure," Walt attempts to have his lab partner Gale killed by Jesse, and indeed he takes responsibility for that action as well.

In being authentic, Walt is also attempting to escape from his bad faith. Before becoming Heisenberg, Walt let other people define him and along with not acting freely he also failed to take any responsibility for his life. After becoming Heisenberg, Walt attempts to find the balance between what his friends and family think and what he wants.

Sometimes Walt has tendencies to consider his own desires more than anyone else's, swinging in the other direction of bad faith in his relations with others, as when he wanted to move back into the house and live with the family and wouldn't listen to Skyler's wishes (Season Three, "I.F.T."). He simply moved back in and didn't care what she wanted or said, and tried not to care that she was sleeping with her boss, Ted. Occasionally with Jesse, Walt has pushed him into things against his will, such as taking care of the meth theft from Skinny Pete, or taking care of Gale. But overall, Walt has made an immense transformation in becoming Heisenberg, and those changes are seen in every facet of his life. Heisenberg isn't an alter ego; he is Walt being an absurd, authentic hero. Walt owns his rock, climbs onward, and defines his life.

That Revolt Gives Life Its Value

When Walt became Heisenberg and put on that black pork pie hat, he began a revolution in his life. Walt starts to live his own life, create his own essence, and become an authentic person. He becomes an absurd hero when he starts cooking meth and takes on the name Heisenberg: knowing he has lung cancer and knowing his days are numbered, Walt recreates himself like a phoenix from the ashes and pushes on with his rebellion against death, social norms, and his old life.

Just like Sisyphus and his rock, Walt has a silent joy because within his revolt he owns his fate and he owns his essence. And just like Sisyphus, we must imagine Walt happy . . . with a black pork pie hat and sunglasses on, of course.

5

Hurtling Towards Death

CRAIG SIMPSON

> There is a tendency of plots to move towards death . . . the idea of death is built into the nature of the plot. A narrative plot is no less a conspiracy of armed men. The tighter the plot of the story, the more likely it will come to death.
>
> —Don DeLillo

Breaking Bad is a show that's first and foremost about *reactions*. These reactions can be chemical, as when pseudoephedrine is mixed with iodine crystals and red phosphorus, which then react to make crystalline methamphetamine. They can be physical, as when cells in human bodies grow uncontrollably and metastasize into malignant cancers due to reactions with toxins in the environment or our DNA. These reactions can also be human, as with the overwhelming feeling of despair that follows in the wake of being told that you're going to die.

All of these reactions in *Breaking Bad*, this interplay between the chemical, the physical, and the human, can be linked in one way or another to the show's antihero, Walter White, an overqualified high-school chemistry teacher who's been told that he's suffering from a rare and deadly form of lung cancer. After the initial shock of this news, he formulates a plan of action that will safeguard the financial security of his pregnant wife, Skyler, and their cerebral palsy-stricken son, Walt Jr.

What this drama presents us with is a man who's been thrown into a seemingly hopeless situation and who must come to terms with not only his own mortality, but also the knowledge that he'll be leaving behind the ones he loves in a potentially precarious situation. Walt's realization that he'll soon die from cancer, that his lifespan has now been drastically shortened (barring a miraculous recovery), means that death is now for him not an abstract or distant limit to life, but rather an over-whelming presence in every waking moment of his existence.

Walt is from the very get-go propelled towards death. The German philosopher Martin Heidegger claimed that all human existence is what he called *being towards death*, "the possibil-ity of our own impossibility."

An Authentic Life

Death, as Heidegger sees it, is the most personal life experience that a human being could have. It's ours and ours alone: once we die we cannot share our experience of it with anyone else because it dies along with us. Heidegger thinks that *being towards death* can define authentic human existence and provide us with the grounds to question the very meaning of our existence.

Heidegger argues that human categories of experience are built on the knowledge that we're ultimately finite, historically situated, and grounded in a *life towards death*. When one real-izes and accepts this reality of life towards death, then one is living an authentic existence. Authenticity also includes living every moment to the fullest while at the same time being mind-ful of life's transitory place in the stream of time. Heidegger attempts to find the healthiest relationship human beings could have with their own mortality—the best way that a human being could live a life in the face of an unstoppable, cer-tain death.

Heidegger believes that we human beings have chosen pro-foundly *inauthentic* ways of living our lives in the face of this threat of unavoidable mortality. In fact, he accuses traditional Western philosophy of being guilty of a dereliction of duty when dealing with the question of death. Philosophy has been more concerned with death-less truths than with the truth of death. For example, the notion of the immortal mind or soul has been privileged over the decaying, finite matter of the body.

Thrown into Time

For Heidegger, the only true facts of life are that we're born and that we die. Being is what happens in between. We always find ourselves already at a certain point in time and have no control over when we enter into its stream. Our existence on Earth is thus heavily influenced by time. Heidegger isn't referring to ordinary clock time—which we imagine progressing forward in a series of nows and where a human being is seen merely to exist in a long line of successive, passing moment—but rather time viewed as a *limited space* (because of its status as a historically conditioned environment) that opens up the possibilities for the emergence of what he would call authentic being, or *Dasein*.

Humans, says Heidegger, are thrown into time, and there's something very Heideggerian about the way we're "thrown" into the narrative timeline of *Breaking Bad* with the explosive opening scene of the pilot episode when Walt is shown driving a careening Winnebago in nothing but tighty whities and a gas mask. The rest of the episode is then told in flashbacks as we come to learn how Walt came to be in this odd situation.

Flashbacks

Flashbacks are an important storytelling device in *Breaking Bad*, and we can use them to explain some of Heidegger's ideas about being and time. Heidegger believes that being emerges from a unity of past, present, and future, with our actions in the past setting out a number of possible futures for us. He says that a human being's past is never really left behind; it lingers and influences who we are in the present and who we might possibly be in the future.

Breaking Bad's flashbacks show us the moments in Walt's life before he became the mythical, meth making and dealing Heisenberg. When viewed in this light, the flashbacks become more than just a means of telling the story. Their philosophical significance comes from the fact that we're given brief but telling glimpses of the man that Walter once aspired to be (for Heidegger this is one of Walt's possibilities): the renowned chemist who could provide for Skyler and Walt Jr. while at the same time enjoying all the material trappings that the American Dream has to offer.

Though in some twisted way Walt manages to achieve these aspirations, it's fair to say that it wasn't in the manner that he had envisioned! In the Season One episode ". . . And the Bag's in the River," a flashback is triggered when Walt is cleaning up the acid-dissolved remains of Krazy-8's partner, Emilio, whom Walt had killed when Kracy-8 and Emilio had attacked Walt and Jesse at their mobile desert laboratory. Here we're shown Walt in his younger days at the Sandia Labs as he tries to quantify the chemical makeup of the human body with his enthusiastic lab assistant, both of them clearly reveling in the joys of scientific leaning. Walt's past as a skilled chemist has become intertwined, in a comically macabre fashion, with his present situation as a man who has committed murder and who must now actually rid himself of human remains.

In the Season Three episode, "Full Measure," we see Walt in happier times, this time with his pregnant wife Skyler, as they both imagine what the future holds for them now that Walt can afford to provide for the large family they both desire: "We've got nowhere to go but up," gushes an optimistic Walt. There's a certain poignancy to these flashbacks because of what the viewer already knows about Walt and Skyler's life and the very different paths that they have taken together.

Heidegger believes that what has already happened in the past is then at the same time already inscribed into our present and our future. Walt's hubris or arrogance at planning his life (something that we all do when we mark a calendar or diary) along a linear time line (modern clock-time) means that he's attempting to separate past, present, and future along a flat, unified line of existence. For Heidegger, it's futile for us to behave this way towards temporality because we don't exist in such a way that can allow us to see all three—past, present, and future—at the *same time*, as separate and distinct blocks of time.

By planning or organizing our lives like this we're actually living inauthentically because we're passively longing for a future point of time. We can see in Walt's statement, "We've got nowhere to go but up," that he believes that his status in society and the future happiness of his family is secure. Flashbacks in *Breaking Bad* serve to remind us that Walt's past has had an influence on his present condition—he's still, after all, practicing chemistry and looking out for his family's well being—as well as on his possible futures. Heidegger would call this Walt's *futurity*, his *Dasein* directed towards the future that always contains the past—his *has-been*.

This has-been of Walt's past (his passion for chemistry while at Sandia labs, his love for his family, and his desire for happiness) doesn't just disappear once he learns of the cancer that has resulted in his life taking a drastic new direction. While it would be impossible to argue that Walt's life hasn't changed because of these new circumstances, these flashbacks to his former life show us that the man he is now was always a *possibility* on the horizon of his existence.

Towards Our Own Annihilation

Everything that Walt was before he learned of his impending death, his former life, with its hopes and aspirations of not just a happy family life but also his desire for upward mobility (which is intimately tied up with this notion of the American Dream) is an element of the unified whole rather than a segment of what has passed. This idea of the whole is a very important aspect of Heidegger's ideas about temporality because he sees the past, present, and future as *one and the same*. In other words, the future shouldn't be viewed as being *later* than the past and the past *earlier* than the present (which is more in line with this modern, vulgar conception of time). For Heidegger, it is through this unified whole that temporality reveals itself as past-actualizing-future.

As with everything in Heidegger's philosophy, death is never far away, even when we make plans. When we plan for the future, as Walt does, we're always moving ever closer towards death because to make plans of this nature and project ourselves into a time that hasn't yet arrived is always a movement towards our own annihilation because death is, at some point in our lives, a certain, undeniable fact. Yet in our everyday plan-making Heidegger feels that we ignore the possibility of death and live our lives as if all the goals we make will be reached without its possible intrusion. If he were alive today he would no doubt balk at our attitudes towards our own mortality. Western culture remains in a state of abject denial as to the reality of death where, deep down, we refuse to accept that we're all going to die.

We live in a culture of widespread death anxiety, where we try to fend off the aging process with cosmetic surgery and even dream of being able to download our conscious minds into sophisticated computer hard drives. When Walt is told of his cancer, he's in a sense made aware of his own embodied existence as a finite being who, like all of us, is vulnerable to suffering and death. If disease does anything for us today, it's perhaps to remind us of the material nature of our bodies; that we are, when push comes to shove, the same decaying, organic matter as everything else. This is perhaps why we hear Walt say that, "There's got to be more to human being than that." He finds it difficult to accept that there may be nothing more to a human being than our flesh and blood make-up.

Calculative Thinking

But this death denial anxiety, denial, and repression are also apparent in Walt's calculative thinking before he learned of his cancer. For Heidegger, calculative thinking was a way of viewing the world that, in a strange way, took flight from thinking itself. It's a form of thinking so intent on achieving goals and getting results that it can never really stop to think about everything that is, to slow down and ponder the everyday. We can view it then as a form of thinking about the world that leads to *thoughtlessness*. Heidegger believes that it is the sciences of the modern technological age that have used this kind of thinking most because it serves specific purposes. While he sees it as beneficial to human needs in the technological world, he laments the fact it is narrow and limited when it comes to thinking and *being* in the world.

Remember that Walt is a scientist at heart. We can see for ourselves that Walt's calculative thinking, his planning ahead, didn't achieve the goals it had set out when he states, "We've got nowhere to go but up." Maybe this is the reason we're presented with a man in *Breaking Bad* who seems desperately unhappy even before he's told about his cancer. He's shown to be an ineffectual chemistry teacher and is humiliated when one of his students sees him moonlighting at a car wash for additional income. Calculative thinkers are only able to take into account the present circumstances, from which they then plan and set out to achieve goals in the future. Walt's initial disappointment comes from a belief that he hasn't achieved all that he set out to with his life. His expectations are dashed when things didn't work out as he'd planned.

Heidegger believes that there's a possible remedy to this very modern, rational way of thinking: meditative thinking. It's perhaps easier for us to view meditative thinking as the polar opposite of calculative thinking because for Heidegger, it means to take notice, to observe, pause, and focus on the moments that make up one's life, "to awaken an awareness of what is actually taking place around us and in us." Calculative thinking's main limitation seems to be a lack of awareness and a restlessness that comes about because of a narrow focus on the pursuit of goals and (what we believe) to be beneficial results. If meditative thinking has a goal, it's thinking itself, which Heidegger believed required patience, care, and determination. Rather than mock this kind of thinking for its lack of practicality and usefulness, Heidegger actively encouraged it because it can allow us to focus on the here and now.

Walt the Meditator?

Having learned of his cancer and his own impending death, Walt actually becomes more meditative in his own thinking by dwelling on what is closest and of most concern to him. In the Season Three episode, "Fly," both Jesse and Walt are working in Gus's hi-tech meth lab when Walt sees a fly towards the end of their cooking session, leading him to embark on an Ahab-like mission to kill it because he views it as a possible contaminant risk. Walt quickly becomes obsessed, resulting in a number of humorous, slapstick situations between Walt and Jesse as well as drug-induced revelations by Walt about his life, and perhaps most intriguingly of all, his death.

After Jesse spikes Walt's coffee with sleeping pills to try and calm him down, we see him open up to Jesse with a remarkable frankness and clarity. In a poignant monologue, Walt outlines the seeming lack of control that he has over his life (killing the fly would perhaps have been a minor symbolic victory for him, yet even this alludes him). He talks about how "it wasn't meant to be this way," how the perfect moment for him to die was months back, before Skyler became aware of his secret life.

What we can read into this is that Walt has realized that his calculative thinking has failed him. Behaving like the rational scientific man that he is, he always believed that the best result was to make enough money for his family and then to die without revealing to them the man he had to become in order to this. But now this is all tainted, particularly with Skyler, who learns in Season Three of his deception.

This realization brings him into the realm of Heidegger's meditative thinking. Walt's reflections on his life and all that he feels has gone wrong with it have now led him to become a more meditative being: he's now thinking about his existence in a manner that allows him to dwell upon that which is closest and of most concern to him. This (admittedly drug-induced!) moment of clarity with Jesse results in the kind of awakening and awareness that Heidegger believes meditative thinking enables. Walt's admission to Jesse about his own death and the moment it should have happened is startling because it's not something we would expect any human being to talk so openly about.

Yet, this is what Heidegger sees as meditative thinking's particular strength and why he openly encourages this as a way of thinking for all of us. It helps us to think outside the box of modern, rational, calculated thinking and look beyond that which we would see as being merely useful to us. By thinking about his own death, Walt has realized that he's a finite being who will one day die. And it's this meditation that pushes Walt closer to what Heidegger would call a more authentic way of living. By talking about the moment he should have died, we can also say Walt is acknowledging his own temporality—his 'thrownness' in time as a historically situated being—where each present moment is one of transition because it's *always already* fading into the past.

Reflections on The End

The real crux of Heidegger's *authentic-being-towards-death* is that we should live every moment as if it will be our last. When we think meditatively about these moments in our lives, as Walt does here (even though it's obviously tinged with regret), we begin to acknowledge their everyday significance because we realize just how fleeting they are. Calculative thinking reinforces an inauthentic being-towards-death because we ignore the possibility of death when we make plans and set goals for ourselves. It pushes the everyday aside and humans become, as Heidegger says, uprooted from reality, and ultimately, from themselves.

Martin Heidegger has a particular relevance in light of an American TV landscape that's awash with death and populated by characters who, like Walter White, must often come to terms with their own mortality. If Don DeLillo is correct to say that there's a tendency for all plots to inevitably hurtle towards death, then perhaps there's no better man for the job.[1]

---

[1] Dedicated to Robbie. . . . My heart now beats for two.

6

Macbeth on Ice

RAY BOSSERT

Things bad begun make strong themselves by ill.

Macbeth, Act 3, Scene 2

Shakespeare made a career out of breaking bad tales. *Hamlet*'s a play about a graduate student who goes on a homicidal rampage (Oh, what a falling off was there!). In *Othello*, a hopelessly romantic husband murders his innocent wife. In the *Henry IV* plays, Sir John Falstaff is a knight who robs carriages when he should be defending the kingdom. Falstaff declares that his accomplice has corrupted him, but his accomplice is Harry, the Prince of Wales. Obviously, the prince hasn't been behaving very princely.

Then there's Macbeth, the loyal, super-heroic warrior who goes berserk and slaughters his own king and people. Out of all of Shakespeare's bad boys, it's Macbeth who can most help us understand Walter White.

Seeing Is Not Believing

Shakespeare's examples of breaking bad provoke us because they feel unexpected. They're the stuff of tabloid journalism: "Prince of Wales Seen Drunk in Eastcheap—News at 11." Such a headline defines a person based on his social role and then tells us how that person violates our assumptions of his or her role.

When Shakespeare considered the effects of breaking audience expectations this way, he would most likely have had Aristotle's theory of tragedy in mind. Aristotle argues that tragedy describes poetic *universals* rather than historic *particulars*: art ought to convey how things *should* be rather than how they are. We believe in characters when they behave as we expect them to behave (or want them to behave); we doubt them when they behave otherwise.

On stage, teachers should be selfless; drug dealers should be selfish. More subtly, the *idea* of a teacher should always inspire self-sacrifice; the *idea* of a drug dealer should evoke exploitation. Of course, Aristotle knew that real people do not live up to expectations—*particular* teachers are self-serving; *particular* criminals might be generous—but he didn't think dramatists should talk about those particular teachers and criminals.

For Aristotle, the distinction between universal and particular helps an audience maintain suspension of disbelief—the ability to accept the fictional reality of what occurs on the stage while knowing that it is only a simulation, the ability to play make-believe. Aristotle would hate for an audience to think, "But the high school teachers I imagine would never do *that!*" (even if the audience knows of teachers who have).

This creates a problem for any author writing about historical figures (like Macbeth) or a character who defies stereotypes (like Walter White). If a playwright wants to describe a particular but an audience wants to see a universal, is there a way to do both? Can you make a particular seem like a universal? Can we believe that a loyal Scottish warrior who just saved the king's life would assassinate his king a moment later? Do we believe that a high school chemistry teacher can turn into an underworld drug supplier?

In the real world, I *know* that it apparently doesn't take much to make a Walter White. An Internet search on "teachers selling drugs" leads to enough cases across the USA to make one think there is some kind of epidemic. Yet, the idea of "teachers selling drugs" is still shocking to my sensibilities. I *know* it happens, but I don't *expect* it to happen. Just because it's plausible, that doesn't mean it's believable to stage. And it's not enough to say that people sometimes just "break bad." In drama, an audience demands some explanation beyond chance and tautology.

Aristotle hates stories that end with *deus ex machina*—random, supernatural, or completely unforeseeable events that change the plot. Outside of a Michael Bay movie, logic must prevail or the audience feels as though it has wasted its time. One way Shakespeare (and Vince Gilligan for that matter) attempts to satisfy this need is to convey a sense of what's inside the character, to expose the character's psychological development or—as the case may be—his psychological break-down. Among Shakespeare's "breaking bad" characters, Macbeth's internal mind—guilt-ridden, insecure in its mas-culinity, and thoroughly preoccupied with patriarchal duties—will most help us understand why we believe in Walter White as a character.

Spoilers Ahead

At the beginning of Shakespeare's Scottish play, a violent rebel-lion wreaks havoc in medieval Scotland. The battle looks grim for Scottish King, Duncan, until Macbeth, along with his friend Banquo, valiantly overthrows the rebel forces, defending the king and restoring peace. Macbeth FTW! As the two warriors leave the battlefield, however, they encounter a group of scruffy witches who foretell that Macbeth will become king and that Banquo's sons will succeed him. There's usually some spooky noises and special effects at this point, as the witches exit the stage.

When Macbeth later informs his wife about the prophecy, she convinces him to kill Duncan at the next opportunity and seize the throne for himself. Conveniently, the king invites him-self to Macbeth's castle for a sleepover only to be murdered in his bed. Macbeth frames the king's bodyguards and is promptly elected the new monarch. Breaking bad doesn't particularly suit Macbeth, however. Plagued with guilt, troubled with paranoia, Macbeth quickly descends into madness, which—in a king—translates into tyranny. Macbeth's goons murder his friend, Banquo (who later haunts him during a dinner party), but the henchmen fail to kill Banquo's son. Macbeth goes on to annoy the heck out of his people, and the people revolt against the new king. Lady Macbeth, in the meantime, falls into dementia, com-pulsively trying to wash away bloodstains no one else can see. Although Macbeth put down the revolt against his predecessor, he dies in battle at the hands of the rebel lord, Macduff.

So much for the plot, which Shakespeare mostly borrows from British chronicles. Shakespeare's original artistic contri-bution is more subtle: he must convince an audience that

Macbeth *would* do the things that Macbeth *did* do. Drama sim-ulates life and its actions, but with Shakespeare, it also simu-lates psychology and thought. Shakespeare's Macbeth is believable to us because Shakespeare creates a convincing illu-sion of Macbeth's mind.

It's What's Inside that Counts

Macbeth's betrayal and tyranny shock us because they seems to contradict everything that Macbeth appears to value: self-sacrifice, honor, loyalty, patriarchy, and masculinity. These all seem good enough values to hold in medieval Scotland where King Duncan describes Macbeth's ability to cut a man in half as making him a "gentleman," but they also end up being the things that turn Macbeth into a monster. When King Duncan promotes him, the honor and recognition of loyalty pleases Macbeth. But when Duncan's son is promoted over Macbeth despite Macbeth's superiority on the battlefield, it offends Macbeth's sense of loyalty and honor.

Later, Lady Macbeth speaks in sexualized language to turn Macbeth against the king. She suggests that a real man—a manly man—would take the witches' prophecy as an excuse to usurp the throne. A real husband will sacrifice everything for his family's future, even his reputation and his life. Here, she pits Macbeth's value of patriarchy against itself—he wants to respect the powerful male figure, but he also wants to be rec-ognized *as* the powerful male figure himself.

Shakespeare's Macbeth could have assassinated the king out of sheer greed, ambition, or villainy like an evil-musta-chioed villain from a Hanna-Barbera cartoon. Instead, Shakespeare's Macbeth has a sympathetic anxiety—he's still insecure in his manhood despite his muscular physique. He assassinates the king to prove his masculinity to himself. This doesn't excuse Macbeth's actions, but it does help us under-stand why he does it. We can more easily imagine a "good guy" becoming a "bad guy" if we focus on what it means to be a "guy."

As the play progresses, Macbeth devolves into a tyrant over the Scottish people because his old values come back to haunt him—literally, in the case of Banquo's ghost. Macbeth isn't sim-ply paranoid that one of his own people will do to him what he did to Duncan; Macbeth is deeply guilt-ridden and troubled by his deeds. His sense of honor stabs him in his heart.

Despite the fact that almost everyone suspects what Macbeth has done, his own inability to confess his crimes means that his turmoil is completely interiorized; but this kind of interiority makes him feel fearful and cowardly. The act which was supposed to prove his manliness turns him into a wimp, compelling him to behave even more viciously to his people in order to reassert his power over them. At first, Macbeth at least tries to keep up appearances; by the end, he doesn't care who knows what. Aristotle calls this "reversal"—an action that has the opposite of its intended consequence—and Macbeth buys his reversals in bulk lots.

Aristotle links reversals with the concept of *hamartia*, the tragic flaw. Tragic heroes need to do something wrong, make some mistake, to justify their tragic end. We need to feel pity for them, but we should not feel they are complete victims. The most commonly observed *hamartia* is *hubris*, or excessive pride. Pride depends on your view of yourself; it plays out in a character's interior. That's where the most exciting things happen on a Shakespearean stage. It's also where the most interesting struggles play out in Vince Gilligan's series, *Breaking Bad*. Gilligan's protagonist, Walter White, is so complex that he embodies not only the internal conflicts of Shakespeare's titular Macbeth, but those of Lady Macbeth and Macduff as well.

Walt as Macbeth

We only believe Walt's behavior if we believe his simulated psychology. Walt's initial values, though less military than Macbeth's, share similar patriarchal tendencies. Both men initially seek traditional male roles as self-sacrificing providers and protectors for their families. Walt verbally claims that he cooks crystal meth in order to spare his family from the expenses of his cancer treatments and to keep them financed after his seemingly inevitable death.

Although this is a plausible enough excuse, the script hints that other thoughts might motivate Walter. In our first encounter with him, a pantless Walter White leaves a potential suicide note on a camcorder. He tells his family, "No matter how it may look, I only had you in my heart." This is Walt, as he wants to be remembered. His use of the preposition "in" figuratively suggests that he is revealing his interior psychology.

Do we believe him? Is his family the *only* thing in his heart? How can we know? In *Hamlet*, the title character professes "I have that within which passeth show." Much Shakespearean drama relies precisely on this illusion of depth—a character telling us there is more going on inside them than we can see. It forces us to conjecture the secrets that move characters and to suspect them when they tell us their motivations.

Other characters also consider what is "in" Walter White. When the chemistry teacher recounts the story of how he courted his wife, his brother-in-law Hank tells Walter, Jr., "Didn't think your old man had it in him." It's a common expression, but what does Hank's pronoun "it" refer to? Hank's version of "it" embodies male libido, aggressiveness—the masculine traits of the barbaric Scottish warrior that led Walt to go out and get what he wanted—what Macbeth refers to as "ambition." No one looks at Walt and thinks that he carries ambitions or could achieve them.

When Walt gives the drug dealer, Krazy-8, the opportunity to beg for his life, Walt says "You keep telling me that I don't have it in me." This "it" is the heart of a cold-blooded killer—someone who can overcome scruples and fear to do something that they know is morally wrong. But Krazy-8's plea backfires. On the one hand, Krazy-8 means to say that Walt does not possess evil, badness, or cruelty in his soul. On the other hand, it might also suggest that he lacks courage. Krazy-8 inadvertently challenges Walt's masculinity.

The episode of Krazy-8's murder is framed by a flashback to a much younger Walt contemplating a chemical equation for the human body with the character, Gretchen. When the formula appears incomplete, Gretchen conjectures the missing percentage might be the soul—an expression of an interior life. Walt rejects Gretchen's theory, asserting with erotic confidence that "There's nothing but chemistry here." This masculinist, scientific materialism combines with machismo to show a Walt far different from the bumbling, nervous, and effeminized male that began the series. This is a Macbethian man who has been buried within Walter White, impossible to perceive except in his own internal memory.

So, what's inside Walt is not merely love for his family. What's inside him is a deep, troubled insecurity about his own lost masculinity. The entire first episode runs Walt through a gauntlet of effeminizing experiences. He is forced to wash the luxury sports car of the student who disrespects him in class. When Hank shows off his gun at Walter's fiftieth birthday party, Walt becomes skittish, handling the gun weakly. Hank responds by saying "That's why they hire men." Walt's guests ignore him at his own party to watch a television news segment on Hank's heroic drug bust. Walt's left alone with his thoughts, apart from the guests, feeling inferior to his brazen, boarish, hypermasculinized relative.

After the party, he experiences a bout of erectile dysfunction when his wife, Skyler, lamely offers him manual pleasure while she simultaneously checks eBay on a laptop. His wife's disinterest in him sexually, as well as the failure of his male genitalia, make Walt even more insecure. After Walt's first crime, however, Walt aggressively initiates sex with his wife: he perceives himself as the patriarchal male again.

Wimpy Walter White and Aristotle's "Reversal"

Crime restores Walt's sense of masculinity, and therefore restores his interior sense of pride—the *hubris* that often leads to *hamartia*. During Skyler's intervention sequence in Season One, Hank interprets Walt's dilemma in just such terms. Walt's wife has asked the family to take turns expressing their frustrations over Walt's refusal to undergo treatment. When Hank reluctantly holds the "talking pillow," he tells Walt: "You got your pride, man, I get it."

Referring to Walt as a generic masculine noun, "man," Hank links the masculine identity with hubris. Of course, Hank's line is ironic; he might understand "male pride," but he doesn't "get" Walt, at least not as completely as he thinks at this point. Still, Hank's interpretation threatens Walter; Walter likes to think he's superior to Hank's barbarian worldview, but perhaps he isn't.

If Walt's dramatic conflict were merely material—honoring financial obligations to his upper middle-class family—then Walt could resolve his conflict in a number of less criminal ways. Most notably, Walt's wealthy, successful friend from graduate school, Elliot Schwartz, offers to hire Walt with full medical coverage or even just to pay Walt's bills outright. But Walt refuses the assistance. Likewise, Walt rejects a suggestion to ask his mother for financial help. An audience can easily conclude that Walt's rejection of help stems from a masculine desire for financial independence and self-sufficiency. Indeed, much of Walter's reluctance to pursue treatment arises from resentment towards his wife's dominance and assertiveness: she researches the options for him, calls the doctors for him, and infantilizes her husband.

But if saving face and dignity motivate Walter White, then the putrid, vile, blood-dripping world he chooses to slink off to seems self-defeating. Does having to sponge up the partially-dissolved remains of a meth cook from a drug dealer's floor really enhance a masculine sense of pride? Is exploiting addicts who are slowly poisoning themselves with meth really that much more noble than taking charity from friends? Besides, as Gretchen points out, Walt tells his family that he *is* taking the charity. His actions contradict his stated motives. Walt's continued dilemma, like that of Macbeth, means that the very acts that make Walt feel more masculine simultaneously make him more shameful. His shame, however, feeds his insecurity, thus leading him to repeat the cycle of crime. His choices more often than not prove counter-productive: he experiences a series of reversals.

Walt is self-conscious of these tragic reversals, particularly in terms of his family's safety. When he writes his ludicrous pro-con assessment on murdering Krazy-8, his sole "pro" reason to kill the drug dealer is to protect his wife and children from harm. After witnessing the kingpin Tuco murder a gang member, Walt suspects that Tuco will come for his own family. Walt spends a night watching by the window with a knife in anticipation of Tuco's attack. He also steals Pinkman's revolver expecting a showdown, after having explained to Pinkman that a single revolver will not be adequate to take out Tuco and his minions. While Walt's behavior certainly can be compared to Macbeth's paranoia and sleepless nights, Walt temporarily surrenders his role as a Macbeth analogue to the psychopathically violent Tuco. Walt, at this point, is more the victim of a blood-thirsty tyrant than the tyrant himself. In this regard, Walt might be likened more to another character in *Macbeth*: the rebel Macduff.

Walt as Macduff

Shakespeare's Macduff leaves a psychological riddle for Shakespearean scholars. Knowing that the king has been killing lords left and right, Macduff abandons home to seek other potential rebels. In Shakespeare's version, though, he leaves his wife and son behind. Macbeth's thugs brutally murder the woman and boy, and the murders eventually enflame Macduff to destroy Macbeth once and for all. The puzzle is figuring out why Macduff doesn't just bring his family with him. Macduff's wife and son have similar questions, and both speak shamefully of Macduff's flight. They react similarly to the frustrated Skyler and Walter, Jr. when Walt starts disappearing for whole days.

On the one hand, audiences sympathize with Macduff's losses; his suffering makes him an underdog to the tyrant. On the other hand, some shrewd theatergoers tend to wonder if maybe Macduff wasn't quite as invested in his family's safety as he could have been. Does Macduff set his family up to die? Might he sacrifice them for political capital, to make him look more victimized and appear the better leader? Might he masochistically want to suffer their loss so that he can fight with greater ferocity and abandon?

It's the kind of unsolvable question that teachers put on midterms, but Walter's choices beg similar questions. Does he really think he can save his family with a kitchen knife? While Walt's pathetic strategy might simply result from irrational panic, one wonders if his feeble preparations are self-handicapping. In the fourth season, Skyler and Pinkman plea with Walt to turn himself in and join a witness protection program. He refuses. He'll protect his family from danger but not at the cost of his revealing his secret.

Despite his claims to have had nothing but his family in his heart, might Walt, in some recess of his interior mind, desire his family's destruction? If Tuco's goons had shown up at the house, he might be able to die looking like a hero defending his family, not like a petty crook who brought his loved ones pain. This would let him keep up appearances of the self-sacrificing teacher and father. Or does such a self-sacrifice actually become a form of spiting those for whom he sacrifices? Either way, the henchmen might have killed everyone at home.

After Walt stages his own temporary insanity by appearing naked at a minimart, he's sent to psychotherapy. Here, he engages in a double bluff with the psychiatrist. Walt confesses that he staged his madness, but lies about the cause. Superficially, Walt is concocting an alibi to cover for his time as Tuco's hostage. His lie is that he ran away from his family out of resentment towards them. But everything Walt claims to resent—his over-qualification for his job, his family's interference, his friends' success—are all things we have seen him resent previously. He also expresses a suicidal resentment towards his family during the "talking pillow" intervention scene, passive-aggressively complaining that he feels as though he has been offered no choices in life (not even marriage to his wife?). Again, he's lying to conceal his secret, but by crafting the lie this way, Walt attempts to deceive himself. If resenting his family is part of the lie, then does this mean (to him, at least) that the resentment isn't real? Walt suppresses the part of himself that disdains his loved ones. He sacrifices for his family to prove to himself that he loves them, but his sacrifices also harm his family, satiating a subconscious resentment towards them because they limit him. He's desperate to prove his love because on some level he doubts it.

Lady Macbeth in *Breaking Bad*

Although Macbeth and Macduff are mortal enemies, their most tragic and perhaps relatable moments overlap when each learns that his wife has died. Lady Macbeth is a critical element of Macbeth's self-identity. She enables him to define himself in patriarchal roles—as husband, lover, and chivalric warrior. Thus, he justifies much of his action as done for her sake. At her death, Macbeth launches into a speech of existential crisis.

Walt, who similarly justifies his actions as being for the sake of his wife and household, finds that his actions have driven them apart. This tragic reversal manifests in Season Three, when his wife separates from him. Without his family, Walt loses his most sympathetic motivation for breaking bad.

Skyler functions as a humanizing agent for Walt, and she even briefly tries to become his accomplice after she offers to launder money for him. Still, she hardly fulfills the more complex functions of Lady Macbeth. It's actually Jesse Pinkman who mostly serves the same dramatic role of Macbeth's consort. Both Pinkman and Lady Macbeth spur on the protagonists (Macbeth actually calls Lady Macbeth his "spur"), providing the resources, inspiration, and sometimes simply the additional manpower needed to conduct crime. Like Lady Macbeth, Pinkman's role as accomplice also binds him to the protagonist: through the beginning of their stories, they're the only characters that share the protagonist's secret as well as guilt. Furthermore, both characters reflect glimmers of the protagonist's remaining morality during otherwise dark moments.

Macbeth's interactions with his co-conspirator express concern for her, and Walt displays protectiveness towards Pinkman, whom he calls his "partner" (a term he also uses for his wife). When Tuco severely beats Pinkman, Walt forces Tuco to pay restitution. Walt later intercedes for Pinkman when they are Tuco's hostages. Walt yet again intervenes for Pinkman when they run afoul of the kingpin Gus and when he interrupts Pinkman's attempt at revenge against Gus's child-abusing drug dealers. Walt "needs him" professionally and emotionally. When Walt adopts the Heisenberg persona, he becomes a tough, confident, aggressive male. However, Pinkman's vulnerability draws a lingering humanity out of Heisenberg, proving Walt retains the capacity to be a "good guy" even when he appears to be bad.

And yet, Walter also serves as Pinkman's own Lady Macbeth. Part of the series' complexity is that Walter is not easily pigeonholed. He's practically a one-man show of *Macbeth*. Walt drives Pinkman into going deeper into the underworld, challenging his masculinity like Lady Macbeth. It's a perversion of Walt's teacherly values to improve his student. When one of Pinkman's henchmen is mugged, Walter bullies Pinkman into retaliation. Even the freedom that Walter envies in Pinkman resonates with Lady Macbeth, who fantasizes about being a man.

In Season Two, when Pinkman begins to assert himself and claim the role of kingpin, Walter submits to his subordinate role as "cook." Walter is now the woman in the kitchen, while Pinkman goes out to make the money. This echoes Walter's role-reversal at home, as his wife begins literally to leave him in the kitchen when she goes out. Although Skyler intends to give Walter a taste of his own medicine, he instead feels the effeminized victim again. Walt had seemed to break bad to become more of a man, but then accepts a submissive role in both of his worlds. In Season Four, Walter guilt-trips Jesse into plotting against Gus's life. Walter even tries to play Lady Macbeth to Gus's hitman, Mike, attempting to convince Mike to help assassinate their boss. Mike gives Walt a black eye instead. The hitman has, apparently, seen *Macbeth*.

Walter White's plans consistently fail. For a while, Walter is King Duncan, betrayed by Jesse at the instigation of his blackmailing, heroin-addict girlfriend (Pinkman, it seems, has several Lady Macbeths in his life). For a while, he is Banquo, hunted by Gus's henchmen (although Walt is quick to flip the role onto rival chemist Gale). For a while, Walter has been almost every character in *Macbeth*, even a bearded witch stirring exotic ingredients in a cauldron.

Breaking Worst—Evil for Its Own Sake

At the end of *Macbeth*, the rebel Macduff gives the tyrant one last opportunity to surrender. Macbeth could submit, perhaps even redeem himself a bit. He could apologize for the horrors he has done and acknowledge his shame, but, instead, he decides to die fighting. Would it be more "manly" to willingly offer restitution, or is it more "manly" to fight even when you are doomed (and wrong)?

And what does Macbeth fight for in the end? His kingdom lost, his wife dead, and his reputation ruined—Macbeth has nothing. Macduff will carry his decapitated head around a stage. Not much dignity there. Macbeth becomes so accustomed to evil that it is a natural default. He no longer seeks excuses or cost-benefit analysis. He no longer even derives pleasure from evil. Macbeth chooses evil for the sake of evil. We accept this at the end because Shakespeare gave us a series of believable psychological conflicts and then stripped them away.

Unlike *Macbeth*'s witches, I can't predict how things will end for Walter White, nor can I predict how his motivations might change. If Walt's story is a tragedy, then Aristotle would predict his final reversal will come from a *recognition*—a discovery of knowledge, usually about himself. Perhaps Walter White will acknowledge what else is in him. Perhaps he will realize that what he thought was there is gone or was never was there at all.

We've witnessed various plausible alternatives as to what "it" is that he has "in" him—his family, his former life, his lust, his pride. But as Walt loses each of his external connections, his motives seem weaker and weaker. Like Macbeth, he stops taking pleasure from the forbidden fruit. Motivations slip away. What moves Walt tantalizes us as it becomes more depraved and less comprehensible. "Didn't think your old man had it in him" takes on new meaning. Watching Macbeth and Walter White do as they please, part of us wants what they have inside them and part of us fears we already do.

Walter White does have something evil inside of him: lung cancer. Cancer is both plot device and metaphor. It nudges him towards a life of crime, to seize his fate and remaining days, but it also signifies the corruption of his soul. Lung cancer resides in the interior: it shows no sign except when something horrible comes out—a cough, a wheeze, a drop of blood in sputum. But Walt embraces cancer rather than rejecting it; self-sacrifice blurs with self-destruction. Fatal disease makes him, in his words, "awake"—it gives him a plausible motive, a mask under which he can act on illicit desires.

That mask becomes almost literal in the black-hat-wearing Heisenberg. When Walter White adopts his pseudonym, we no longer see him as just a teacher who turns criminal. We see him as competing identities within one mind, as Macbeth *and* Lady Macbeth *and* Macduff *and* Duncan *and* Banquo *and* witch. We believe in him because, in our own thoughts, we, too, resent being limited to a single role on life's stage. We pity Walter White, and we fear that we might make similar mistakes because we're like him. This is what Aristotle calls *catharsis*, pity and fear for the protagonist, and it's the very purpose of tragedy.

7

Walter White's Will to Power

MEGAN WRIGHT

From the first scene of the first episode of *Breaking Bad*, I was hooked. I think what I liked about it was that this guy, Walter White, was prepared to have a showdown with the police in his underwear. That takes some kind of courage, or stupidity.

But then the scene cuts to three weeks earlier and this same man is nothing like the man who is so confident and prepared to die at the beginning of the episode. Why did Walt change?

Walt's Unsuccessful Will to Power

One reason why Walt is able to change is by using his *will to power*, which the philosopher Friedrich Nietzsche says is imposing your will over another living being. At first Walt isn't using his will to power effectively. In the scene of the pilot episode where Walt is lecturing on science and how exciting it is, one of his students (Chad) is disrupting class by flirting with a beautiful young woman in the back of the classroom. At first, Walt's the only person who notices they aren't paying attention, and he tries to ignore them. When their talking becomes so loud that everyone in the class turns to look at them Walt finally says something. He interrupts them by saying "Chad, is there something wrong with your table?" Feeling that he's regained control of his classroom, Walt begins to resume his lecture. However, as Chad begins to move back to his seat, he doesn't go silently; he drags his chair back to his table. The chair makes a loud screeching noise that's even more disruptive than Chad's flirting was. In fact, Walt doesn't even try to talk over it.

Once Chad is back to his regular assigned seat, he sits down and looks smugly at Walt. "Are you done?" says Walt. Though we know he's angry, he sounds quiet, almost like he's caving in to Chad. This seems to be reinforced by Chad nodding at Walt like the student is the teacher giving permission to continue with his lecture. Because of this, it appears to all of the students in the classroom (and to everyone watching the show at home) that Walt has allowed Chad to dominate him, or *out will* him, as Nietzsche might have said.

Working at the Car Wash

Unfortunately, there are several other times in the show where Walt doesn't use his will to power. A case in point is in the pilot episode when Walt shows his inability to use his will to power effectively when he's at his second job as a cashier at the car wash. Even before we see him at work, we hear Walt and his wife, Skyler, discussing his job. Skyler says, "I don't want him"—meaning Walt's boss—"dicking you around tonight. You get paid till five. You work till five. No later." Even before we see Walt working at the car wash, this tells us that Walt's boss must take regular advantage of Walt's weak will to power by either intimidating or guilting him into working after hours for free. Later, when we see Walt at his second job, we get to see how his boss, Bogdan, manipulates Walt.

Later in the show, when we see Walt at his second job, Bogdan is in the background talking on the phone. We can't hear what he is saying but it's clear he was yelling at someone. Eventually he ends the call, comes to the register, and approaches Walt. "He's not coming," says Bogdan. "He says he quits. I'm gonna run the register." Right away we can see Bogdan is very blunt with Walt. In fact, he sounds quite rude, but Walt, who is probably recalling what Skyler said earlier at breakfast, tries to fight Bogdan's strong will by saying, "Bogdan, no. We talked about this." Unfortunately Walt's reply comes out quietly—especially compared to Bogdan who is louder and more direct about what he wants. Still, Bogdan changes his strategy and casts himself as the helpless and desperate boss when he tells Walt, "I'm short-handed Walt. What am I to do? Walt?" Bogdan taps the cordless phone twice as if he is trying to tell Walt to "Hurry up and wash the cars!" without using words. His strategy works, and as Walt abruptly turns and begins to walk out of the camera frame, Bogdan calls after Walt saying, "What am I to do?"

Bacon and Birthdays

Poor Walt. Even when he's at home, Walt can't use his will. We first see this towards the beginning of the pilot episode when the White family is sitting at the breakfast table. Skyler brings him a plate of scrambled eggs and strange-looking bacon. When Walt sees the bacon and says, "Look at that," Skyler replies, "That is veggie bacon. Believe it or not. Zero cholesterol. And you won't even taste the difference." He grunts and then cautiously sniffs the bacon. A few moments later, when Skyler is distracted by their son's (Walt Jr.) arrival at the breakfast table, we see Walt take a bite of the bacon, make a face, and gently put the veggie bacon back on his plate. Though it's clear that Walt doesn't like the bacon, he continues to eat it. When Walt Jr. sees the bacon he asks, "What the hell is this?" Walt replies, "It's veggie bacon. We're watching our cholesterol. I guess." Walt Jr. says, "Whew! This smells like Band-Aids." Skyler says, "That's too bad. Eat it." Walt Jr. turns to his father and the two exchange some banter before Walt ends the scene by saying, "Eat your veggie bacon." Despite the fact that we see Walt and his son clearly don't like the veggie bacon, Walt encourages his son to eat it to please Skyler.

The next time we see Walt at home is after his day at the car wash with Bogdan. Unbeknownst to Walt, Skyler has decided to throw him a surprise birthday party. Unfortunately, Walt doesn't even have a good time at his own birthday party. Throughout the whole thing Walt looks like he's uncomfortable, and his brother-in-law Hank (a DEA agent) seems to be the source of his anxiety. It begins when Hank lets Walt Jr. hold his gun, a police-issued Glock .22. Walt is visibly unhappy with the situation, but his son is thrilled, "This is awesome," he says. "Dad, come check this out." Walt says, "Yeah, I see it," but doesn't make a move to take the gun. "*Come on*. Take it!" says Walt Jr. Finally Walt takes and handles the gun awkwardly while commenting about how heavy the gun is. Hank taunts Walt by saying, "That's why they hire men." Everyone laughs at this comment. Hank sees his brother-in-law is still very nervous holding the Glock .22 and says, "Geez, it's not gonna bite you. He looks like Keith Richards with a glass of warm milk." Again, Hank's jokes make everyone (with the exception of Walt) laugh.

Hank continues making fun of his brother-in-law, saying, "Walt, you gotta brain the size of Wisconsin. But we're not gonna hold that against you." This creates more laughter. Hank continues on a more serious note, "But your heart's in the right place, man. Your heart's in the right place. We love you man. We love you." It appears that Hank has decided to give Walt a break, until we see him take Walt's drink from his hand and says, "To Walt!" So while everyone else toasts Walt and takes a drink, Walt awkwardly waves the gun. We see that, so far, Hank has no reservations about using his will to power to make himself the center of attention while at the same time making Walt look like a lesser man at his own birthday party.

At this point it seems like Hank can't push his will any further, but then Hank says suddenly, "Hey! Turn on Channel Three!" In the next scene, we see everyone at the party is gathered around the television watching Hank being interviewed by the local news station about a major meth lab bust. The only person who isn't glued to the screen is Walt, who's standing towards the back of the living room drinking and staring at the carpet. Hank has used his will to power to make himself the ultimate center of attention, and Walt's only sign of protest is his refusal to join the group.

Yet, Walt eventually submits to Hank's will by joining everyone else at the television. Walt asks his brother-in-law, "Hank, how much money is that?" Hank replies, "Ah, that's about seven hundred grand. Pretty good haul." Walt is impressed and says, "Wow. That's unusual isn't it? That kind of cash?" Hank says, "Hm, that's not the most we ever took. It's easy money—till we catch ya. Walt, just say the word and I'll take you on a ride-along. Watch us knock down a meth lab. Get a little excitement in your life!"

Walt Is Superman?

So far we've seen that Walt has a weak will. He lets everybody tell him what to do—Bogdan, Skyler, Hank, and his students. The question is how does Walt transform from the soft-spoken high-school chemistry teacher into the pantless man at the beginning of the show who's prepared to have a shootout with the police? Well, if we look at another idea of Nietzsche's, we might be to explain this. Among his many writings, Nietzsche talks about something he calls the *Übermensch*, or Overman or Superman. We'll use 'Superman' here.

Nietzsche's not talking about an alien who's sent to Earth and runs around in spandex trying to save people. The only difference between normal humans, like you and me, and Nietzsche's Superman is in the mind. Nietzsche believed that the Superman will be a step above other men because the Superman will create his own morality apart from mankind. Now let's be clear: Nietzsche, for all his complaints about modern morality, doesn't want to do away with morality; he simply wants to redefine it. And this is what Nietzsche believes the Superman will do: the Superman will define his own morality apart from man's and, thus, be superior to man—hence why Nietzsche labels this creation the "Superman" because he's above other men.

What does all of this have to do with Walt White? Well, let's look at the next scene in the pilot episode. Sometime after the birthday party, we see Walt working at the car wash. It appears Bogdan has taken Walt off the cash register again. As Walt is moving a barrel of chemicals around on a dolly, he stops and begins to have a coughing fit. Instead of his coughing subsiding, Walt passes out. Shortly after this scene, Walt is told that he has inoperable lung cancer and has, at most, only a few more years to live. This news of his impending death begins to transform Walt in some way.

We see the first step of this transformation when Walt is at the car wash. This is also the first time we see Walt's successful exertion of his will to power. The scene begins with Walt looking very distracted. Then Bogdan appears and demands that Walt wipe down cars like he did earlier in the episode. "Walt!" says Bogdan. "Come on, man. I'm short-handed. I need you outside to do some wipe-downs. Come on!" Walt, sounding far away, responds "What?" Impatiently, Bogdan says, "I said, 'I need you outside to do some wipe-downs!' Are you here to work or to be staring at the skies! Come on, let's go. Come on, man."

Unlike the last time Bogdan took Walt off the register, Walt doesn't meekly accept his boss' order. Instead, Walt says, "Fuck you, Bogdan," and turns away to leave. Bogdan is stunned by

Walt's reaction, "What?" he asks. Walt turns around. "I said, 'Fuck you!' And your eyebrows!" he exclaims. Then Walt violently slaps the car accessories dangling from the wall opposite the cash register, sending them flying through the air onto the floor. "Wipe down this" Walt yells as he grabs his crotch

The next time we see Walt, it's early in the morning, and he's very calm. He sits beside his pool, lighting a match. He stares at the flame for a moment before throwing it into the water. We see there are many other matches in the pool, which means he has been doing this for a while, maybe for hours. The matches are symbolic of Walt's life. They burn brightly but are extinguished before they are done burning, just like Walt. He should have at lest twenty or thirty more years to live, but the cancer will end his life sooner than expected—like the water ends the burning matches. It's in this scene that Walt makes a critical decision and exercises his will to power again by calling Hank and taking him up on his offer to do the ride along so he can learn about the meth business.

Now, let's stop and think about how this relates back to the Superman. Remember, Nietzsche believes that the Superman will create his or her own morality. This is exactly what Walt does. After all, meth is illegal and society says it's immoral to make, sell, or use meth. However, Walt knows that he will die soon, and his family will be left will a pile of bills to pay. He knows that meth is a lucrative business, but it is illegal.

In his mind, Walt weighs the choices: to make meth and thus make enough money so his family will be taken care of after he dies, or obey the law and die leaving his family heavily in debt. Walt creates his own morality by deciding that making meth, even though it's illegal, is the right thing to do. His family is ultimately more important than obeying a rule created by society. This realization is the beginning of Walt's transformation from "mild mannered" Walt White into Nietzsche's Superman.

This epiphany I have described is best summed up in a conversation he has with Jesse Pinkman in the pilot episode. This dialogue takes place after Walt gives Jesse the money to buy a trailer that they can cook meth in. Jesse says, "Tell me why you're doing this. Seriously." Walt replies by asking, "Why do you do it?" Jesse says, "Money, mainly." Walt says, "There you go." Jesse is not convinced and says, "Nah. Come on man. Some straight like you, giant stick up his ass all of a sudden at age, what, sixty, he's just gonna break bad?" Walt says, "Fifty." Jesse says, "It's weird, is all. Okay, it doesn't compute. If you've gone crazy, or something. If you've gone crazy or depressed—I'm just sayin' that—that's something I need to know about, okay. That affects me!"

Walt sums up his revelation, saying, "I am awake." This only confuses Jesse further, but for Walt and the audience, these three words tell us his acceptance that certain societal moralities like "Drugs are bad" can be cast aside. Walt realizes this and so he creates the new morality of, "Drugs are not bad because selling them will enable my family to be financially secure after I die." This creates a chain of events that unfold in the rest of the *Breaking Bad* series.

Walt Asserts His Will to Power

After Walt's call to Hank in the pilot episode, there are numerous examples of Walt successfully exercising his will to power: Walt not telling Hank that Emilio's partner got away, Walt telling Jesse how they will cook meth even though Jesse protests, and Walt beating up the man making fun of his son at the clothing store.

Another example of this is in the scene where Walt confronts Jesse after the meth lab bust from which Jesse escapes. Walt looks up Jesse address in the school computer and goes to his house to confront him. At first, Jesse believes that Walt has come to preach to him about turning himself in to the police. He says, "Look, I don't know what you're doing here Mr. White, but if you're plannin' on giving me some bull-winder about getting right with Jesus or turnin' myself in—" Walt interrupts, "Not really." Jesse continues, "High school was a long time ago, 'kay. And you ain't *Welcome Back Kotter* so step off. No speeches."

Walt says, "Short speech. You lost your partner today. What's his name? Emilio? Emilio is going to prison. The DEA took all your money, your lab. You got nothin'. Square one. But you know the business, and I know the chemistry. I'm thinking, maybe you and I could partner up." Jesse laughs, shakes his head and says, "You, ah, you wanna cook crystal meth. You— you an' me." Walt says, "That's right." Jesse laughs "Wow."

Walt, realizing he isn't being taken seriously, says, "Either that, or I turn you in." The next scenes in which Walt appears, we see him stealing chemistry equipment from the school where he works. Then he arrives at Jesse's house with the equipment, the two begin to plot their next steps. Thus we see that Walt has successfully used his will to power to get Jesse to become his partner—even though Jesse isn't too terribly happy about being blackmailed into this.

And so, Walt and Jesse begin to cook together, and they discover Walt has a talent for cooking meth. Jesse even calls Walt's meth 'art'. Things appear to be going well until the end of the episode, when we see the ultimate exertion of Walt's will to power. It begins when Jesse is forced by two drug dealers, Emilio (who believes Jesse snitched on him) and Krazy-8 (Emilio's cousin and bad-ass drug dealer), to go to the site where Walt and Jesse have planned to cook meth for the day. Emilio recognizes Walt from when he was arrested and tells his cousin that he's with the DEA. Believing that Jesse has snitched on them, the cousins are about to murder Walt and Jesse until Walt offers to show the two men how to cook like him. Krazy-8 agrees since he's very impressed with the quality of meth Walt has made.

While he's cooking, we see Walt pause for a split-second, as if he's debating. Krazy-8 tells him to hurry up and Emilio caresses Walt's cheek with the tip of his gun. Walt dumps a canister of red phosphorus into the mixture he is making. The combination of chemicals causes an explosion. While Emilio and Krazy-8 are stunned, Walt runs from the trailer and locks the door behind him. The pair attempt to escape, but Walt holds the door closed even when they shoot at the door. Walt grabs Jesse and flees. This is where the show picks up from where it left off at the beginning, and we discover that the sirens we heard are fire engines, not police cars. Jesse (who was beaten unconscious by the two men earlier) wakes up and asks Walt what he did to Emilio and Kazy-8, and Walt replies, "Red phosphorous in the presence of moisture and accelerated by heat yields pho . . . sphine gas. One good whiff and poof." Immediately after saying this, Walt vomits. And so, Walt has committed the ultimate expression of his will to power: The killing of two men. Well, technically Krazy-8 isn't dead yet, but that's another episode.

Superman, a Superfan

The episode ends with Walt coming home. As he slips into bed, his wife tells him that she's upset he disappeared and won't talk to her. In response, Walt has sex with her. This is so unexpected and out of character that Skyler says, "Walt? Walt is that you?"

What I've said about the will to power and the Superman can be seen in later *Breaking Bad* episodes. If you re-watch the series from the beginning until the last season, you can see just how much Walt has evolved. I think Nietzsche would have been proud—or at least a fan of the show.

8

Better than Human

STEPHEN GLASS

At the center of the two TV shows, *Breaking Bad* and *Mad Men*, are two fascinating guys, Walter White and Don Draper. Both are trapped between two identities, and can't figure out which they prefer.

Is Walt a spineless chemistry teacher, or a ruthless drug lord? Is Don a suave advertising exec, or a motherless man-child? Which identity should these men embrace, and why do their identity crises make them so watchable?

Both Walter White and Don Draper struggle to free themselves from the rules of society so that they can make something more of themselves. The philosopher Friedrich Nietzsche foretold the coming of a superior being, the Overman, who will live according to his own rules, not the rules of the common herd. Walt and Don each have impulses to become Overmen.

Most people are weak creatures, happy with easy comforts, who conform to the status quo they're born into. They see the Overman as evil, because his new values contradict theirs. His good is their evil, and they can't understand that the world is apparent—it's all a matter of personal perspective, and we should accept all that's good and bad equally. Being able to do this is the root of happiness. It's a steep hill to climb, but Walt and Don are struggling up it.

Last Man Standing

The opposite of Nietzsche's Overman is the Last Man. Don and Walt certainly don't qualify as Last Men. Last Men are unheroic, pitiable and actually detrimental to humanity. They avoid exertion, are unable to dream, don't consider the meaning of their existence, merely earn a living and keep warm, and are proud of this nihilistic mindset.

Roger Sterling in *Mad Men* fits this model quite snugly. His life is all cheap jokes and expensive drinks, and thankfully he's being left behind by younger generations, led by Peggy and Pete—think of the cut from Peggy smoking marijuana to Roger singing in blackface ("My Old Kentucky Home"), or Roger's racism towards the Japanese ("The Chrysanthemum and the Sword"). Roger is self-absorbed, hedonistic, and has no goal besides staying wealthy, and his is a dying breed.

In opposition, Don Draper wants to work—he wants to build something of his own. Work is his passion and main priority, but his weakness for what society tells him is good—a beautiful wife, a big house with a white picket fence—holds him back. Not to mention his indulgence in poison like a Last Man, namely, drinking and smoking heavily to deal with his anxiety. Ironically, this only worsens his issues, but he can't stay on the wagon. When he has a drunken vision of dead friend Anna, he's devastated and quits drinking ("The Summer Man"). But he can't stay sober, life becomes dull, so he relapses into drinking.

Walt is definitely no Last Man. Immediately after being diagnosed with lung cancer he embraces his mortality and breaks the law, desperately cooking crystal meth with ex-student Jesse. Even when, after a botched deal with rival producers, he thinks he's caught, he videotapes a goodbye to his family and denies to any law enforcement that he's admitting guilt. He's chosen to break the law because it's now necessary to protect his family. For the first time in his life, Walt is exercising his own will.

It's a long time before he really enjoys his work, though. Mostly he's under constant stress to preserve his life and freedom. Three episodes into Season One ("And the Bag's in the River"), the stress is the reason for his second murder—a grueling asphyxiation of Krazy-8—and the camera lingers on his tearful, apologetic face. We see his similar despair when he allows Jane to choke to death on her own vomit, his hand over his mouth in disbelief of himself ("Phoenix"); and in the Season Three episode, "Fly," when he considers when it would've been best for him to die. He isn't wishing for death, however. He learns to "let it go,"—"it" being the past he harbors guilt over. An Overman has to accept that all that's happened, good and bad, was a consequence of their will. Only then can they truly move forward.

The reason Walt can choose to move on is because unlike Don, who hurts himself with booze and cigarettes, Walt's poison (his cancer) was forced on him. Peculiarly, it helps him to transform and realize that he has the power and will to choose for himself.

Jesse is more *Breaking Bad*'s Last Man. Seasons One to Three highlight his laziness in life and work, a lifestyle which indirectly causes Jane's death, as her influence on him conflicts with Walt's. Jesse's love of Jane is symbolic of his laziness, and the clearest image of this is Walt's frantically shaking Jesse from a heroin-induced stupor, a perfect example of their active-passive dynamic. Jane's death doesn't change Jesse as Walt would've liked, but it does make Jesse realize self-loathing (unlike a Last Man), as he blames himself. He worsens in Season Four, hiding in his house, surrounding himself with strangers and using drugs again. Only through Walt and Gus's manipulation of his perspective does he gain a sense of purpose and will to work so as to care for Andrea and Brock.

So neither of our lead characters are Last Men, but how far are they true creators, real Nietzschean Overmen?

Walt's Will to Become an Overman

We're introduced to Walt speeding through the New Mexico desert, corpses sliding around his RV, readying to shoot at police. What could possible lead to this?

After the title in the pilot episode of *Breaking Bad*, the first person we see is Skyler, who's sleeping peacefully while Walt lies awake. He exercises weakly on a stair-stepper, staring down at it from his Contributor to Research Nobel Prize certificate. Come morning, Skyler feeds him veggie bacon and he parrot-talks her advice ("We're watching our cholesterol, apparently"). Walt isn't living. He's barely surviving and he knows it. He's weak and submissive to his loving but overbearing wife.

Upon his diagnosis and fearing for his family's finances, Walt "wakes up" and recognizes that his life is transient, and only his fear and weakness has kept him from achieving his potential. This is the first step to becoming an Overman, and the first shift in perspective—one that says *no* to the accepted values of the status quo. Walt does so by breaking the law in order to make money for his family, and it's this central conceit of the show which attracts our viewership first and foremost: we ask ourselves the question, is it right to disrespect and hurt others in order to safeguard what I love?

Walt has had the urge to reject the status quo since before his cancer diagnosis, suggesting that we always have the will to become Overmen. In the pilot episode, when he sees a video of Hank's meth lab bust at his birthday party, Walt immediately asks about the money made rather than the illegal drugs themselves. Think also of the flashback in the Season Three episode, "Full Measure," when Walt tells Skyler he wants to aim higher than a mediocre house: "why be cautious? We've got nowhere to go but up." One episode earlier ("Half Measures"), he killed two men to protect Jesse, and in this episode he makes Jesse kill Gale, to protect himself. This is where Walt's will to aim higher has brought him.

Walt takes time to affirm his law-breaking choices however. Here, *Breaking Bad* adapts Nietzsche's work. Nietzsche tells us that an Overman moves past simply negating the accepted values of good and bad, and chooses (affirms) his own. This makes him happy. Until the end of Season Four, Walt is far from happy, and thinks he has made bad decisions. He has acted out of desperation, not an affirmative will to succeed, but this doesn't necessarily mean he's not acting as an Overman. As Gus says in the Season Three episode, "Mas," Walt's decisions weren't bad: "a man provides for his family . . . even when he's not appreciated, or respected, or even loved. He simply bears up." Walt needs to realize that even if his family can't see his decisions as good, he still can. This realization would be a final change in perspective that would make him happy and indicate his becoming an Overman, as it would be affirming his work as good for him. In the finale of the fourth season ("Face Off"), Walt reaches this point.

Before Season Four, Walt's happiness came in brief spurts, and came from hurting others. He would prove to them (more than himself) that he was exceeding their expectations—he gloats about his multi-million dollar deal with Gus to Jesse ("I'm in, you're out"). The ever-selfish Saul responds, "Go with the winner" and proves that Walt's pride and ego do make others admire him. But Jesse shows that this perspective isn't as strong as it seems, by symbolically breaking Walt's windshield ("Mas").

Nietzsche would agree that Walt's pride and smugness is not a sign of power, but insecurity and weakness. To be an Overman, Walt needs to be happy regardless of other peoples' opinions. In contrast to most common people who abide by the morality of society and traditional religions, the Overman designs the image of himself. He creates his own morals and values. He chooses what's necessary for himself and lives happily according to his own will, not the will of the people or of some god. Because of these unsettling ideas, Friedrich Nietzsche has become the most notorious thinker in the whole of Western philosophy. His ideas have been used and abused by some of history's famous and infamous people, as different as Albert Camus and Adolf Hitler.

Jesse turns against Walt in the fourth season, giving Walt the space to realize that he is living for himself. Even Jesse, who admired him in the past, now thinks he's selfish and sides with Gus. This makes Walt realize that he can't rely on others to make him truly happy. He needs to create his own happiness, and Gus is his only obstacle.

Going Under

The end of the episode, "Crawl Space," cleverly subverts the image of Walt dead and buried to show his "going under," the phrase Nietzsche uses to explain the route to overcoming man and becoming an Overman. This shot makes us expect him to die, because the image of burial signals an end, but *Breaking Bad* makes it the start of an inspiring season finale.

Walt becomes an Overman by overcoming everyone, including us, the audience. Like Jesse, we're in the dark about Walt's master plan, and it's the first time in the series we're not kept up with what's going through his head. Season Four's last shot ("Face Off") reveals that he poisoned Brock, creating an elaborate double-bluff to engineer Jesse's perspective of who's on his side, turning him against Gus.

Walt's morality has unexpectedly changed. Now, to do what's good for him includes doing what he recently saw as

despicable—hurting, maybe even killing, a child. He has realized that doing this isn't inherently bad, and it's become necessary. We all think child abuse is wrong, and considering Walt's
response to Tomas's murder in the episode, "Half Measures," we
don't expect him to ever partake. It's this assumption that
makes the revelation so shocking. He has exceeded our expectations and overcome us.

In making Jesse think that Gus poisoned Brock, Walt wins,
outplaying Gus by becoming him, and at the end of the season
he stands atop a building, literally "over" humanity, smiling
quietly to himself. Finally he affirms for himself that he's
achieving his potential.

Breaking Bad adapts Nietzsche again here, making a different philosophical point. Nietzsche says that an Overman
wants other creators around him, so that they can create new
values together and move past the status quo. Walt's competition with Gus disputes this. It suggests that in a modern-day,
capitalist scenario, two creators can't co-exist. Walt's and Gus's
reasons for breaking the law are very similar, but with one
slight difference in perspective—how to treat Jesse—they
become competitors.

Growth, Decay . . . then Transformation!

By killing Gus, Walt embraces an important part of Nietzsche's
Overman doctrine: the Eternal Recurrence. This explains that
all life occurs in moments that have happened infinite times
before and will repeat infinitely. The Overman, the creator,
reorders elements of life that recur, according to their personal
will. They shape life according to what they think is good.

The final episodes of the third and fourth seasons are about
Walt and Gus trying to neutralize one another, and they share
notable plot motifs. Most important is the dead or dying child
as emotional leverage against Jesse. What's important though,
is what changes between the two seasons. In Season Four, Walt
uses the knowledge that killing Tomas hurt Jesse against him.
Walt chooses to recount that hurtful event, risking a huge
amount of personal guilt, in order to manipulate Jesse's perspective. This is Walt accepting the Eternal Recurrence of all
joy and sorrow, as Nietzsche puts it. He happily acknowledges
that he willed all good and bad, and has overcome his own

weak affection for Jesse. Walt has reached true self-affirmation—he has been transformed into an Overman.

Don's Will to Become an Overman

Mad Men's Don Draper is more difficult to characterize as an Overman, but in exploring this idea we can try to explain his popularity. Nietzsche's work is theoretical, and in applying it to a real-life scenario, sacrifices to the weaker side of our nature are made, because of our relationships with others whose will to excel isn't as potent. Don's enthusiasm for working by his own rules is often sacrificed for a colleague's benefit, which is necessary if he's to reach the top of the capitalist pyramid (a system which is rooted in conformers, not Overman).

After years of employment without a contract, Conrad Hilton's account demands Don's obligation to Sterling Cooper, and Don gives in. When Hilton pulls out and Sterling Cooper is dissolved, Don is agitated and aims to be an individualist again, suggesting the building of a new company, Sterling Cooper Draper Pryce. This Season Three finale ("Shut the Door. Have a Seat") almost suggests Don's accepting Eternal Recurrence, as he joyously begins a new company and simultaneously divorces Betty, who represents the prevalent values of 1963. He accepts happiness and sorrow in one go.

Despite this, Season Four of *Mad Men* is Don's relapse into weakness and unhappiness. In the end it looks like he's deluding himself by becoming engaged to Megan—an "upgrade" of Betty in that she understands his weakness for one-night-stands, and is better with his kids. But Peggy sees through Don's happiness because she's so similar to him, only more self-aware. At the end of Season Four ("Tomorrowland"), Don lies awake while Megan sleeps. (When he assumed Betty's happiness in their marriage he had no trouble sleeping, but having been through a painful separation from her, he knows her pain, and this engagement is uncomfortable). Don's weakness for a boring and comfortable marriage has led him to a rash decision.

Don's not wanting to be "had" applies to his personal life. Rarely is he not having an affair, and more than once he has asked his partner to escape with him. All of Don's relationships are doomed because his partner's will to excel is either weaker or more powerful than his. Midge and Rachel both refuse to leave town with him because they have ties to friends and business (so they're conforming), and Don is too desperate for the unfulfilling love of his family that he can't stay with Joy and her baseless, hedonistic family.

To avoid breaking down completely over this anxiety, Don visits Anna Draper, the only person who knows about his troubled identity transformation. Don calls Anna "the only person in the world who really knew me" ("The Suitcase"). Peggy disagrees, and it's true that if Don were to couple himself with a contemporary Nietzschean Overman "creator," it'd be her. Her suggestion that she really knows him is correct—she knows the difficulty of applying her feminist choices in the 1960s, what with the patriarchy opposing those values. Again though, Peggy's will is stronger than Don's, so they can't be together. Her strength is at odds with his weakness to be a dominant man.

Don is the uncomfortable mid-point between the dying generation of Roger Sterling and the politically progressive generation of Peggy. He doesn't realize the irony of calling Peggy "an extension" of himself. While they share character traits, Peggy doesn't resort to conforming to a submissive feminine role. Her unplanned baby with Pete Campbell signals what this pitfall might entail, so she wants to struggle through everything trying to subjugate her ("The New Girl"). Don can conform and stay comfortable, what with his being a white man, a powerful position.

This shouldn't imply that Don is completely non-creative and never affirms his actions. Good or bad, his actions are situational. They benefit him momentarily, with whatever perspective he has at any given moment. Look at how he treats Sal—discovering Sal's gay, Don advises, "limit your exposure" ("Out of Town"). It'd be pointless to let such a trivial matter lose Sterling Cooper an art director, correct? Up to a point. Don's perspective changes after Sal refuses a come-on from Lee Garner Jr., threatening the loss of a huge account. In this situation it's necessary for Sal to go ("Wee Small Hours"). It's him or the business, and to not choose the business would be a weak act. Don, like anyone trying to become an Overman, must be selfish. They also need to remember that actions are momentary, as are their reasons. In other words, "People do things."

Don fails as an Overman more so than Walt White because he negates values much more than he ever creates and affirms his own. And this isn't unexpected: he's built a life for himself in the world of business, in which it's incredibly difficult to be an individualist when you've so many responsibilities to colleagues and clients.

Nietzsche describes man as a "rope, tied between beast and overman . . . a bridge and not an end." Don is literally a bridge for us, the audience. We can see his mistakes, his faults, and overcome them; hence, *Mad Men*'s period setting. But a period setting is a double-edged sword. It does two things: first, it reminds us of what has passed and makes us feel superior, it makes us feel that we can overcome the problems of the past; but second, it makes us nostalgic. *Mad Men* is a staggeringly good-looking show, and we can't help but wish, even ever so slightly, that we lived in 1960s Manhattan. (Particularly if we're men, what with our gendered ancestors having everything we, and they could possibly want at their fingertips).

Empathy and Inspiration

Why do we keep watching Don Draper? Because we empathize with him. We can see his mistakes, we can see what's stopping him from excelling and being happy with himself, but generally we reflect his weakness. We have problems with our jobs, our families, the political sphere—but at least we're comfortable. Our moods are up and down, but at least we're not alone in that. We have Don to empathize with. And, given that Don embodies much of Nietzsche's Overman, there's a part of us that empathizes with a man who is the victim of his own attempt to design and create himself and his own morality.

Walt is more inspiring to many people, probably because he embodies Nietzsche's Overman (even more so than Don Draper) by actually re-creating himself as Heisenberg as well as living by his own moral code, a code that provides him with what he and his family need to survive. *Breaking Bad* takes a middle-aged man and imbues him with purpose, with power, with will, and he succeeds in building a new life for himself, no matter the cost. If fifty-year-old Walt can do this, surely we can, too! Or, at least there's a part of us that wishes we could live like Heisenberg, an example of the Overman. As TV viewers, we're passive in a sense, and if we want genuinely to become Overmen, that is, to be happy with ourselves and recreate our identity, then we need to be active. We need to get up from our sofas, for a start.

9

The Riddle of Godfather Gus

JEFFREY A. HINZMANN

Gustavo Fring is an enigmatic figure, to say the least, and we knew precious little about him. All we're sure of is that he's a meticulous and careful businessman whose main business successes are the Los Pollos Hermanos fast-food chain and near-total domination of the meth market in the southwestern US. We also know that he lives in Albuquerque and sponsored the DEA fun run. Ironically, this review of the facts only deepens the enigma.

One thing that's especially interesting about Gus is how his approach to his business sheds light on some key ideas underlying business, and makes us think about the line that divides the legitimate businessperson from a criminal. It's a finer line than most people think, as a close look at Gus will show.

We do know that Gus had a serious personal grudge against the Mexican cartel that used to dominate the meth trade. Beyond this, we have strong suspicions about a number of things: he was regarded as Chilean, though positive evidence that he actually was born or lived in Chile is suspiciously thin. This also clashes a bit with his apparent black blood; mixed-race individuals (such as Giancarlo Esposito, who plays Gus) are fairly common in the Caribbean and Brazil, but less common in Chile and Argentina.

His sexual orientation is also indeterminate. It's not clear whether he was married or had a family, though we know he was extremely upset over the brutal murder of his friend, Max Arsiniega. While brutal murders by gangs of hardened criminals are understandably upsetting, most don't hold grudges for over twenty years: far less common still to establish a chemistry scholarship in Max's honor at the University of New Mexico. Gus used that scholarship to groom chemists such as Gale Boetticher, to carry on Max's legacy of being an excellent meth cook for Gus' drug business.

Gus is described as being "very careful" ("Bug"), an assessment confirmed by Gus's refusal to meet with Walt and Jesse to discuss the meth business because Jesse is five minutes late and a junkie. While waiting for the meeting, Walt and Jesse are visited by a man answering to the description of someone very careful, the manager of the restaurant who asks, in an almost corporate tone, "Is everything to your satisfaction?" before moving on. That man was indeed Gustavo Fring, and his carefulness is by far his most dominant trait ("Mandala").

It's Gus's carefulness that makes him philosophically interesting. Unlike most drug lords or other criminals, Gus isn't a flashy guy. He dresses impeccably; glasses, a shirt, and tie (tucked in of course), never any bold patterns or loud colors. He wears glasses and has his hair cut short in an almost military style. His bearing is also reminiscent of a military man, and perhaps we can't rule out time in the military since we know so little of the overall story of Gus's life.

This also fits with another aspect of Gus that's as important as his appearance and demeanor, his extraordinary personal discipline. Here, Gus clearly surpasses both Walt, who's a bit undisciplined for a scientist, and Hank, who is quite undisciplined (in some ways) for a police officer. Gus's sense of self-discipline contributes heavily to his patina of mystery. He gives away so little about himself through his body language or words that we are left with only the scantest scraps of information to work with. He doesn't betray a smile, a look of recognition or a slip of the tongue under even the most stressful circumstances. These traits aren't merely idiosyncrasies of Gus's though, they're the product of a ruthless logic most often employed in an activity very often not mentioned in the same breath as drug-dealing: legitimate business.

CEO Path

Gus's entire criminal enterprise is modeled much more on corporate business than most criminal endeavors. He's certainly no Tony Montana, as he's too careful and not flashy. He's also not really a good candidate to be a Corleone; though their criminal empire had some corporate aspects, it was too overtly nepotistic and violent to truly be a business in the conventional sense of the term. More than any of these, Gus runs his business professionally, producing meth in a state-of-the-art laboratory with the best help money can buy and keeping production on a tight schedule. He's also not attached to any chemist that he works with, willing to replace even his most important employee if a slightly improved person arrives on the scene. It was Walt's suspicion that Gus was planning to replace him with fellow chemist, Gale Boetticher, that resulted in Gale's murder; but had Gus been more loyal and less businesslike, it might also have been avoided.

Gus launders his money through numerous legitimate businesses he owns, and benefits from some other elements of these legitimate businesses as well. He ships his meth in specially marked drums of chicken batter though the distribution network of his Los Pollos Hermanos chain. His meth lab is hidden underneath a laundry facility he owns, concealing not only the lab itself but also effectively concealing the exhaust and providing a plausible rationale for the frequent shipments of strange chemicals needed to keep it in operation. This too is an order of thoughtfulness and care rarely seen in traditional criminal enterprise.

Gus is careful, an effective criminal, and a good businessman because he's disciplined his emotions, almost stoically, to not make the mistakes that usually doom most criminals. He doesn't attract attention, he doesn't lose control, he doesn't arouse suspicion, and he doesn't make mistakes. It's interesting that I said *almost* stoically, as stoicism is an ancient Greco-Roman philosophy that emphasizes the discipline of emotions in order to cope with the tragedies of life. Gus is no stoic— though he quite ably passes for one.

Sociopath

Gus is a sociopath. He kills one of his henchmen in front of Walt and Jesse in order to intimidate them, and he does so with his usual care. He carefully removes his jacket, tie, and glasses, and puts on a pair of work overalls before he kills his own bodyguard in cold blood ("Box Cutter"). We also know that Gus has ordered the murder of a child ("Full Measure"). No stoic would approve of this. Sociopathy is no philosophy; instead, it's the result of powerful defense mechanisms that direct rage to the emotionless use of reason, for the purpose of gradually accumulating instrumental power over one's surroundings. The emotions are almost completely suppressed so that the rational mind can better do its job of giving rage the tools needed to gain power. This tends to suppress the natural human tendency to empathize with other humans, especially those suffering or those seen as fellow members of a privileged group. And the result then is an extremely unstable person (as in the case of numerous serial killers). But Gus's ability to discipline his emotions and himself in spite of the instability that lurks beneath is what makes him so very chilling.

In all these cases of amoral behavior and lack of empathy, the unifying feature is what the members of the Critical Theory tradition in Western philosophy—which has such figures as Theodor Adorno (1903–1969) and Jürgen Habermas (born 1929)—call *instrumental rationality*. Instrumental rationality is the use of reason to solve problems and achieve goals, all while doing so utterly amorally. Thus, the use of instrumental reason involves making no assumptions about the nature of morality or the moral status of specific actions. It's the pursuit of what Immanuel Kant (1724–1804) called *hypothetical imperatives*, goals that are calculated and prudential, rather than *categorical imperatives*, which are absolute moral requirements.

What's significant here is that while morality might be detached from certain conceptions of reason, most healthy humans are still possessed of some moral tendencies, which are thought to be in need of cultivation and care, not neglect and abandonment. The disciple of pure instrumental reason is very likely to not feel that they owe others any humane treatment beyond what advances their interests, if they extend their commitment beyond certain types of research, data-gathering, or puzzle-solving and on into the realm of interpersonal relations. They violate, at the deepest level, Kant's injunction to "always treat people as an end in themselves and not as a means only," and they have none of the usual feelings of empathy that may be responsible for a reluctance to be cruel to others.

If all this is true, then a thoroughgoing commitment to instrumental reason seems like a red-flag for sociopathy: a place where the normal and healthy commitment to not always deal with others through the lens of ruthless rationality is set aside in favor of a bottomless commitment to some sense of effectiveness in the pursuit of personal gain. Gus is bottomlessly committed to effectiveness, lacks empathy for those around him, and doesn't behave morally unless it is an instrumental aid to the accomplishment of his goals. His goal is the elimination of a major Mexican cartel.

Toward a Criminal Theory of the State

Before Niccolo Machiavelli (1469–1527) and Thomas Hobbes (1588–1679), the state had sometimes been conceived as a brutal entity that exists primarily to consolidate the power of the ruler. But these two are the great popularizers of the idea in modern times.

Talk of benevolence to citizens or promoting social growth are, at best, afterthoughts. Machiavelli thought it was better to be feared than loved, and Hobbes thought that the king was entitled to whatever he wanted in exchange for providing some modicum of safety to people who's only alternative is the state of nature where life would be "solitary, poor, nasty, brutish, and short."

The lives of Gus's employees aren't much better than this if they cross his path. The Mexican cartels are even better at amassing power than Gus is, albeit in a more overt form. As the name and the rich history of organized crime associated with it suggest, a cartel is a powerful crime organization that is similar to an autonomous political organization. In Mexico, in particular, this suggestion is more than mere hyperbole. The authority of the legitimate Mexican government has struggled over the past decade to maintain control of its own territory, as the cartels grow ever more powerful. Possessed of an almost bottomless source of income once they inherited the drug trade to the US following the demise of the Colombian cartels, the Mexican cartels have increasingly been able to buy off Mexican law-enforcement officials and remain stocked with weapons that challenge the firepower of the Mexican marines. Even the elite Mexican anti-cartel elite force *Los Zetas* is either corruptable by the cartel influence or defeatable by cartel firepower.

Given this state of affairs, Gus is up against some stiff competition. It's here that we can see the full benefits of the way Gus's use of instrumental rationality and the corporate ethos allows him to effectively crush his rivals. While the cartels explicitly clash with recognized and powerful governments, such as those of Mexico, the US, and others, Gus's embrace of instrumental rationality counsels a corporate approach.

Corporations are multi-national organizations with no essential tie to any specific government (though they favor some countries which recognize corporate personhood). They nonetheless benefit from a voluntary co-operation with the laws of the land (for the most part). Even the shadiest corporation is still ultimately a white-collar endeavor, and a symbiotic relationship with a major government seems ideal. Corporations make more money focusing on a specific type of product sold to a specific type of market-niche, and specifically avoid providing for their own defense and infrastructure, for example.

Gus sells his drugs in exactly the same way. He recognized long ago that a highly refined form of meth, produced by an exceptional chemist, would allow him to dominate a certain sector of the drug trade. Using a corporate model of delivering a superior product at a lower price (and with a distinctive brand no less: blue meth) would allow him to dominate the market relatively non-violently. His carefulness is a further commitment to his lack of violence, by being careful, not being seen or even so much as arousing suspicion, Gus can grow, prosper, and launder his millions completely under the noses of a self-righteous DEA and US government.

Since he has no hope of challenging the government's authority, and little interest in doing so, his business functions more smoothly and earns far greater profits simply being innocuous. As far as anyone in legitimate society is concerned, he's an uptight purveyor of a small fried-chicken chain called Los Pollos Hermanos and of no further interest. Only Hank Shrader has the wherewithal to think otherwise, and he (unofficially) plants a tracking device on Gus's car to see if his suspicions are justified. Gus turns up clean, his carefulness saves him from suspicion by the normal standards of the law, but Hank, aware as he is that it pays to be a careful criminal, concludes that, "anyone this clean has to be dirty" ("Bug"). He's right, of course, but in any case Gus's fate is nearly sealed by this point.

Goodbye Godfather Gus

Though Gus is a strange species of criminal, one who makes us rethink our simplistic understanding of the nature and motives of crime, he turns out to be a criminal all the same. He certainly meets an end appropriate to a criminal, blown-up by a bomb planted by Walt on Tio Salamanca's wheelchair, this as a result of Walt's unshakable paranoid (but nonetheless justi-fied) fear that Gus was ready to eliminate him at any moment. We learn a great deal about Gus, including his past, the history of his grudge with the cartel, and how he comes to meet his end, starting in the Season Four episode, "Hermanos."

Early in "Hermanos" Gus is called in for questioning by Hank when his fingerprints are found at the apartment of the murdered Gail Boetticher. Gus is at his rational, composed, sociopathic best, displaying an unseen creativity by adroitly spinning a story about how he knew Gale through the Max Arsiniega chemistry scholarship Gale received at UNM. Gus's Chilean origins are also investigated, but precious little is revealed. The absence of records of Gus's life in Chile is blamed on the poor record keeping of the Pinochet regime. Nonetheless, Hank's suspicions kick in all the stronger, as he's attuned, in a remarkable way, to the artifice that Gus uses to mediate his interactions with legitimate society. He begins investigating Gus, and this sets in motion a chain of events that contributes to Gus's downfall and death.

In a flashback at the end of the episode, we learn how Gus came to be a bitter, sworn enemy of the Mexican cartel. We see Gus, nervous in a business suit, sitting poolside at the cartel's villa along with Max Arsiniega. They're meeting with the car-tel to offer to make the same high-quality meth that Gus has gone on to so effectively build his empire around for the cartel. The meeting begins promisingly enough, the men are congrat-ulated for their chicken recipe and their proposal is listened to with interest.

Only at the end of the meeting does it abruptly turn bad. Don Eladio is insulted by Gus's way of arranging the meeting, which was to give samples of his improved meth to cartel henchmen as free samples. Though they profusely apologize, the cartel doesn't display the control Gus is so famous for in addressing this problem. Instead, they abruptly kill Max (and thereby provoke a reaction of extraordinary rage from Gus, probably the only time we see such a thing from him) in response.

The only reason Gus isn't killed too is that Don Eladio tells him, "I know who you are," perhaps insinuating that Gus is somehow protected by powerful interests, plausibly stretching back to the Pinochet regime but ultimately the meaning of this cryptic statement is unknown, even by the show's writers. What this flashback makes clear, though, is that Gus's construction of his criminal empire is largely driven by a desire to destroy the cartel and avenge Max's murder, a fact that is required to understand the next episode, "Salud."

Salud

In "Salud" Gus takes Jesse down to Mexico to show the cartel how to make meth as part of a truce worked out between the mafia organizations. Jesse is, in spite of being rather unprepared for such a risky gambit, successful. Later, Gus, Jesse, and Mike (Gus's bodyguard) are at the cartel's villa, by the same pool where Max was murdered so long ago. Here, in this poetically appropriate setting, Gus exacts his revenge by giving Don Eladio and all of his men poisoned Tequila. In an ultimate, almost mythic display of his rational self-control, Gus ingests some of the same ricin-poisoned Tequila that kills Don Eladio's men. The move is exactly the right one to gain the trust of a group quite conscious of Gus's resentment and appropriately suspicious of being poisoned. Gus simply goes to the bathroom to throw up the poison (with the same eerie calm he does so many other disgusting things) only to walk out and find everyone in the villa dead: exactly as he had planned.

This is Gus's moment of great triumph, but in just a few episodes, his attempt to pit Jesse against Walt will backfire. Walt will find Tio Salamanca, now living in a retirement community and confined to a wheelchair, and only able to respond to questions by ringing a bell, a willing ally in his attempt to bring Gus down. Tio's bell becomes the detonator that explodes the pipe bomb strapped under his wheelchair. Tio is killed, sacrificing himself in the blast because Gus has spent years tormenting him with sadistic and condescending visits, exploiting his incapacity.

For a moment, Gus seems to be unscathed, walking out the room apparently intact. This is a side shot, however, and when we see Gus from head on we see him looking a lot like the Batman villain Two-Face. Half his body is badly disfigured and looks of death, the other half remains clean and presentable; a perfect visual representation for the inner division that permeated Gus's character. Gus always seemed like a disciplined, unified force acting in his own interests, but he was in fact an almost split-personality: a badly damaged real self driven by rage and vengeance wearing a carefully crafted mask of banal respectability.

A Trail of Destruction

In the end, Gus appeared to be a rather typical criminal after all. Dare I say, even an almost human character. What has been illuminating is to see how effectively Gus was able to advance his agenda by being as inhuman as possible. Gus's self-discipline and lack of empathy allowed him to build a criminal empire, stay one step ahead of his enemies, ruthlessly manipulate subordinates like Jesse, Walt, and Gale, and leave a trail of destruction behind him. His most significant legacy, however, is to foreshadow the monster that Walt seems to be transforming into as the series progresses.

10

If Walt's Breaking Bad, Maybe We Are Too

J.C. Donhauser

Chemistry innovator turned high school chemistry teacher, Walter White goes to incredible lengths to ensure that his wife, disabled teen son, and infant daughter will be well off after he dies of what medical experts diagnose as terminal lung cancer.

At first Walt convinces himself that his obviously illegal actions are justifiable, given his diagnosis—enough so that he pursues them right under the nose of his DEA agent brother-in-law, Hank. Yet, given the precarious situations he always ends up in, we have to ask: Is Walt, a seeming genius, acting in rational ways? And even if he is ensuring the wellbeing of loved ones, surely it's still morally wrong to manufacture and distribute meth. Isn't it?

After crashing his mobile meth lab in what seems to be a high-speed chase, the very first words Walt utters in the pilot episode reveal his motivations for cooking and selling meth. Frantically rummaging around after the crash, Walt picks up a camcorder to record himself:

> To all law enforcement entities, this is not an admission of guilt; I am speaking to my family now. Skyler, you are the love of my life—I hope you know that. Walter Jr. (voice wavering), you're my big man. There are going to be some . . . *things* . . . things that you'll come to learn about me in the next few days. I just want you to know that no matter how it may look, I only had you in my heart.

We're introduced to Walt as someone who's intelligent, practical, and primarily concerned with doing good things for his loved ones. But looking back with hindsight, we have to wonder whether Walt is actually acting in a practical or rational way to achieve *good* ends.

Rational Acts and Beneficial Consequences

We judge our decisions, in large part, by the consequences we should expect to result from them—and deem decisions as better or worse relative to the desirability of their consequences. For example, we might refrain from going out to eat multiple times a week, to save money for a cruise vacation in the future. This is a good decision if our goal is to go on a cruise; it's a rational way to get the desired consequence.

On the flip side, consider instant gratification. Weak in the face of temptation, we may regret eating too many chips or cookies when our pants start feeling a bit snug (pesky consequences). Being honest with ourselves, we see that eating many unhealthy things is irrational and not in our interest—if our interest is fitting in our pants. Expectations of probable consequences guide the ways we act, and the extent to which someone considers likely consequences of their actions leads us to see him or her as a better or worse decision maker.

Chemistry Geniuses and Meth Addicts as Decision Makers

Prior to Jesse's personal transformation following the death of his girlfriend, Jane, he and Walt fall on opposite ends of the spectrum of being better or worse decision makers. Walt carefully weighs options and tries to find maximally efficient ways to produce the consequences he wants with whatever resources he has available. Jesse opts for quick fixes, and where those aren't available he often simply gives up and hits the pipe.

In the pilot episode, even seconds after being informed that he has inoperable lung cancer, forgoing any shock or fear response, Walt promptly assesses the reality of his situation. The doctor, stunned at Walt's lack of emotion, asks if he fully understands what he's being told. Visibly annoyed by a spot of mustard on the doctor's coat (details), Walt nonchalantly replies, "Best case scenario, with chemo, I'll live maybe another couple of years." Consequently, after some brief research as a tag along on a DEA bust with Hank, he reasons that producing meth is the most efficient way that he, as a skilled chemist, can leave his family a nest egg in the short time he probably has left.

Jesse's approach is less than reasoned and methodical. None of us can forget what happens when he fails to heed Walt's advice to dissolve Emilio's corpse with hydrofluoric acid in polyethylene bins; instead turning to the quick fix of attempting the dissolving of the body in his clearly non-plastic bathtub. His shortsightedness in making decisions is similarly shown by his failure to realize his dreams of drumming and singing in "*his* band" Twaüght Hammër. Typical of his character, Jesse feigns success, merely pretending he's the great drumming front man of the band, while in reality his friend Badger is the front man and Jesse has been replaced on drums after failing to show up for practice due to his busy meth cooking and smoking regimen. Rather than acting in rational ways to achieve his goals—like (duh!) rehearsing—often the old Jesse assures himself that his situation is hopeless and then gets high while trying to maintain only an outward illusion of success; he's an expert poser.

Cost-Benefit Analysis

Walt and Jesse make decisions, for better or worse, according to a *cost-benefit analysis*—the thought process we use to choose some particular thing or action over alternatives by weighing the benefits against the losses required to get what we want. We use cost-benefit analysis for tasks as common as grocery shopping or buying insurance. We might buy in bulk, incurring a greater immediate cost for a long-term savings, or purchase insurance at an immediate cost that will result in the benefit of reduction of costs in an emergency.

Walt's and Jesse's opposite approaches to cost-benefit analysis show in their conversation after an addict nicknamed Spooge robs their foot soldier, Skinny Pete, of one thousand dollars and some of their product. Jesse rationalizes the loss and Walt points out that his rationale is irrational:

> **JESSE:** Dude, it's called breakage. Okay, like K-mart, shit breaks. It's the cost of business okay, yo. You're sweatin' me over a grand.

> **WALT:** Hey, look I'm just the chemist here, I'm not the street guy, yo. But it seems to me what you call breakage is just you making a fool of yourself. I've got another technical term for you: *non-sustainable business model*.
>
> **JESSE:** You're focusing on the negative. Six grand a day we're making. What's your problem?
>
> **WALT:** What happens when the word gets out on the clowns you hired? Once everyone knows that Jesse Pinkman, drug lord, can be robbed with impunity. . . .

Walt sees the big picture; a trend of minor losses and chinks in their street cred will probably lead to major losses over time. From the start of his career in the meth business, this is Walt's outlook. When Jesse returns having sold only an ounce of their first successfully cooked pound of blue meth for $2,600, and Walt says, "This is unacceptable! I am breaking the law here, this return is too little for the risk." His cost-benefit analysis is that the risks are too high for the relatively small benefit—so he proceeds to up their game. Walt makes rational decisions to get desirable consequences by objectively assessing the probable consequences of every action (even the small stuff). But is acting rationally to get what he wants for his family doing *good*?

Actual Consequences or Rules of Thumb

When we judge an act as right or wrong based primarily upon its consequences we're accepting the ethical theory called *consequentialism*, which has historical ties to the writings of the nineteenth-century thinkers Jeremy Bentham and John Stuart Mill. Consequentialists use rational cost-benefit analysis as the primary way to determine whether an action is good or bad. For them, if it "costs" more to be truthful or to not murder, then one should lie or murder to bring about the benefits—what's good is accruing benefits on the cheap.

Walt's approach to ethical dilemmas shows that he's a consequentialist thinker. In the first season, he very clearly does a reasoned cost-benefit analysis prior to killing Krazy-8—writing out a list of the reasons to let him live versus reasons to kill him. On the *let him live* side he writes, lastly, "Murder is wrong!" Murder often comes with bad consequences for all involved parties, and Walt can't carry through with the murder until he's assured that it's the most rational option. The consequences of letting Krazy-8 live—"He'll kill your entire family if you let him go" as Walt writes on the *kill him* side of his list—guide Walt to carry through with the murder only after that he notices that Krazy-8 has made a shank out of a piece of broken plate (". . . And the Bag's in the River").

In line with Walt's behavior in this situation, consequentialist theory reflects one way that we naturally tend to assess the rightness or wrongness of our actions. Actions with good consequences are obviously good and those with bad consequences obviously bad. But we all know that life's not that simple. The increasingly complicated situations in which Walt and Jesse find themselves, our own mixed feelings as viewers show, and even Walt's choice of the alias Heisenberg suggest this much. Walt's alias is a nod to physicist Werner Heisenberg's *uncertainty principle*, which says that we can never be completely sure of what will happen in any situation because there are always variables which we don't know about—like Gustavo Fring's ignorance of Walt and mutual enemy Hector Salamanca conspiring to assassinate him. Often it isn't cut and dried how things are actually connected, which consequences are good and which are bad, or which consequences we're responsible for causing. Some philosophers argue that such complications show that the most basic form of consequentialism, *act consequentialism*, is flawed.

Acts and Rules

Act-consequentialists judge actions by their actual consequences; actions that produce undesirable consequences are bad, ones that produce good consequences are good. The problem with this approach is that we can cause things to happen that most of us agree we shouldn't be blamed for. Hank, for example, often unintentionally aids Heisenberg (the number one criminal Hank's trying to stop)—whom we know *is* Walt. Notably, Hank kills Tuco Salamanca, which allows Jesse and Walt to escape with their lives, eliminates one of their major competitors and threats in the meth business, and, thus, allows them to produce and distribute meth more efficiently ("ABQ").

Similarly, in the pilot episode, a stoic Native American man helps Walt and Jesse by towing their crashed meth-lab on wheels out of the ditch. He unknowingly helps Walt and Jesse transport Emilio's corpse and an unconscious Krazy-8, whom they imprison and Walt later kills. Like Hank, he's contributing to negative consequences for some people, but we're inclined to think that he himself is doing nothing wrong—he's just trying to help some strangers who are stranded in the desert. We can't always gauge a person's actions based solely on their actual consequences, because we can contribute to bringing to fruition events that we don't intend or can't anticipate.

Some ethicists suggest that because of such complicating factors the most objective way to judge any action is to focus on general rules dictated by what is reasonable to expect if everyone acted in the way being considered. Such *rule consequentialists* argue that actions are better or worse, not in relation to their actual consequences, but in proportion to how far afield they fall from a rule that would be best for most people *if* everyone followed it. It's reasonable to expect that we would all be better off if everyone, as a rule of thumb, helps people who are stranded or incapacitate violent gun wielding criminals. Thus, according to *rule consequentialists*, Hank and the Native American guy are good-doers, even though each contributes to bringing to fruition insidious events.

Acting Like Tuco

Even if we agree that we should do what's best for the most people possible when we can, it also seems to make sense that what's good for us and our loved ones takes precedence over what's good for complete strangers or known criminals. Walt must be of this opinion when he decides that he should make meth for strangers for his family's benefit. *Agent-centered consequentialism* is the variation of consequentialism that appears to be consistent with Walt's actions in this regard.

Agent-centered consequentialists judge actions based on their consequences (as consequentialists), but they also argue that the most important consequences are those *for the person carrying out the actions* that produce those consequences—the "agent." Morally good actions thus benefit the agent and everyone else or benefit the agent without harming everyone else.

This view of morality accords with our intuitions for the preservation of ourselves, our families, or our country.

Yet, if we agree that rule consequentialism makes better sense of our moral intuitions than act consequentialism, agent-centered consequentialism looks more difficult to accept. Why? Because some actions that produce preferable consequences for their "agent" *and everyone else* would be bad for most people if followed as a rule of thumb. Though this sounds confusing, considering the actions of a sociopath like Tuco makes this clear.

Even within the counter-culture of people active in making, distributing, and using meth—the community for whom Tuco increases overall desired consequences by succeeding in widely distributing the drug—he's not a good guy. Rule consequentialism accounts for this, and agent centered consequentialism does not. Tuco's self-interested actions tend to provide the drug community with what they take to be good, but his behavior isn't desirable as a rule. If everyone acted like Tuco, the overall "good" for everyone (a supply of meth) would probably not increase or even remain stable. If *everyone* in that community were actively trying to gain control by instilling fear in everyone else with gratuitous violence, meth distribution would likely suffer—as it does when the cartel is at war with Gus Fring.

But wait! Isn't Tuco just a bad example of someone whose actions tend to promote personal and overall good but which are bad for everyone if followed as a rule, because he's not *rationally* achieving his ends to begin with? If so, then agent-focused consequentialism might be okay, and we might justify Walt's new career. Though we may think him insane, it's arguable that Tuco's behavior is rational! His goal is *to maintain control* by instilling fear in his competitors. And relative to this goal he *is* acting in ways that do the job quite well. Tuco's violent wild-card approach is so rational that Walt (as Heisenberg) turns the tables on Tuco, and later Gus, by copying his tactics and blowing things up to gain the upper hand in the finales of Seasons One and Four.

Still, even if it's a rational way of gaining control, surely there's something morally wrong with the way Walt strikes back at Tuco and Gus—just as there's something wrong with Tuco's *modus operandi*. Again we might justify our feeling that taking extremely violent measures, even in retaliation or defense, is wrong because most people would be worse off if we all acted like that as a rule. If so, Walt's actions are not okay, *even if* they benefit him and his family without serious negative consequences for society at large.

Doing Good Is Doing Less Harm

Breaking a neighbor's window for no reason in the context of an ordinary day would be considered wrong. But, breaking a neighbor's window to save their baby from dying in a house fire would clearly be more right than wrong. Likewise, after murdering Krazy-8 Walt makes Jesse a promise, "No matter what happens, no more bloodshed. No more violence" ("A Crazy Handful of Nothin'"). But Walt relaxes his no-violence rule in high-stakes situations, just like the "Don't break the neighbor's window" rule is relaxed in emergencies.

The idea that good is minimizing harm to the extent you're able is central to consequentialist ideologies of all kinds. If we agree that rule consequentialism makes sense, it's the rule that supersedes all others. Sometimes Walt behaves in ways suggesting that he adheres to the associated idea that it's wrong to allow harm or suffering that one could easily attempt to prevent. In the days before he kills Krazy-8, while Mr. 8 is suffering from chemical lung damage in Jesse's basement, Walt brings him food, water, and a bucket to relieve himself in to lessen his suffering a bit—he even cuts the crust off of Krazy-8's sandwiches (". . . And the Bag's in the River"). It appears that he's doing *some* good by acting to lessen harm and suffering.

On the flip side, we have what some fans take to be a pivotal tipping point in Walt's moral demise. When he watches Jesse's love, Jane, choke to death on her own vomit, our intuition is that Walt has done wrong—arguably since he could have easily rolled her over ("Phoenix"). We rationalize what he's done in this situation only by coming up with reasons why letting Jane live *would probably contribute to the harm of others*—namely Jesse. He's done wrong if letting Jane die will probably bring about more harms than if he prevented her death.

What's Wrong with Distributing Meth?

Most people regard smoking meth as more wrong than eating pizza, ice cream, or coffee. We must imagine that this is because of the expected harmful consequences of smoking meth, as it can't be that ingesting chemicals is somehow inherently wrong—everything we ingest is made of chemicals.

Even the obvious possibility of addiction doesn't seem to make meth use automatically bad. Why? For one thing, it's not a necessary consequence—one *could* smoke meth in moderation and not abuse it. For another, there's the possibility of addiction with pizza or chocolate or coffee. But "chocoholism" and caffeine addiction don't seem to be as badly wrong as meth addiction. So, it must be more than the possibility of addiction that makes us judge meth use as more badly wrong than other ingesting actions.

Some events of *Breaking Bad* suggest that it's more distant consequences associated with stigmatized actions like smoking meth that lead us to judge them as wrong. On the misguided suspicion that Walt Jr. is smoking pot (after Skyler finds what we know is Walt Sr.'s weed), Hank takes him to the Crystal Palace—a seedy motel junkies and prostitutes frequent—to show him that doing drugs is wrong (". . . And the Bag's in the River"). Why? The implication is that it's because pot-smoking often leads to a degenerate and criminal sort of life. Hank's showing Walt Jr. the distant, supposedly statistically likely, consequences of using gateway drugs to convince him that smoking marijuana is wrong. We may think it unlikely that gateway drug usage seals our fate as a degenerate. Still, the idea that decidedly bad distant possibilities made more probable by some type of action warrants our judging that action negatively, seems to be a keeper.

If this rationale is right, distributing meth is wrong if it contributes to the overall increase of harmful consequences. By succeeding in the meth business, Walt is fueling the low-quality lifestyle of addicts and those they in turn harm. And even if this does end up benefiting his family—which is questionable—it appears that he's contributing to the harm and death of many more people than he's helping. Sometimes it even seems that Walt, like Jesse, is shortsighted as to the consequences of his actions. The ripple effects of his actions propel the increasing seriousness of the situation Walt and his family are in.

By the fourth season, if the high *incidental* death toll associated with Walt's actions weren't enough, the gravity of the consequences of his actions are made transparent. Gus drags

Walt into the desert at gunpoint, strongly encourages him to vanish (to put it politely), and punctuates his point by exclaiming, "I will kill your infant daughter!" ("Crawl Space"). Honestly, the bad ramifications of one's actions don't get much clearer than that.

Can We Please Not Break Bad?

According to some consequentialists, even if moral perfection is impossible, we can each easily act at least morally better by lessening expectable harmful consequences of our actions. We can follow this very simple rule: If we can prevent something bad from occurring without sacrificing anything of comparable significance to ourselves, then we ought to do it. For instance, it would always be better to save a drowning child and get your clothes wet than to let her die just to keep your clothes dry. It's hard to argue otherwise.

If we agree that this is a good, common-sense, rule then it becomes clear that Walt *is* "breaking bad." Yet, it also appears that we each may be, too. Walt could've easily saved Jane's life by rolling her over. Likewise he could've easily belayed his pride and accepted the charity of his former colleagues, Elliot and Gretchen Schwartz, rather than contributing to the harm of very many other people by producing meth and continuing to do so.

Also, we, like Hank, also often fail to see the whole of the consequences to which we contribute—even in carrying out mundane everyday actions like shopping. And, perhaps surprisingly, each of us can often do much better than we actually do at little inconvenience to ourselves. To show just how simple it might be to be much morally better than we each are right now, in closing I'd like to suggest just one way that we could lessen a lot of harm and suffering without any appreciable personal loss.

It's reasonable to expect that the worst-off people in the world—like starving children in third-world countries—would be much better off given only a very small portion of the resources that we currently waste every day. If we can't argue with the thought that we should prevent whatever bad things we're able to at little or no personal sacrifice, then we should each save and redistribute those merely wasted resources since it would be better to do than not. Rather than buying one beer for $2, we would do better to buy six for $6 and use the saved $6 to somehow lessen harm and suffering in the world.

We could lessen the suffering of very many people by donating such easily saved money to lifesaving organizations like Children's Safe Drinking Water (CSDW) or Oxford Committee for Famine Relief (OXFAM)—donating on someone's behalf can even get some Christmas or birthday shopping out of the way. And if we could each do so much better, lessening the suffering of innocent children rather than wasting money, by being slightly smarter shoppers—what might we do with cash like Hank or Gus?

Just as we could lessen harm by redistributing our wasted money, Walt could do the same on a very large scale by being a successful drug lord. If Walt were lessening overall harm in the world in this way—much more so than most of us—we have to wonder whether he'd be doing something morally right. I leave you with this query, for your own further philosophizing.

11

I Appreciate the Strategy

SARA WALLER

One day in the midst of a normal but somewhat disappointing life, Walter White finds himself staring into the abyss of terminal cancer. Believing he has months to live, he chooses to pursue what is easy to consider an immoral activity—cooking and selling meth.

Meth, after all, can hurt people, make them violent, kill them, or make them kill others. But, then again, what kind of a father would let his children live in poverty when he has the knowhow to provide for them? What kind of a husband would leave his wife with bills she can't pay when he's able to pay them? Given his situation, we can see that there are moral reasons for his choice.

So, is Walt a bad guy or a good guy? And do the moral rules we use to guide our lives change when we see our lives coming to an end?

Promoting Benefit, Pleasure, and Happiness

Utilitarian principles advise us that good actions are those that produce the greatest happiness for the greatest number of people. Many institutions in the United States are founded on utilitarian principles,

We determine the president according to a majority of votes; we import goods that the majority of people wish to buy, and we offer public education and social security for the intended benefit of the majority of citizens.

Utilitarianism, advocated most forcefully by John Stuart Mill (1806–1873), is a moral system that treats everyone equally. No one person's benefit, pleasure, and happiness, or loss, pain, and misery are more important than anyone else's. When we're attempting to do what's moral in the world, we should maximize the happiness of as many individuals as possible. The more happiness our deeds bring about, the more good we've done in the world, and the more pain our deeds cause, intentionally or unintentionally, the more evil we've created.

For utilitarians, happiness and pleasure are often taken to be the same or about the same, and this makes the question of alcohol or drug use an important one. After all, many people enjoy taking drugs, and can consume some drugs, in one form or another, for years, without major mental or physical health problems. It's legal to sell beer in America for roughly utilitarian reasons—it pleases a lot of people most of the time. While some suffer from alcoholism or are victimized by drunk drivers or alcohol abuse, most people, most of the time, benefit from the pleasures of the drink and the profits it supports.

In early twentieth-century America there was something called Prohibition. The drinking, selling, or production of alcoholic drinks were banned. Prohibition certainly didn't produce happiness for the greatest number of people.

Since many drugs also have the potential to create the greatest amount of happiness for the greatest number of people, the legal status of many controlled substances is hotly debated. Marijuana, if legalized, may increase the profits of farmers as well as bring pleasure to many users. Generally peaceful potheads would increase in the population, suffering from short term memory deficits and reduced lung capacity, and the question before us is one of whether the benefits outweigh the potentially problematic consequences of forgetful folks at work fumbling over what non-potheads might consider to be relatively simple tasks.

But never mind about marijuana; let's talk about crystal meth. Studies show that occasional, short term meth use increases mood, productivity, and allows people to work efficiently for hours on little sleep while enjoying boring, tedious, or unpleasant tasks. So here's a strong potential for increasing happiness by allowing for meth use. However, meth is very addictive, with a high percentage of occasional users becoming habitual, if not daily users. Prolonged use results almost inevitably in a reduction of brain size and brain cell count, and with that, a reduction in IQ, general functionality, and memory. Meth rots the teeth and easily damages the cardiovascular system as well as the lungs. People on meth for long periods of time often become both violent and delusional (in contrast to the more peaceful delusional states of the potheads).

Act Utilitarianism

A good utilitarian must weigh, and decide, whether the potential for long-term positive consequences outweighs the potential for negative consequences in the consideration of the morality of legalizing, or even cooking, crystal meth. Act utilitarianism is a form of utilitarianism where every single *act* you commit must be weighed according to how much pleasure and how much pain it produces.

In Walt's case, cooking about six months' worth of meth and selling it might be a morally good act, by the standard of act utilitarianism. The profits will increase his own pleasure—since he can view himself as a good provider—as well as increase the well being of his wife and son, and provide for his unborn daughter. Although meth is certainly a potentially dangerous drug, six months' worth of production builds in a limit to how much havoc it can wreak on the streets and in the local community. Walt can hope that the pleasures afforded to his family will outweigh the damage caused to the consumers. Perhaps no one will become violent; perhaps no one will die. A few people will get high, in which case, they'll also enjoy themselves, and Walt has surely maximized pleasure and minimized pain all around. He can die a good man.

If Walt believes he has fifteen or twenty-five years to live, the utilitarian calculus used to determine whether or not he should cook meth will change. Suddenly the likelihood of users dying, or being harmed by violence or by the drug itself, rises. Providing a constant supply of meth to the streets of his community over an extended period of time could fundamentally change that community for the worse, and increase the amount of pain so profoundly that the pleasures enjoyed by his family and himself would be far outweighed by overall sorrow. According to an act-utilitarian calculation, cooking meth is something that could be a morally good action for a short time, but is probably not a morally good action for a longer period of time.

So then, it seems that we—if we're utilitarians—can't be too morally outraged at Walt for breaking bad. He believes, at first, that no one will be harmed, that he'll use his vast knowledge of chemistry, that his partner Jesse will make some money, a few meth-heads will buy some high-quality product, and that he'll die before any really terrible consequences emerge. Sounds like a great choice!

But in the first three seasons, he kills Emilio and Krazy-8 Molina, goads Jesse into developing a dangerous partnership that results in Jesse's hospitalization, blows up Tuco's dealership, alienates Skyler and Walt Jr., inadvertently gets Tuco and Combo killed, and stands by as Jesse's beloved Jane slowly chokes on her own vomit. The overall pain probably has outweighed the pleasure by the end of Season Two, if not far sooner!

And, this illustrates one of the classic problems for utilitarianism. If we measure the good we'll do by imagining the consequent happiness our actions have brought, we're always trapped in the limits of our imagination. We can't really do good if we can't predict the consequences of our actions with certainty or at least with a really, really high degree of probability. We don't always know what those consequences will be, obviously, because we can't foresee the future!

Existentialism

But there's one thing we can foresee with certainty in everyone's future: death. That we'll all die and that life's short both are the primary focus of *existentialism*. Existentialists highlight the fact that we're all dying—some more quickly, and some more slowly—and because of this we should exist in the moment and live our lives to the fullest.

Existentialists measure goodness differently than utilitarians do. For the most part, existentialists agree that pleasure and happiness are important for human beings, but they're far less likely to consider the pleasures of all people equally, or place pleasure as the ultimate value, simply because they're committed to making decisions in light of the brevity of life.

Existentialists also generally reject religious comforts and believe that this is the one and only life we have. Given the fact that there's no god or afterlife, they believe that we're completely free beings. We're in charge of our lives and we choose, and are responsible for, all of our actions. There's no built-in purpose for us in this existence; we have to make our own purpose in this purposeless existence through our actions and choices. While in some ways we are *thrown* into this existence—for example, we don't choose all aspects of our lives, such as what culture or time period we were born into, or what nationality or race we are—the human condition is still one in which we navigate around the fixed aspects of our lives to make our existence meaningful and develop who we are in every action we perform.

Walt the Existentialist

Walt is without question a man confronted with a classic existential problem: facing his own death, he must make choices and decisions regarding the moral thing to do. He could leave his family in financial disarray; he could run off and die by himself. He could (and tries to) refuse treatment so as to minimize the impact on his family (both financially and in terms of remembering him as weak, emaciated, and bald). But his love for his family is, at least at the outset of the series, the meaning that he gives to his life in a world that has otherwise been rather meaningless for him.

Like most existentialists, Walt doesn't appear to be a very religious man; if anything, he's a scientist who probably believes that there's no life after death. With no commandment from a god or gods to preserve his own life, he's ready to let it go. Skyler convinces him to get treatment, but with that decision comes Walt's commitment to leave his family better off rather than worse off. And since he knows that they'll suffer, too, with his cancer, that they'll see him lose his hair, become even less effectual as a man in the world, and physically waste away, he decides that he must do something to rectify their vision of him and his vision of himself.

Walt doesn't worry about going to Hell. He worries about the all too short lives of the people around him, and improving the quality of those lives. In an absurd and godless world, money really does seem to be the answer, and that's what Walt chooses to get. Money becomes the new family value because it will genuinely improve the brief lives of his loved ones. And with money comes personal power and masculine efficacy—all parts of the new meaning of Walt's life.

The existentialist wouldn't encourage Walt to change his moral values and actions at the end of his life; rather, existentialism reminds us to be aware of our mortality at each moment. Walt, upon realizing that life is short, has shifted his moral views. If life is infinite, then it's easy to continue to suffer at a low level and mildly degrading job, and to be rather unsatisfied with one's life. But when life is short, every moment counts. Cooking meth becomes an avenue to enhancing every moment he has left, and it's definitely time to quit working at the car wash. Cancer is his wake-up call.

Skyler the Utilitarian

Walt the existentialist has a way of viewing what's moral and immoral from the perspective of a man who knows his time on this planet is short. But what about the moral viewpoint of Skyler, who doesn't face the same existential problem?

In her decisions, Skyler seems to follow a sort of act-utilitarianism. For example, she chooses not to tell her sister, Marie, that it's Walt, rather than Walter Jr., who's smoking marijuana. Indeed, she tells Marie a white lie, saying that she is working on a short story about a pothead, rather than confess her concerns about her husband. We can see that she doesn't really want her sister involved in her marital business because she imagines that Marie will only make matters worse for all involved. Also, she never reports Jesse to the police, even though she's very angry with him, perhaps for similar reasons. It would make Walt unhappy to see Jesse in jail and be without marijuana, and that could have negative consequences for her and for Walt Jr.

But when Marie steals an expensive white gold tiara for Skyler's baby shower, Skyler demands both a confession and an apology. Why are some lies acceptable for Skyler but not others? Because in this case, the lie Marie tells has huge consequences for their relationship as sisters and (as far as Skyler knows) for the financial state of affairs of the White family.

Walt's treatments are expensive, and a good six hundred dollars would help them all; a tiara helps no one—not even the unwitting baby girl meant to wear it.

Skyler needs the money rather than the fashion show, and she needs a sister who'll help her through Walt's medical crisis rather than a sister who's busy acting out and getting in trouble. Marie's theft increased unhappiness, and her confession and continued honesty at least appears to suggest better consequences.

This reasoning helps to explain why Skyler then lets (and even helps) her boss, Ted, "fudge" his accounting records for his business. As a single action, it keeps people employed, provides for Ted's daughters (and perhaps Skyler's job), keeps investors and customers happy, and perhaps helps a worthy business stay alive until the economy shifts and allows it to flourish more honestly. She could blow the whistle, but if she did, many people would suffer, including her! Skyler likes her relationship with Ted (a little too much, since they start having an affair), and given her home situation at the end of Season Two, she has every reason to keep her romantic options open (which, it seems, would increase the happiness of two people while decreasing the happiness of none).

Skyler the Existentialist

So, Skyler's decisions fit well with the ethics put forth by act utilitarianism. Could they be considered existential as well? Is she making her own life meaningful by making choices in light of her own mortality? Skyler is shaken by Walt's health news, but her response is to fight—she's not willing to believe that Walt's bound to die. Her focus is (at first) on keeping Walt alive and continuing their family as it has been; indeed, she is attending to the immanent birth of their daughter and the new life and new hope embodied in that event. Skyler isn't always making choices by looking at life as all-too-short.

But Skyler seems to have made some existential decisions about how to live that Walt only comes to as his health breaks down. She's willing to break some rules, to confront people (like Jesse, or Ted, or Marie), and to lie or withhold the truth (even though she often experiences moral outrage at others). When she's detained on suspicion of stealing the tiara, she has no trouble making a scene in order to be released. She even threatens to create discomfort for all the workers in the store, and their customers, by calling the news media about her treatment. She's willing to maximize the unhappiness of multiple other people in order to preserve meaningful things in her life—sometimes she gives up her *act utilitarianism* in favor of *existential* concerns.

When Skyler finally decides that there's something Walt is hiding from her, she quickly and easily packs a bag and orders Walt out of the house. Skyler does make decisions, and perform actions, that aren't the actions of a cautious utilitarian woman who thinks she will live forever. She does have a few existential notes to play, and she's honest with herself about what she needs and what is important to her for a good life.

Hank the Utilitarian-Existentialist

Hank serves the greater good every day as a DEA agent, making sure that drugs don't harm people, that criminals are not a danger to the general public, and that the poisons that come from meth production are not inhaled by too many innocents. Yet the occasional Cuban cigar is on Hank's life list of simple pleasures, and he doesn't mind doing favors for people in the right places in order to receive certain illegal treats such as these. His notion of the right way to behave when his beloved Marie has a shoplifting problem is to keep quiet about it, and then if necessary ask those impacted (like Skyler) for their patience and understanding.

Hank isn't working for the DEA because he believes that the law should be upheld unwaveringly at all times. Rather, he seems to think that keeping many drugs off the streets promotes the greater good for the community, and apparently, so does allowing himself and others to enjoy an occasional illegal cigar or the thrill of stealing. Who's really hurt by those cigars? They provide pleasure for the smokers and profit for the manufacturers, and if used sparingly, don't create a health risk. And Marie's thievery? Well, it helps her so much, and the places she steals from can write it off as a business loss—no harm done. And she's in therapy after all.

But Hank's decisions aren't only based on utilitarian concerns; they have a little existentialism in them, too. Hank enjoys his cigars as much as his drug busts; the little rewards, the big moments of excitement, these are what make life living for Hank. He likes the danger, he likes being a hero, and he thinks he deserves small transgressions like the cigars because he does do a good job out in a dangerous field. He confronts his own death (and the deaths of many drug dealers and players) far more often than Skyler, Walt Jr., or Marie, and so he has a sense of the potential brevity of life. He wants to enjoy what he has, to call in sick to brew beer, to make good Margaritas, and to live life to the fullest, because he knows that the next day brings a battle with guns and criminals and perhaps his last breath.

Hank has a good idea of what he wants his life to be like (and it has something to do with alcohol and a scantily clad Shania Twain), and he chooses to help people fulfill their life-desires and meanings, too. He tries to give Walt Jr. a role model who's not so unbearably geeky as he imagines Walt to be. He tries to help Marie mend her relationship with her sister. He tries to support both Walt and Skyler as their marriage disintegrates. He seems to understand what each character wants in his or her life, and is willing to extend himself a bit to help them get it. Hank lives his life with existential knowledge and a willingness to make life meaningful with his actions.

Marie the Existentialist?

Marie, on the other hand, seems in most cases to be rather unaware of the brevity of her own life. She sees that Hank has a dangerous job, but somehow that doesn't apply to her. She sees Walt struggle with cancer, but that isn't about her either. She enjoys her life, her job, her sister and friends, and her stealing and mild meddling, but her actions for the most part suggest not a conscious making of self and meaning with an eye toward death, but a pleasure-driven code of conduct that even diverges from act utilitarianism.

Marie steals the tiara, probably not with the idea in mind that Skyler will love the gift, but that it will be a big, spectacular gift that will draw lots of attention toward Marie. She tells Hank that Walt Jr. is smoking pot not because she's concerned about the greatest good for the greatest number of people, but because she can claim to be the one who cared enough to do something about her nephew's drug problem. (Maybe she can even be seen as raising Skyler's child better than Sklyer). Marie could easily be seen as a simple moral egoist—she does what she thinks is good for her, and other people aren't considered much one way or the other.

But Marie takes a stand when we find out that Walt has cancer, and her words show a surprising existential depth in her character. When the whole family meets to discuss the issue of Walt's treatment, assisted by the talking pillow, suddenly Marie calls attention to the importance of Walt's choices and his right to control and be responsible for his own life. He should not do what makes the greatest number of people happy, rather he should do what he wishes, because he's the only one really facing his own immediate death.

Skyler is shocked; Marie doesn't care. And while Marie certainly upsets the apple cart once again and gains some scandalous attention for herself by standing up for Walt's freedom of choice, she's also bringing to the fore that great existential notion that *your death is your own*. This is all Walt has left, and we shouldn't make utilitarian demands of pleasing the group on the person who confronts something so serious, and so final, as the end of his own existence.

Waking Up

Is Walt a great example of an existentialist? We could argue that in fact Walt should've been living his life with an eye toward his own death for many years; that he has only recognized his real values upon seeing the brevity of his life. As Walt says in the pilot episode, "I am awake." For the first time, he sees his own life clearly.

Walt converts from act utilitarian to existentialist. Or, perhaps his utilitarianism actually contains his existentialism, and in that case, the moral rules we hold dear don't really change as our chances to experience life run out.

Consider a marathon runner with twenty-six-point-two miles before her. She'll make choices to conserve her energy, stay warm and hydrated, and keep to a well-thought-out pace. She has plenty of time to make moves in the race, to pass her competitors, and to strategize, as she sets out on her journey. To win, she must consider all the miles she will run equally, and the consequences of her actions and choices for each mile, carefully preserving her ability to run, the general happiness and well-being of her body, the temperature and hydration of her muscles.

The situation at the start of the race suggests caution and conservative behavior. In the final mile, she should behave differently, if she wants to win. It's time to take off the jacket and shed the extra weight, to forego the sip of water, and to make her move on the runner ahead of her. She won't get another chance. Her muscles have been hydrated and cared for, and they're ready now to achieve that last burst of energy needed to ascend to the winner's circle. Now, she expends all her energy, and her choices are not conservative, but extreme. She has no more miles to worry about, and she has no reason to hold back. Indeed, the earlier holding back was in the service of this mile and the decisions now made, at the end of the run.

To be a utilitarian in early life is to make an existential decision. When the final mile appears, we simply need to "wake up," like Walter White.

No W Y ou're Co O king

12

What's So Bad about Meth?

Patricia Brace and Robert Arp

At certain semi-reflective times, Walter White and Jesse Pinkman actually placate their guilty consciences about producing and selling crystal meth with a common argument that most of us have heard many times: adults should be able to make adult decisions about what they want to do—including doing drugs like meth—and the government or cops should mind their own business and, in the words of Peter Tosh, "legalize it . . ." Let's take a serious look at this argument by "breaking" (pun intended!) it down. And, in the process, we'll see that there are probably several things we can point to as being "what's bad about doing meth."

Adult Decisions

"Adults should be able to make adult decisions about what they want to do." We've all heard this a million times before, but what exactly is the justification for this claim?

There's a long and strong tradition in the history of Western philosophy—going back to at least Immanuel Kant (1724–1804) —in which rational beings are seen as *autonomous*, that is, free to make choices for themselves unimpeded by any coercion. Fundamental rights to privacy and the use of one's body as one sees fit are viewed as elements of this autonomy. It may be true that the right to ownership over one's own body in exercising decisions is the most fundamental of these rights. So, "adults making adult decisions" can mean something like a fully rational person, who understands the risks of a decision, being morally justified in making that decision, provided that the decision produces no harm to anyone else.

If someone is autonomous in this sense, then surely she can choose to do crystal meth. It's her body, and she can do with her body whatever she sees fit to do with it. In fact, this is the idea behind the United States Supreme Court's 1973 ruling in *Roe v. Wade*. The court ruled that, until the fetus is viable (able to live on its own outside of the womb around the third trimester of pregnancy), a woman's decision to have an abortion is her own personal, private matter, and is akin to other privacy rights afforded a full-fledged American citizen.

However, is someone justified in doing something like meth, which may not harm anyone else, but probably will cause harm (addiction and/or even death) to the person doing the meth? There's another argument that can be traced back to Kant, and others, that engaging in an action that knowingly causes harm or death involves that person in a kind of "performative contradiction" and shouldn't be performed by a rational adult. Rational persons pursue things that bring about happiness and life; but doing something that will harm or kill that person is wholly irrational (and would be a performative contradiction), and so shouldn't be performed by the rational adult. Thus, rational adults shouldn't do crystal meth.

Another way to think about this is the following: death by drugs ends a person's desire for the drug itself (obviously, because you're dead, Einstein!), so this seems pretty contradictory! So, despite being an adult who can make her own decisions, the performative contradiction of basically killing yourself in the process of getting that fix is the first bad thing about doing meth.

Good Consequences

There's also the view that someone shouldn't engage in some action if it will cause harm to oneself or others, period. This is a view embodied in the philosophy of the utilitarian, John Stuart Mill (1806–1873), where the consequences of actions become significant when making a moral decision. The rule for the utilitarian is this: if an action likely will bring about good consequences for the person or persons affected, then that action is moral, and you can and indeed should do it. On the

other hand, if an action likely will bring about bad consequences, then such an action is deemed immoral, and you
shouldn't do it. Doing meth likely will bring about bad consequences for the person doing it (addiction and death among
them), so it shouldn't be performed. So, the bad consequences
of meth are another bad thing about doing meth.

But there's a catch here. The production and selling of meth
allows Walt to make large amounts of money very quickly with
a minimum investment of time and resources. He needs the
money because he's just found out that he has lung cancer. A
high school chemistry teacher, even one as respected as Mr.
White, will never be able to accumulate enough cash to provide
for his family after he's dead. Walt actually makes the utilitarian argument that making and selling meth allows the "good
consequence" of providing for his family.

The flaw in Walt's argument and reasoning, however, is that
according to the utilitarian, if an action will affect several persons, then the good and bad consequences to *all* must be considered and weighed, so to speak. The effects of meth on people
have been consistently shown to be negative, whether it's simple physical detriment, emotional turmoil, or dysfunctional
intrapersonal dynamics. So, if the meth user is acting immoral
by causing harm to herself or himself, then the meth producer
and meth dealer are also acting immorally because they are
contributing to the harm of many people. The "good" of Walt
providing for his family in death does not outweigh the "bad" to
a whole heck of a lot more people whose lives are destroyed
because of meth. In fact, it could be argued that the meth producers and meth dealers in this case really are doubly
immoral! And Jesse may qualify as a triple threat since,
despite Walt's scolding, he's not only a cooker and dealer of the
product, but also a user! So, harming lots of people is another
bad thing about doing, and selling, meth. So, the bad consequences of meth to all people, in general, *still* are another bad
thing about doing meth.

Meth as Cancer of the Soul?

But there's more bad stuff associated with doing, or dealing,
meth. As it stands, the meth industry is illegal and chock full
of degenerates who think nothing of deceiving, stealing, or even

killing. And it's as if the meth industry actually breeds scum-bags. After all, Walt does become Heisenberg as a result of his association with this illegal activity.

A perfect illustration of the continuing detrimental effect that his involvement in the criminal world of meth has had on Walt's relation to the "straight" or non-criminal world takes place in the season one episode, "Cancer Man." Throughout the episode, Walt has been crossing paths with an arrogant yuppie in a very expensive, red BMW convertible with the license plate "KEN WINS." Ken steals a parking place from Walt and then talks loudly on his blue tooth about his business dealings, mentioning large sums of money and basically establishing himself as a jerk.

Walt hasn't had a good day even before encountering Ken. He's had a confrontation with Jesse over continuing their business arrangement; then after being told he has to make a $5,000 deposit to even see the doctor, his oncologist announces that his cancer is "treatable, not curable." To top it off, the treatment isn't covered by his insurance and will cost over $90,000 out of pocket—money he has no hope of ever acquiring through legitimate means. As Walt drives along a highway later that day, he begins coughing up blood and is forced to pull into a gas station. Who should already be there but Ken, his gleaming car parked at the pump unattended while he is inside chatting with the clerk.

Walt has become a criminal chemist who killed two people a few days ago and disposed of their bodies by dissolving them in acid. That's, as Jesse would say, "Some serious shit." It's meth lord Heisenberg-to-be who breaks bad on Ken's BMW. He gets his revenge by using science, putting a metal squeegee under the car's hood to short out the battery, causing it to explode and set the car on fire. Part of you cheers for him—standing up to a bully, defending his interests against a rich arrogant jerk—but if we *really* look at what he's done, he's crossed another line.

How many people's safety and even lives does he put in danger by deliberately setting a car on fire next to a gas pump? Why does he do it? To save his own life? To help his family? No—it's a pure ego reaction. It's as if the criminal thought process has infected his everyday life, and possibly his soul. He doesn't consider the safety of the many, only his own needs. It could be argued, too, that setting Ken's car on fire is the moral equivalent of dealing meth—it's a criminal act for his own benefit that could cause irreparable harm to others. Again, we have another bad thing associated with doing, and selling, meth; namely, the criminal lifestyle associated with the meth world is acting like a cancer that's spreading to other parts of Walt's life.

More Cancer for the Soul

In part for revenge, but also because he needs a deal with Tuco to go through, Walt adopts a second persona, calling himself *Heisenberg* (as in the physicist who developed the Uncertainty Principle). Shaving his head, he becomes the "bad ass" that his son addresses him as when he sees the chemo-induced haircut. Heisenberg succeeds in getting the deal by being even scarier than the drug lord is and literally blowing up Tuco's head quarters ("A Crazy Handful of Nothin'").

Science wins the day again. Fulminated mercury—which looks exactly like larger crystals of meth—is his weapon of choice. Returning to his car with the bag of money, he returns to himself and as "Walter" at first seems to freak out, screaming and banging on the car's interior until he gets a nosebleed. Then he comes off the adrenalin high and we see Heisenberg emerge as a self-satisfied smile slips across his face as he drives away. He won—but at what cost? He showed his face to Tuco and a multitude of witnesses. He drove his own car to a major drug deal. For someone who should be working hard at remaining incognito this was a reckless move.

What's happening here? The high he gets isn't from *smoking* meth—Walt has become addicted to the rush of power the drug culture provides him. Despite every other part of his life careening out of control, as Heisenberg, he just bested the most vicious dealer in Albuquerque at his own game. More bad things associated with doing, and selling, meth.

It's Like a Greek Tragedy

In the Season One episode, "Gray Matter," Walt's pride becomes hubris, affirming that *Breaking Bad* is, despite its moments of dark humor, truly a tragedy. If, as he's maintained, the only reason to continue to cook and sell meth is the need to make money for his family, (to pay for his cancer treatment so they aren't left with a huge debt), he's actually given a chance to escape that need. His former partner, Elliot, now a rich and famous businessman first offers Walt a job, then when that's refused, promises to pay for all of his cancer treatment. Walt's pride won't let him accept the help; at first he's even willing to forgo treatment, telling his loved ones during a brilliantly acted intervention scene, "All I have left is how to deal with this . . . I choose not to do it." He changes his mind the next morning as he takes in the familiar details of his life, the smell of his wife's pillow and hand cream, and the baby books next to cancer books on the nightstand. He tells Skyler he will go for treatment and accept Elliot's offer.

After his harrowing first treatment, however, where they shrink wrap him to the table and burn his chest with radiation, he again refuses Elliot's help, instead showing up at Jesse's, asking, "Wanna cook?" Walt had a real choice this time—a way out of his moral dilemma, and he chose the unethical path. If one's moral life is based in always choosing the correct center path, Walt continually breaks sinister, to the bad side.

Legalize It?

We've seen enough of what's bad about doing meth to at least call into question the standard line, "adults should be able to make adult decisions about what they want to do—including doing drugs like meth." So much for that claim's apparent truth.

But what about the claim that "the government or cops should mind their own business, and let adults do what they want to do." We've all heard this before. It naturally follows from the "I'm an autonomous adult" kind of claim. Now, it's one thing to talk about drugs that aren't destructive if taken moderately (like caffeine, alcohol, and possibly even THC). It's another thing, however, when we talk about drugs that are destructive even if taken moderately (like meth, cocaine, and heroine). Should the government or cops allow rational adults to take a drug like meth, even if it kills them? Further, should the government or cops allow people to make and sell a drug like meth to meth users?

In his work, *On Liberty* (1859), John Stuart Mill makes the claim that the "struggle between Liberty and Authority is the most conspicuous feature in the portions of history with which we are earliest familiar." Mill is correct as the tension between governor and governed has endured a timeless existence. It would seem that the laws enacted by the government exist as a limitation on the freedom of the members of the society so that the common needs of the society can be met. At the same time, the members of the society must have enough freedom to be able to fulfill their own needs. It's then arguable that an injustice is done either if the government of the society enacts laws that prevent the fulfillment of individual needs or, if the governed of a society, in the individual pursuit of happiness, prevent the fulfillment of the common good.

Freedom, then, becomes the central concern of a society—the freedom to pursue what's conducive to individual and collective happiness, as well as the freedom from oppression in order to achieve this happiness. More specifically, the government can maintain a patriarchical or paternalistic authority over its citizens, and the prospects of liberty are called into question; or the government can maintain a *laissez-faire* kind of authority over its citizens, and the prospects of authority are called into question.

Animals?

Yet, a balance of paternalism and *laissez-faire* kind of authority seem necessary in a society such as that of the US. If someone chooses to do meth to such an extent that he will likely be harming him or die, then that person has lost his autonomy and abilities to make fully rational, adult decisions. Thus, with the meth user there ceases to be the being that's autonomous. If that's the case, then someone else can step in and make decisions for that person. A meth user is kind of like an animal in that sense—another bad thing about doing meth!—and needs to be directed, guided, or even "caged" by the appropriate authorities. Also, the meth producer and meth dealer must be stopped by the appropriate authorities, too, since these actions contribute directly to the meth users irrationality, and are thus irrational actions themselves.

Further, on utilitarian grounds, since the meth user is harming himself, and since the meth producer and meth dealer are harming others, all of these actions can be condemned, and the government has the right to come in and defend innocents (and animalistic addicts) from the harmful effects of such behavior. Again, animalistic or destructive behavior can't go on unchecked in social situations, and it's up to the governing body and cops of a society to enact laws (governing body) and enforce laws (cops) that prevent such behavior.

Forbidden Fruit Tastes the Sweetest

By the end of Season One, Walt has broken bad, and this is clear in the episode, "A No-Rough-Stuff-Type Deal." After a PTA meeting to discuss the theft of the lab equipment, Walt and Skyler end up having car sex in the school lot while parked right next to a police car. When a surprised Sky asks her husband, "Where did that come from and why was it so damn good?" Walt's reply: "Because it was illegal," broadcasts his corruption and disregard for governmental authority over his life.

In an exchange with Hank at the baby shower the next day, we see Walt's feelings about legalizing drugs are a bit ambiguous as well. When shared Cuban cigars prompt Hank to say, "Forbidden fruit tastes the sweetest," Walt muses on how we decide what's legal. Hank's reply, "Meth used to be legal—sold it over every pharmacy counter in America. Thank God they came to their senses over that one, right?" makes us realize the irony of both their positions relative to the drug. If meth was legal, Hank might be out of his job busting meth labs and Walt certainly couldn't be making the huge profits he is from its sale.

The shoplifting sub plot that's been percolating all season comes to a head when Skyler is almost arrested for trying to return Marie's stolen baby tiara shower gift. In an exchange with Skyler we see that her moral center is still pretty straight down the middle while Walt fishes for reassurance that if he'd committed a crime she would stand by him.

WALT: What would you do if it were me? Divorce? Police?

SKYLER: You don't want to find out.

We know that Walt has just spent the last several days engaged in criminal behavior; he and Jesse robbed a chemical storage facility using thermite from Etch-A-Sketches to blow the locks and cooked a large batch of meth in Jesse's basement while an open house went on upstairs. Stealing a baby tiara isn't sounding all that bad to Walt at this point. Skyler's response foreshadows the second season break in their marriage.

Wreckage and Bodies

The last scene of the Season One episode, "A No-Rough-Stuff-Type Deal," sets up the second season, which will feature Walt and Jesse's continued dealings with Tuco and the fallout from those interactions. After sampling the product they deliver, in a fit of paranoia, Tuco goes off on one of his minions, beating him, possibly to death, right in front of our heroes ("Seven Thirty-Seven"). Again, their criminal enterprise has had the unintentional, but very real consequence, of harm to people—this time very directly.

In Season Two, Walt and Jesse's criminal enterprise will wreak all kinds of havoc with people's lives. In the second season finale, "ABQ," as Jane's father the air traffic controller mourns his daughter's death, his inattention causes two planes to collide in mid air over Albuquerque. The image of plane wreckage and bodies raining down on Walt's house is metaphor for how meth has become the destroyer of everything around him.

So, what's bad about doing meth? Lots, apparently . . .

13

It's Arbitrary?

ADAM BARKMAN

In the Season One episode, "A No-Rough-Stuff-Type Deal," Walt engages in a spirited discussion with his brother-in-law and DEA agent, Hank, about the legality of drug use, sales, and production.

Walt thinks laws that made alcohol illegal during the Prohibition (1920–1933) and current laws that make Cuban cigars and drugs like marijuana and meth illegal are all "arbitrary." Hank dismisses Walt's argument: "You ought to visit lockup; you hear a lot of guys talking like that."

We're left feeling that Walt's probably right: that alcohol, cigars, and other drugs like meth are more or less the same, and that whether they're legal or not is based on mere social whimsy.

But something's being legal is one thing; its being moral is another. There are plenty of things that are moral, but legally questionable, just like there are plenty of things that are legal, but morally questionable. I'm not so much interested in whether it was lawful for booze to have been illegal during the Prohibition or for Cuban cigars and illicit drugs to be illegal right now, so much as whether producing, selling, and using drugs—whether it's alcohol, cigars, caffeine, aspirin, marijuana, or meth—is moral or immoral.

Objective Moral Principles

Many would argue that there are some moral laws or principles—like "You shouldn't murder," "You shouldn't steal," "You should tell the truth," or "You should treat people fairly"—that all people should follow no matter what culture or circumstances they're in. I'll call these *objective moral principles*, because any rational person who takes the time to think about a moral situation will see that there are objective, universally binding principles that emerge from the situation and tell us what we should or shouldn't do. For example, Walt Jr. understands the objective moral principle that, all things being equal, "You should respect your superiors," which is what he does when he sets up a website to help his dad, who is dying of cancer. Or again, Hank understands that, all things being equal, "You shouldn't lie," which is why he didn't lie when he had to give his statement about what happened when he assaulted Jesse Pinkman.

Now, why do I say, "all things being equal" in the above examples? It's because objective moral principles hold as a general rule—"all things being equal"—but there can be exceptions to the rule. For example, there's a moral principle that says something like, "You should return things you have borrowed." But if your friend comes banging on your front door after having an intense fight with his wife and demands the ax you borrowed from him last week, you'll definitely want to disregard that particular moral principle!

Also, there might be a situation where a couple of moral principles emerge and conflict with one another, and one trumps or cancels the other out. For example, Walt Jr. should respect his father according to a principle like "You should respect your superiors." But if Walt Sr. wanted Walt Jr. to lie for him about something, the moral principle, "You shouldn't lie" might trump the "You should respect your superiors" principle, and Walt Jr. wouldn't lie for Walt Sr.

Do No Harm and Clear-Headedness

Probably one of the most basic universal moral principles is "Do no harm." We shouldn't just be going around punching the elderly, kicking cats, or insulting children at random because these actions inflict physical or emotional harm. And when we see people, animals, or anything capable of being harmed in pain, suffering, or unhappy in some way we try to minimize or get rid of the harm that's causing the pain, suffering, or unhappiness. On the face of it, then, Walt and Jesse seem to be harming people by producing and selling meth, especially since consistent meth use almost always causes, at the very least, crazy hallucinations (psychological harm) and brain damage (physical harm).

Now most would agree human beings have the potential to become better than they currently are, where "better" refers to characteristics like courage, self-control, justice, and wisdom. And most make becoming better a moral principle: "we *should* strive to become brave, temperate, just, and wise." This is why, after assaulting Jesse, Hank says to Marie, "I'm supposed to be better than that" ("One Minute"). On the other hand, a person who doesn't try to improve himself—a person who doesn't care about virtue and self-actualization in this sense—is generally considered immoral.

Given the do no harm principle and the becoming better principle, we can deduce what I'll call the *clear-headedness principle*, which generally obligates us to shun activities that cloud our minds and engage in activities that illuminate them. Clouding our mind with crazy hallucinations, for example, is actually doing harm to us psychologically since the mind naturally functions best without such diversions. The clear-headedness principle is up for debate, for sure; nevertheless, in its various forms, it's acknowledged by important thinkers as diverse as the Buddha, Mohammed, Jesus, and Immanuel Kant.

What's a Drug Anyway?

Before going any further in exploring the morality of using a drug like meth, it's important to have a working definition of a *drug*. One dictionary says a drug is a "chemical substance that affects the processes of the mind or body." Another says it's a "substance used as medication or in the preparation of medication," while still another claims it's an "illegal substance that causes addiction or marked change in consciousness." It doesn't take the keen mind of a Walter White or an Aristotle to see that none of these definitions are particularly helpful. Since salt mixed in water is, on the first definition, a "chemical substance," should we consider it a drug? Or, on the second definition, if water is used as medication, does this, then, make it a drug? And what about in a country like Saudi Arabia, where pornography, an addictive substance for many, is illegal: should it be considered a "drug" there?

Even if there's no perfect definition of a drug, I think we can work with the first general definition: "a chemical substance that affects the processes of the mind or body." Then we can divide these chemical substances into drugs that cloud the mind and drugs that don't.

Drugs that Do and Don't Cloud the Mind

Certain drugs, usually in fairly unrefined states, are good. After all, the ancient Greeks sacrificed to Dionysius, the god of wine, Shinto priests still pour out libations of sake every New Year's, and Yahweh in the Old Testament required, on certain occasions, "half a hin of wine as a drink offering." Also, opium poppies can be chewed to soothe a toothache, coca can be munched on to stimulate an unfocused mind, psychedelic mushrooms are an ancient anaesthetic, and alcohol is a natural sedative found in over-ripe fruit. And we can well imagine Hank, the home-brew king, drinking his concoction in moderation as a stress-reliever.

But still, these drugs cloud the mind, and if some drugs that cloud the mind can be used for good purposes, how can we reconcile this with the clear-headedness principle? Consider this scenario: let's say for argument's sake that when Hank was shot, the doctor had the choice to give him an anaesthetic that would cloud his mind, such as marijuana, or an anaesthetic, like metoclopramide, that wouldn't. Obviously, insofar as the doctor can more fully obey the do no harm principle by alleviating his patient's pain *and* not clouding his mind, then he should do so. Thus, metoclopramide is better than medical marijuana, in that situation.

However, if, for some reason, the doctor only had a bag of Jesse's weed, then it would be better for Hank to smoke the weed and have a cloudy mind than not to be anaesthetized at all. The reason for this is not only that alleviating serious, unnecessary pain is required by the do no harm principle, but also if Hank were not anaesthetized, he would likely cause harm to those around him—for example, nurses, doctors, and visitors—with flaying arms, curses, and so on. As the saying from the Old Testament goes: "Give beer to those who are perishing, wine to those who are in anguish; let them drink and forget their poverty and remember their misery no more" (Proverbs 31: 4–5). Obviously, my argument isn't a defense of medical marijuana especially since we have drugs that don't cloud the mind and are more medically efficient; rather, it's a very particular case where a mind-clouding drug might be used without doing anything immoral.

It should be apparent, then, why I favor separating drugs into those that cloud the mind and those that don't, rather than into medical drugs and recreational drugs. Marijuana, or Walt's bottle of tequila, for that matter, can have a medical purpose. If we try to divide drugs into medical and recreational, we're faced with a whole host of problems: Is Viagra a medical drug or a recreational one? What about red wine? Better to make the distinction between drugs that cloud the mind and drugs that don't, even if this distinction shouldn't be taken to imply that drugs that cloud the mind are always bad and drugs that don't are always good. Life is too messy for this kind of absolute division.

Meth and Morality

Nevertheless, because of the clear-headedness principle, we have a general rule that helps us to say why in most cases it's immoral to use, sell, and produce drugs that cloud the mind like meth. Alcohol in moderate doses, aspirin, and coffee don't cloud the mind, and can also do some good, such as alleviate stress, relieve pain, and stimulate a tired mind: Hank relaxes with his margaritas, Skyler takes an aspirin when she has a headache, and Walt drinks coffee every morning to help him wake up. But LSD, peyote, ecstasy, cocaine, pot, heroin, and, of course, meth are in virtually all cases taken for no other reason than to cloud the mind, thus leading to a distorted, unjust form of enjoyment.

These illicit drugs create tons of psychological harm: they impair short term memory in the temporal lobe, disrupt communication between the limbs and the cerebellum, and cause the pleasure part of the brain (the nucleus accumbens), the emotional part of the brain (the amygdala) and hormonal part of the brain (the hypothalamus) to overrule the self-control part of the brain (the lateral habenula by way of the fasciculus retroflexus). These illicit drugs also create tons of physical harm: whereas heavy drinking can kill cells in the fasciculus retroflexus in a matter of months to a few years, cocaine does it in a few weeks to a month, and meth in a few days to a week!

In addition, cloudy thinking, whether for a few hours at a party (pot) or for a lifetime through regular abuse (meth), prevents a person from acting appropriately both toward himself and to those around him. Through mind-clouding drugs, reason and wisdom are overthrown by mere instincts, at best lowering humans to the level of beasts (seeking base pleasures above superior ones), and at worst reducing humans to a zombie-like condition, where nothing else matters but a "bump" to increase a spike of dopamine in his brain. You don't need to be a psychiatrist or have a PhD in psychology to see that heavy drug use enslaves the mind and body, and is destructive of one's personality and essential humanity.

Addiction and Abuse: Coffee, Alcohol, and Cigarettes

While the cloudy-mindness factor is the first factor to consider when examining different types of drugs and their misuse, it's not the only factor. Abuse and addiction are two other important factors, and are best looked at in four distinct cases: coffee, alcohol, cigarettes, and meth.

Coffee is likely good in and of itself, but it can be addictive and misused. For example, if Walt couldn't control his coffee intake, then he would be acting intemperately or unjustly since his higher self (his self-control) should be able to control and regulate his lower self (the desire for coffee). Moreover, because caffeine can be addictive, Walt the coffee drinker needs to make sure that he, and not coffee, is in charge. Nevertheless, while coffee abuse can hurt Walt (psychologically, insofar as he wouldn't be able to control himself, and physically, insofar as too much caffeine hurts the body), the abuse of coffee isn't likely to affect others around him in an immoral way.

Alcohol, especially red wine, in small doses is good in and of itself; yet, it can be misused and is addictive as well. Although not all agree what *drunkenness* is, I think we are safe to follow the standard medical practice of measuring blood alcohol content (BAC). A person with .000-.029 percent BAC is normal, while a person with .030-.059 percent will enjoy mild euphoria and relaxation. For a generally healthy adult (alcohol is always harmful to children), neither of these blood alcohol levels would constitute intemperance, and the latter would likely constitute the proper blessing of "wine that gladdens the heart." In concrete terms, a man of Walt's body weight (body weight mattering a great deal in determining BAC) might enjoy two fingers of scotch, a pint or so of beer, or a glass or two of wine without going overboard, while a man of Hank's body weight could enjoy a bit more. Still, because anything in excess of .06 percent probably counts as drunkenness or cloudy-mindedness, that kind of alcohol consumption would be immoral.

Also, just because a person like Walt might not get drunk on two glasses of wine, it doesn't mean that this is good for his *body*: science shows us quite the opposite, and wisdom, importantly, tells us to treat our bodies in a better way. Nevertheless, if over-drinking-but-not-getting-drunk (that is, Walt having two glasses of wine) isn't a regular occurrence (that is, a non-addictive habit), this might well be justified on some occasions, such as at a party or after a particularly stressful day at work: there are many more important factors than the body's optimum health.

Further, because those who abuse alcohol, compared to those who abuse coffee, are much more likely to hurt others around them through brawling, unwanted sexual advances, drunk driving and so on, its benefits are more controversial than those of coffee. Those Old and New Testament folks were pretty sharp when they observed: "Wine is a mocker and beer a brawler; whoever is led astray by them is not wise" (Proverbs 20:1); "Be very careful how you live, not as unwise but as wise . . . Do not get drunk on wine, which leads to debauchery" (Ephesians 5:15–18).

Finally, we all know, and numerous studies have shown, that alcohol is a potential "gateway" to drugs that are bad in and of themselves, and so needs to be used moderately. Even some of those New Testament folks, like St. Paul of Tarsus, were pretty sharp: "All food is clean, but it is wrong for a man to eat anything that causes some to stumble. It is better not to eat meat or drink wine or to do anything else that will cause your brother to fall" (Romans 14:20–21).

Cigars—one of Hank's favorite drugs—aren't obviously good in and of themselves since smoked tobacco is carcinogenic. Yet, because most who smoke them do so with great pleasure and only on very special occasions—as Hank does to celebrate the birth of Holly—they aren't obviously bad either (perhaps no worse than a slice of decadent cake on a birthday). But this isn't true of Skylar's favourite drug, cigarettes, which, while good insofar as they both facilitate group acceptance and don't cloud the mind, are still largely bad. The nicotine in them makes them very addictive, leading to intemperate and overindulgent behavior (including, as with all addictions, financial intemperance), and the carcinogens that a smoker inhales makes lung cancer an increased probability, constituting an obvious immoral action since a person should do no harm to him or herself! Second-hand smoke, moreover, is harmful to all.

Addiction and Abuse: Meth

Lastly, meth—*Breaking Bad*'s drug of choice—has really no proper benefit, and has a string of serious psychological and physical harms surrounding its use. Dopamine is the neurotransmitter in the midbrain that mediates communication between the personality centers, the emotional centers, and the motivational centers of the brain. It's the primary transmitter in the nucleus accumbens (the pleasure center of the brain), and increases with certain stimuli. While the pleasure derived from a delicious meal or an orgasm (hang on!) cause synaptic levels of dopamine to increase around 200–300 percent, meth—the drug with the highest dopamine spike, especially if it's Walt's 99 percent pure ice—can cause increases of up to 1200 percent. When the relevant cells are depleted of dopamine, the person crashes. Because the relevant brain cells are still fairly healthy in a first time user, the person experiences mild depression for a few days; however, because the pleasure is so intense, it's extremely addictive, and as use continues and the brain can't keep up, the crash becomes more intense to the point where nothing can satisfy but the pleasure brought on by the crystal: food that once tasted good now tastes bland and conversation with friends no longer gives joy.

The addictive nature of meth (and many other illicit drugs) ultimately causes a person not only to violate the clear-headedness principle, but also causes one to treat *everything* around him or herself as a means to the next fix. Theft, prostitution, and even murder are resorted to; in Oregon, for example, 85 percent of all theft crimes are related to meth users and meth usage. And there are many other problems associated with meth in several other states in the US. Further, obligations to family are cast aside; again, in Oregon meth is one of the leading reasons children are sent to foster homes. In the Season Two episode, "Peekaboo," we see that not only do Spooge and his woman not give a rat's ass about each other, but they also neglect their own kid, who is dirty and hungry and forced to entertain himself with infomercials on TV. In the Season Three episode "Abiquiu," this neglect causes Jesse to say with righteous indignation, "What kind of mother gets wasted when she has a little kid to take care of?"

The end result of all of this is that using meth is straightforwardly immoral, which means that meth sales and production are immoral as well.

Ruining Lives

Philosopher Douglas Husak may be correct when he says that those who condemn illicit drug use as immoral or unjust "rarely offer a reason in support of their vehement moral condemnation." It's my hope that in this chapter I've met Husak's challenge as well as Walt's, which would have us believe that there's no compelling moral reason or foundation to oppose the legalization of drugs like marijuana, cocaine, or meth. In this way, I agree with Hank, who lucidly sees that mind clouding and addictive drugs "ruin lives."

14

Does Cooking Make Walt a Bad Guy?

GREG LITTMANN

SAUL GOODMAN: Idle hands are the devil's plaything. So, get back on the horse and do what you do best. First step: Talk to our friend and get cooking.

WALTER WHITE: (*Shaking his head*) I can't be the bad guy.

—"Caballo sin Nombre"

Of all of the morally questionable acts committed by Walter White, the most fundamental is his decision to manufacture meth with intent to distribute. In conventional morality, a criminal working in the drug trade is the quintessential "bad guy." DEA agent Hank Schrader certainly feels this way. In his mind, the world is divided between the decent people who need protecting, and the "dirtballs" who need to be knocked into line, and anyone involved in the drug trade is squarely in dirtball territory.

But if cooking meth makes Walt such a bad guy, we ought to be able to explain what sets cooking meth apart from more morally acceptable business ventures. It turns out that the line is extremely hard to draw, a fact that has implications not only for the way that we should deal with the drug trade, but also for the way that we should deal with the production of legal recreational drugs such as alcohol and tobacco, as well as other products that cause harm.

Harming People

So why would anyone think that being a meth cook makes you a bad guy? That one's easy: meth fucks people's lives up. Badly. Despite the fact that your teachers always told you that meth is awful, dangerous stuff, *meth really is awful, dangerous stuff.* Most obviously, it's extremely addictive, meaning that people who only intend to use it casually (that is, *everybody* when they first start to use) frequently find themselves trapped by a serious habit. When Wendy first picked up the pipe, it's unlikely that she intended to end up working the streets night and day just to support her addiction. Common long-term effects of meth use include anorexia, heart damage, memory loss, anxiety, paranoia, aggressive behavior, and the disgusting dental condition known as "meth mouth" (you may recall Wendy presenting her blackened meth mouth for Walt Jr.'s inspection in ". . . And the Bag's in the River"). Overdoses can result in death by organ failure. The DEA motto displayed at Walt Junior's high school stating "Meth = Death" may be an overstatement, but meth sure as hell is *bad* for you!

Given the enormous harm that meth causes, it might seem obvious that anyone manufacturing meth for public consumption is doing something morally wrong. After all, not harming other people seems like a pretty basic standard for behavior. We condemn burglars who harm others by stealing their possessions, and we condemn muggers who harm others by assaulting them in the street, so why shouldn't we condemn those who harm others by providing them with dangerous drugs? If ruining lives for the sake of money doesn't make you a bad guy, what does?

However, Walt's crime differs very significantly from burglary and mugging in at least one extremely important respect: Walt doesn't force anyone to use meth. A burglar won't wait for an invitation before invading your home and a mugger won't ask your permission before kicking your ass, but a meth cook just prepares the product, leaving it up to *you* to decide to use it. There is a sense in which the meth cook does not harm anyone at all, but merely *enables* people to harm themselves. In the Season Three episode, "Sunset," Gale Boetticher explains, "I'm definitely a libertarian. Consenting adults want what they want," making it clear that in his view, the responsibility for any damage caused by meth lies squarely on the consumer, not the producer.

If we don't allow a moral distinction between harming people directly and enabling them to harm themselves, then we must allow that workers in many perfectly legal industries are guilty of inflicting terrible wrongs. Tobacco kills people. If we don't recognize a moral distinction between inflicting harm and merely providing a product with which people harm themselves, then we must accept that the tobacco grower is as morally culpable for growing tobacco that kills someone as they would be if they had picked up a gun and murdered them with it. And speaking of guns, if we don't recognize a moral distinction between harming and enabling harm, then we would have to lay the blame for Gale's murder ("Full Measure") as heavily on the manufacturer of Jesse Pinkman's handgun as on Jesse himself. Further examples are easy to find—we don't blame producers of paint for graffiti, beer brewers for drunk driving, or the makers of lab equipment for the fact that some people will use their beakers to cook meth with.

Enabling People to Cause Harm

Having said this, we would be moving too quickly to let Walt off the hook just because he doesn't hold a gun to anyone's head and order them to smoke. While it's true that Walt doesn't force anyone to use meth, we don't have to *force* someone to do something harmful before we're morally culpable. Consider Saul Goodman's offer to have Badger shanked in prison in the Season Two episode, "Better Call Saul." If Saul had gone through with his offer, he wouldn't have directly done Badger any harm, since he wouldn't have shanked him himself, but he would still have done something morally awful. Similarly, Walt is surely morally culpable for ordering Jesse to murder Gale ("Full Measure"), even though Walt didn't personally pull the trigger.

Morally culpable participation in the harming of another person can be even less direct. If I give you a firearm, knowing that you intend to kill your neighbor with it, then I'm doing something wrong even though I don't personally kill anyone. What I *am* doing in such a case is *wrongfully enabling* you to kill your neighbor. Likewise, when Badger and Skinny Pete attend a support group for recovering heroin addicts, just in order to drum up interest in Walt's blue meth, we can recognize that they're wrongfully exploiting meth addicts by enabling their addictions, despite the fact that they don't force the addicts to take meth or otherwise do them any direct harm ("Crawl Space").

Similarly, though we might judge Walt to be innocent of "doing harm" in any direct sense by cooking meth, we might at the same time condemn him as a bad guy for enabling so many other people to do so much harm. Unlike his dealers, Walt doesn't even encourage people to use his product, but without Walt's cooking skills, Jesse, Badger, and Skinny Pete would have nothing to sell.

But can we even judge Walt guilty of *enabling* meth abuse? We might resist doing so on the grounds that if Walt *wasn't* supplying meth, meth would be no more difficult to buy than if he *was*. After all, someone else would be meeting market demand; for as long as people are willing to pay good money for meth, other people are going to have a go at manufacturing it. As the United States learned during Prohibition (or should have), taking one supplier out of the picture is just a business opportunity for other suppliers. ". . . if I'm not supplying it, they're getting it somewhere else" points out Gale ("Sunset"). Even Hank recognizes that removing a supplier, even a major supplier, won't ultimately reduce supply. After he kills kingpin Tuco Salamanca, he notes in the Season Two episode, "Breakage," that there is "not a lot of crystal on the street right now" but goes on to admit "Of course, that's not going to last. Wait to see who's going to rally the roaches now his turf's up for grabs."

Indeed, it's arguable that by participating in the illegal drug industry, skilled chemists like Walt and Gale not only do no harm, but also make things *better* for everyone. Gale observes, "At least with me, they're getting exactly what they pay for. No added toxins or adulterants." Indeed, from the pilot episode of *Breaking Bad*, Walt has been promising "You and I will not make garbage. We will produce a chemically pure and stable product that performs as advertised. No adulterants." Looked at from the purely utilitarian grounds of producing a greater amount of happiness over unhappiness, Walt might be thought to have a positive *duty* to cook meth, and the same would go for any other criminals out there with a pure product.

If we *do* blame Walt and other meth cooks for enabling meth use, we'll presumably also have to blame many legal industries for enabling other harmful habits. If meth cooks enable meth use, then tobacco farmers enable tobacco use, a significant cause of death in the world. Similarly, alcohol suppliers enable alcoholism, casinos enable gambling addictions, and gun manufacturers enable shooting sprees.

Bad Habits

It might be tempting to resist the analogy between cooking meth and the production of legal substances that cause harm. We might, for instance, insist that cooking meth is in an entirely different category from producing beer or cigarettes, on the grounds that the effects of meth use are so much *worse*. This is a line that Walt rejects explicitly in "A No-Rough-Stuff-Type Deal," in which he insists that a moral distinction between producing meth and producing legal recreational drugs is illusionary. He states, "It's funny, isn't it, . . . how we draw that line? What's legal, what's illegal? Cuban cigars, alcohol. You know, if we were drinking this in 1930, we'd be breaking the law. Another year, we'd be okay. Who knows what will be legal next year? I'm just saying it's arbitrary."

Hank could not disagree more. To his mind, there's a black and white moral distinction between cooking meth and manufacturing legal recreational drugs. He answers Walt just by noting, "You ought to visit lockup. You hear a lot of guys talking like that." In other words, he's saying, "Walt, you are talking like a *bad guy* there!" Hank sees no irony at all in the fact that he spends his time at work hunting for drug suppliers and his spare time brewing homemade beer.

Horrible, Painful, and Lingering Death

But two points must be made in reply to the claim that there's such a black and white distinction. First, it's doubtful that meth really is so much more harmful than some legal products. The obvious example here is tobacco, which is highly addictive, cannot be indulged in safely, and isn't only lethal, but causes a particularly horrible, painful, and lingering death. It's true, tobacco is unlike meth in that not many people go broke from their tobacco habit, and tobacco doesn't generally interfere with people's ability to go to work. All the same, *killing you* is still about the worst negative effect a drug can have, and tobacco use carries a very serious risk of death. The US government's Centers for Disease Control and Prevention (CDC) has concluded that smokers are ten times more likely to die from bronchitis or emphysema. Women who smoke are ten times more likely to die from lung cancer, while men who smoke are twenty-two times more likely to die from lung cancer. And those are just a sampling of all the ways that tobacco can kill you! The CDC estimates that smokers die, on average, fourteen years earlier than non-smokers.

Indeed, it's arguable that meth is *less* dangerous than drugs like tobacco and alcohol, because so many fewer people would be willing to *take* meth. Meth has the virtue that many of its negative effects become apparent relatively quickly. One can often immediately spot that someone on the street is a meth addict, which isn't generally true for those addicted to, say, tobacco. Heavy meth users are walking advertisements against using meth, more powerful than any number of government announcements. Tobacco victims, on the other hand, tend to die relatively discreetly, with their cancer unobvious until they are moved into a hospital ward.

Whether I'm right to blame the relative unpopularity of meth on the obviousness of the downsides of meth usage, there's no doubt that it *is* a good deal less enticing to the public than alcohol and tobacco. The CDC estimates that about forty thousand deaths per year are attributable to alcohol in the US (*excluding* accidents and homicide), and an incredible five hundred thousand attributable to smoking tobacco. (Talk about *mad volume*, yo!). Conversely, the US Department of Health and Human Services' best guess for annual meth deaths is five hundred and other sources give significantly lower figures. So while a heavy meth addiction may usually be worse than, say, a heavy tobacco addiction, the number of people that a tobacco farmer may endanger or kill is significantly greater than would be possible for a meth cook.

More importantly, regardless of how we rate the relative costs of meth against legal drugs like tobacco and alcohol, there's no way to justify treating the cooking of meth as being a fundamentally different *type* of activity from growing tobacco or brewing alcohol. Let's allow for the purposes of argument that meth causes *much* more damage to people than any of these legal drugs. The difference is still one of the *degree* of the damage caused, rather than the sort of business being engaged in. If the meth cook is doing something evil by providing a dangerous addictive drug, then the tobacco farmer is doing something evil, even if it is a *lesser evil*, by growing *their* dangerous addictive drug.

Yet something remains deeply troubling about Walt's willingness to manufacture meth, just as something remains deeply troubling about *anyone's* willingness to manufacture meth. The meth industry, as a whole, *harms people* badly, without providing any sufficiently compensatory good. If only nobody would cook meth, the world would be so much better off. It seems difficult to condone the existence of an industry that causes so much suffering and serves no purpose other than generating money. Walt's meth may be substantially more pure than most of the meth available in New Mexico, but it is still *meth*, and so extremely bad for people. As Jesse points out in the episode "Fly", "we make poison for people who don't care."

Just Standing By

Is it possible that Walt is acting immorally, even if he is neither directly harming people nor enabling people to harm themselves? It seems plausible that we can treat people immorally without doing either of those things. In particular, it seems plausible that we can treat people immorally just by standing by when we should be acting to help them. A perfect example of this occurs in "Phoenix," in which Walt finds Jesse and Jane Margolis sleeping off a heroin high together. As he tries to wake Jesse, Walt accidentally knocks Jane onto her back, at which point she throws up and begins to choke on her own vomit. All that Walt has to do to save Jane's life is to turn her over onto her side to clear her airways, but instead, he stands by and watches her die. Most of us could agree that his inaction is morally inexcusable. He does Jane no direct harm by just standing there, yet it's a terrible thing he is doing simply by doing *nothing* to assist. We can't put the wrongfulness down to the fact that Walt accidentally knocked Jane over in the first place, because all he was trying to do at that point was wake Jesse. Besides, Walt's inaction as he stands and watches Jane die would seem no less monstrous if she had already been on her back and choking to death when he walked in—it's the fact that he *could* save her life but *doesn't* that is so morally repulsive.

Some philosophers insist that there's no moral difference at all between killing someone and standing by allowing them to die. Many Western hospitals practice passive euthanasia; that is, they will allow willing patients to slip into death rather than insisting on giving them life-saving treatment. On the other hand, active euthanasia—that is, doing something to the patient that will cause death, such as giving them a lethal injection—is illegal almost everywhere. In light of the fact that active euthanasia can often provide an easier death, medical ethicists have increasingly questioned whether there is any moral justification for withholding active euthanasia, since the end result, the death of the patient, is exactly the same in either case. If it's true that the end result of our decisions is all that matters, not whether we work actively to achieve these ends or simply allow events to unfold without interfering, then standing by and allowing something bad to happen to someone is just as immoral as directly harming them.

If cooking meth neither directly harms people nor enables them in any significant sense to harm themselves, perhaps cooking meth still constitutes such a morally unacceptable act of "standing by." What makes the act seem so repugnant to us is that it appears to require a callous indifference to the harm that users of the meth will suffer. The profession of "meth cook" lies at the heart of a system that propagates human misery. That having been said, it's too easy to dismiss the meth cook as a "bad guy" for standing by while people suffer. After all, if the meth cook is a "bad guy" for standing by while users suffer, then the same goes for any of us who stand by rather than acting to help those suffering from addiction to meth. The indifference of the meth cook is shocking to us because of their proximity to the people who use their product, but if their sin is standing by when addicts need help, then that's a sin of which most of us are guilty.

It's Who You Know

It's a strange fact of human psychology that the more closely associated we are with someone, the more offensive it seems to harm them or to allow harm to come to them. A clear example of this phenomenon is Walt's reluctance over murdering the gangster, Krazy-8, who is being kept prisoner is Jesse's basement with a bicycle lock around his throat (". . . And the Bag's in the River"). Walt knows that it's in his best interests to kill Krazy-8, and Walt has already shown himself willing to kill people, since he has already killed Krazy-8's partner, Emilio, with phosphine gas. Yet Walt agonizes over this killing. Part of his reluctance may have to do with the fact that there's no direct threat to his own life in this case, but much of his reluctance seems to stem from how *personal* this killing is. He's *talked* to Krazy-8, and this makes it seem worse to him to *murder* Krazy-8. When Walt, tormented by guilt, is looking for an excuse *not* to kill Krazy-8, he resorts to trying to get to know him better by quizzing him about his background. He wants to know about Krazy-8's father, his education, and any other personal details that Krazy-8 can offer.

Why does Walt want to know? What does his interrogation have to do with finding an excuse not to kill Krazy-8? None of the facts Walt uncovers give him any particular reason to spare the gangster, but Walt hopes that if he only gets to know him better, he'll be so repulsed by the idea of killing him that he'll be unable to go through with it. Similarly, whether meth cooks *know* meth consumers or not, they're in close association with them through their work. The dealer may be the meth user's immediate contact, but the cook's place in the chain is only a few links behind (or one link for a small organization, as Walt and Jesse are originally). It's this proximity, rather than any difference the cook makes by cooking or not cooking, that makes their lack of concern about the fate of users seem so much worse than our own.

Good Guys, Bad Guys, and Guys Who Need Our Help

So does cooking meth make Walt a bad guy or not? What the considerations above show is that drug production is too complex a moral issue for any simplistic reduction of people into "good guys" and "bad guys." Any serious attempt to deal with the drug problem must do more than attempt to locate and incarcerate the bad guys in order to protect the good people.

Like tobacco addiction and alcohol addiction, meth addiction is best treated by helping the addict; not by trying to put all of the bad-guy suppliers in prison.

Now of *course* criminal gangs in the meth business do terrible things. I'm not saying that there's no evil in organized crime or that gangsters are mostly sweet little misunderstood angels. Organized crime is brutal and cruel, and not to be romanticized. I'm not even insisting that *Walt* isn't a bad guy for all of the things that he does—he lies to his family, puts them in danger of having their home seized rather than accept charity, blackmails Jesse into breaking the law, kills his rivals, and even orders the murder of poor Gale Boetticher, who never did him any wrong.

But the meth problem stems not from a fundamental moral or psychological difference between the producers of meth and the rest of us. The meth problem stems from the desire to use meth that too many people have. If we want to do any good in dealing with the meth problem, we need to help people to confront their desires, and to confront whatever problems in their life might have made meth seem like an attractive alternative in the first place.

What are the implications for the production of legal substances that cause harm, products such as alcohol or tobacco? As noted above, any attempt to paint producing legal, recreational drugs like these as a fundamentally different type of activity from producing illegal, recreational drugs like meth will fail. We don't need to condemn those who work in these legal industries as "bad guys," but we must recognize that just as in the case of meth cooks, the fact that they don't force anyone to use their product doesn't indicate that there's nothing wrong with the existence of the industries that employ them.

The moral here is that social problems like drug abuse—whether the drug being abused is legal or illegal—are not effectively dealt with by trying to divide humanity into the good guys and the bad guys, and then making sure that the bad guys are locked away where they can't harm us. These problems are complex, and simplistic black and white thinking can only blind us to the terrible dangers of legal, "good guy" products, while simultaneously miring us further in the colossal failure known as the *war on drugs*.

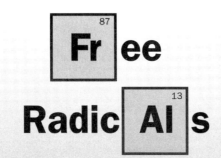

15

Been through the Desert on a Horse with No Name

OLI MOULD

When Walt walks into Tuco's office, there's an unerring steely gaze in his eyes and a sense that there'd be no turning back. As Walt squares up to a nefarious psychopath like Tuco, we're wondering how Walt will ever make it out of there alive.

However, we soon see that Walt has planned his attack, and his business negotiation, using his intricate knowledge of chemistry. By disguising fulminate of mercury as crystal meth, he's actually smuggled a bomb into Tuco's office and used it as a threat, all the while negotiating the business deal that will give him the money he needs. Once leaving Tuco's office, Walt calmly walks through the gathering crowd who seem too awestruck at the devastation to really bother about Walt. He enters his car, and suddenly releases his anger, frustration, and anxiety in a cacophony of contorted countenance.

This scene from the Season One episode, "A No-Rough-Stuff-Type Deal," is dramatic, not only because of its cinematic qualities, but because it marks a tipping point in Walt, a point at which he begins his descent into what can be called the *Desert of the Real*. It's called a *desert* because it's mostly harsh and lifeless.

Walt's world, from the moment he's told he has terminal cancer, unravels, and he begins his descent. Or perhaps, a more apt phrase would be that his world *unveils*. Until that point, we're led to believe that his family life is a solid one, his job, while unfulfilling keeps him afloat, and he has some deal of respect as a father, husband, brother-in-law, teacher, and co-worker. Given that the story of Walt starts with the realization

171

of his own impending demise, the only evidence we have of his life to that point is through conversations, photos, and idiosyncrasies. It would all seem, to him, very *real*.

However, his reality is very different from what some philosophers and psychoanalysts call, the Real. There is a distinct qualitative difference, which needs to be explored to see how Walt enters the Desert of the Real.

Constructed Reality versus the Real

Our reality is constructed by a combination of language, symbols, media, history, culture, and everyday experiences. But this constructed reality is different from the Real.

Figure 15.1 Constructed Reality versus the Real

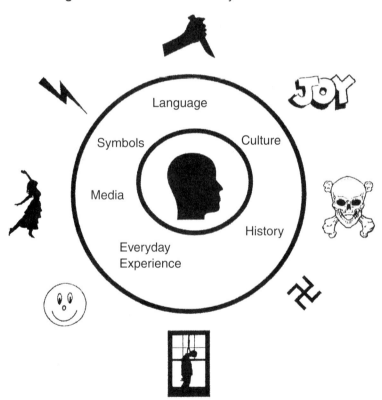

Figure 15.1 gives us a sense of how we tend to insulate ourselves from the Real by our own ideas, perceptions, and con-

structed reality that act as a layer, buffer, or veil between us and the Real, which takes the form of death, traumatic events, horrible experiences, as well as ecstatic experiences, positive interactions, and highly memorable events. Constructed reality is kind of a defense mechanism we almost have to erect so as to not be crushed by the various harsh and lifeless aspects and manifestations of the Real.

Walt's non-cancer, constructed reality becomes punctured by the Real through his cancer diagnosis. Or more accurately, the veils of his constructed reality that have built up over the course of his life lift momentarily and expose the Real, and from that point, his constructed reality changes drastically.

Walt's journey into the Desert of the Real can be articulated through a reading of one of the most famous psychoanalysts, Jacques Lacan (1901–1981). For Lacan, the Real can exist and impinge upon us momentarily, providing instances of what can seem *surreal* given the reference points of our constructed reality.

Here's an example: if a middle-class white male tourist is in a major city and accidently walks into a neighbourhood dominated by ethnic minorities, he may come into contact with a group of young males listening to gansta rap and talking in a lingo that the he doesn't understand. To the tourist, whose constructed reality to that point didn't contain gansta rap and the like, the whole incidence would seem surreal, perhaps even threatening. This is the Real, though, puncturing or irrupting his constructed middle-class white reality.

The difference then between our constructed reality and the Real effects how surreal an irruption can be. In Walt's case, the difference between his reality (husband, teacher, car-washer) and the Real are experiences that are very far apart. The fleetingness of contact with the Real, however, does have the effect of changing the mechanisms of recognition of reality within Walt, collapsing the distance (albeit momentarily) between the Real and Walt's constructed reality.

Disruption

The Real therefore has a habit of disturbing or disrupting Walt, of subverting his constructed perceptions of reality, or the lived everyday experiences of family life. And this disruption is harsh and lifeless, like a desert. The everyday constructed reality that

Walt lives is monotonous and predictable. It's in these disruptions where the subject, Walt, comes into contact with the Real. The Real however isn't a singular entity, as we would understand it.

Some label the Real as *hyperreality*. Therefore, instances of The Real often display characteristics that are attributed to the surreal. This, says Lacan, makes one faint and "unbalanced." And so the Real disrupts, shocks, and surprises—burrowing into the edifices of constructed reality that Walt has built for himself. Throughout the episodes of *Breaking Bad*, these instances of burrowing provide the catalyst for the changes in the narrative—they are the instances of conflict, suspense, and drama.

Overtaking and Altering

As Walt gets more involved with Jesse, Tuco, and then Gus, his involvement with the meth drug trade becomes more about survival and gaining an income by whatever means possible—and the life of a meth cooker and meth dealer becomes his accepted constructed reality.

It wasn't always like this. Walt is understandably reluctant before deciding to cook with Jesse so as to obtain enough money to pay for this cancer treatment. He battles with his conscience many times and as his actions lead to further criminal actions (some with some rather nauseating consequences, such as mopping up the decomposed body of a drug dealer).

The irruptions of the Real that burrow into the constructed reality Walt has built up for himself start to bubble up, and it's the murder of Krazy-8 in Jesse's basement that shows this. Before Walt walked into Tuco's office and his journey into the Desert of the Real was really underway, there's another instance of the Real puncturing Walt's reality. As Walt approaches Krazy-8, he's still attempting to convince himself that it will all be okay. "All I want to do is go home" says Krazy-8. "So do I," retorts Walt.

Walt does want to go home. More than this, he wants to return to his reality of home life, perhaps despairing that he got involved with the drug trade in the first place. When he realizes that Krazy-8 does intend to kill him with a piece of broken plate, Walt kills Krazy-8. Upon the death of the victim, Walt is heard crying, "I'm sorry" (". . . And the Bag's in the

River"). As Walt sits sobbing in the basement, it's because of the realization that his reality has ultimately shifted in response to the Real.

Our constructed realities shift all the time. Lacan says that constructed reality is made up of language, symbols, signs and experiences, and as such, our realities are coded and recoded on a continual basis. Those philosophers who argue that reality isn't an absolute object suggest that reality is a construct, and as such, is constantly manipulated by the actions of our everyday lives. For Walt however, his reality shifts dramatically after killing Krazy-8; in other words, his reality has been well and truly subverted by an attack of the Real.

As the Real penetrates (often violently) into realities, inbuilt coping mechanisms fail, and so, we see Walt breaking bad. The Real has left a mark on Walt's consciousness and his reality has shifted terminally. However, there's always a choice. At this point, Walt could come clean, admit to his crimes, and face the consequences. He chooses instead (or convinces himself that it is his *only* option) to continue cooking and so the degradation of his life into criminality continues. The Real begins to interject into his reality, it overtakes him and alters his reality, and those of the people around him.

The True Self?

As Walt continues to cook, he commits more and more criminal and immoral acts. Stealing school lab equipment with which he can cook more substantial and better quality meth is bad enough, but then to pin the blame on the janitor exemplifies the way in which Walt is allowing the Real to irrupt into his reality and his actions ("Cat's in the Bag . . ."). Walt abhors the illegal activity that he's being "forced" to undertake by his insistence that it's the only way to get the money he needs. His refusal to take the job offered to him by Gretchen and Elliot is reasoned by Walt, albeit consciously, as not being able to fend for himself. By not accepting the hand out (which it effectively is), he's exposing his reality to further irruptions from The Real.

Once you recognize that your reality is constructed, and that there exists the Real beyond your constructed reality, you've achieved a kind of nirvana state of awareness of your true self. For Walt, it may be that his true self actually is

Heisenberg's tendencies for criminality and a more subversive lifestyle. For instance, his reinvigorated sex drive seems to correlate with his cooking. When Walt and his wife Skyler attend the school meeting to discuss the arrest of the janitor (which Walt was responsible for), there's another example of the Real breaking into Walt's (and Skyler's) reality. The discussion of the missing lab equipment that was taken by Walt is juxtaposed with his more aggressive sexual encounter with Skyler in the back of their car. Walt indicates that it was the illegality of the act that heightened its enjoyment, and with a clear relation to his cooking indicates that illegality is spurring Walt's journey into that harsh and lifeless Desert of the Real.

There's also an attempt in the doctor's office to pass off the increased sexual potency as an effect of the cancer treatment. But more tellingly, when Walt is sharing a Cuban cigar with Hank, his brother-in-law from the DEA, he's discussing the boundaries of legality ("A No-Rough-Stuff-Type Deal"). The discussion however leaves Walt with a sense of unease, clearly evident by the realization that meth used to be legal and Hank's satisfaction that the opposite is now true. Here, Walt is attempting to excuse his cooking, arguing that the boundaries of legality are arbitrary and that what could be illegal today may be legal in the future. Maybe he thinks that cooking meth will be legal before too long. Walt's reality is attempting to justify his new found fondness for cooking, an attempt by his consciousness to become more aware of his true self as Heisenberg.

This justification is further explored by Walt with a conversation he has with Skyler after she tells him about her sister Marie's shoplifting. He asks her what she would do if it were Walt accused of shoplifting. "People sometimes do things for their families" Walt says, in an attempt to excuse his own, far worse, criminal activities. He's trying to explain away his lust for criminality (a consequence of the Real's impact on his reality) as a desire to help his family. Her response of clear contempt for his suggestion brings Walt's constructed reality crashing back down.

The False Self?

Yet, Walt's reality is still very much constructed of his family relationships, his conscious justification of his cooking as helping him get obtain the treatment he needs to recover. The deal with Tuco in the scrapyard will provide him, he hopes, with the ultimate justification that The Real will not be allowed much more irruption into his perceived reality. But when Tuco ruthlessly murders his associate in the scrapyard, Walt and Jesse look on in bafflement, bemused by Tuco's shear belligerence and flippant disregard for human life ("Crazy Handful of Nothin'").

What effect does this have on Walt's reality? His meeting with Tuco originally was to set up the business deal that would get him the cash he needed. You would think then, that once he obtained the money, he could return to some semblance of his previously conceived reality, however constructed. Tuco's brutal actions show how unlike Walt's previous reality is the drug world he has entered—a stark reminder that the slippage of Walt's reality is continuing, his journey into the Desert of the Real is now no longer under the motivation of his own unconscious desires for illegality, but something much more than that.

Memory Lapse

The Real then, as is argued by philosophers and psychoanalysts like Lacan is ultimately indescribable and undecipherable. It exists beyond our constructed realities. Walt's reality is constantly adjusting, responding to the presence of the Real. Lacan argues that reality adjusts through the variation in our language and symbols in accordance with its encounter with the Real.

We see this clearly in Walt, as he has to tell more lies to keep his reality in place. The biggest lie he tells, in terms of the effort he goes through to make it appear as part of his family's reality, is that of his "memory lapse" ("Bit By a Dead Bee"). His abduction by Tuco meant that he could no longer maintain the usual lies he told his wife about his whereabouts when he was cooking, and so he's forced to come up with a bigger lie which leads to him spending some time in hospital.

The lie he tells about his memory lapse means that his family have to adjust their realities, too, in order to compensate for the fact that Walt may incur another memory lapse in the future. The ever-increasing size of the shift of realities (in other words, the more surreal it seems, and what could be more surreal that being found in a supermarket naked?) is further evidence that Walt is being effected, transformed if you will, by the Real.

Shattering Reality

Philosophers who discuss the Real point out that it's never experienced directly. This, however, isn't always the case. Traumatic encounters have a way of shattering reality, no doubt. The Real has a raw power that can shift the realities that we surround ourselves with. Such trauma is often a large scale.

In the aftermath of the 9/11 attacks, many talked about that event as an exposure to the Real, as our realities failed to cope with such a cataclysmic event. Events like these truly do hit home the harshness and lifelessness of the Real.

For Walt, the trauma isn't a singular event, but more of a continual attack by the Real. As his reality fails momentarily, he reconstructs it in a different manner, hence altering his reality as well as the realities of his family and friends. The memory lapse that Walt lies about is just another example, albeit a significant one, of his reality attempting to cope with the onslaught of The Real. We've seen how he tries to explain away his cooking by saying that it's his only way to obtain the money for his treatment, and then for helping his family. As the Real interjects even further, his reality explains it further by attempting to rationalize the legality. With the escalation of cooking, the business deal offered to him by Gus, Walt's reality slips further and further into the Desert of the Real (Season Two, "Mandala"). He's running out of normal excuses.

Consider the killing of Krazy-8 by Walt and his conscious regret of such an action. That's in stark contrast to when Walt hands a revolver to Jesse and proclaims, "I want you to handle it." He's referring to the problem that one of the distributors employed by Jesse to peddle the meth was robbed ("Breakage"). Not to be seen as weak, Walt makes the decision that the crime must be punished. From the regret of a self-defense killing to the commissioning of the murder as a show of strength is a monumental leap in behavior.

The Real has altered Walt's reality to such a degree that he has changed irrevocably. His reality and all that entails—his relationships, his behavior, his language and experience—has shifted to reflect the Real. Walt, it can now be said with some degree of certainty, has shifted from a being a family man to becoming his alter ego, Heisenberg. Is he beginning to realize that the Real is unavoidable? Perhaps that's why he advises Hank, after his close shave with an exploded tortoise, to "get up, get out in the Real world and you kick that bastard as hard as you can right in the teeth" ("Better Call Saul"). Walt's constructed reality has changed forever.

Not Even an It

Through Walt, we see that the Real is a philosophical concept that's more than unconscious desire. It's not even what could be considered fate or destiny. It's an existence that can't be experienced or sensed; it can't even really be referred to as an *it*—although that is all our language can hope for. We construct realities based on the whole range of emotions, experiences, memories, and idiosyncrasies that pervade our everyday lives. When we encounter events, traumas, or other irruptions that shake our reality, we are exposed to harshness and lifelessness of the Real, and that's why we call this exposure desert-like. But the desert metaphor is just that—a metaphor for an ultimately un-experience-able reality.

The seismic shifts we experience in our own constructed realities are more jarring than the daily fluctuations in our realities, but have no less transformative effect. *Breaking Bad* shows just how realities change in response to an exposure to the Real. Walt's journey into the Desert of the Real is a series of traumatic and disruptive events that as a whole, shifts his reality from family man with a steady teaching job, to drug lord.

A Horse with No Name

So, in the Season Three episode, "Caballo sin Nombre," when Walt sings to himself the lyrics from that most esoteric of *America* songs, "I've been through the desert on a horse with no name," perhaps the horse with no name is reflective of the Real, which is itself nameless. The ways in which constructed realities are shown to change continually through irruptions of the Real—not just for Walt, but for the other characters as well—is what makes *Breaking Bad* a great show to express this philosophically rich idea.

We construct our own realities around our daily lives and experiences, at times disrupted by the Real. When the Real comes crashing in, will we, like Walt, decide to break bad?

16

You're Supposed to Be a Scientist

LISA KADONAGA

You're not dealing with rocket scientists.

> —Missouri State Highway Patrol officer, Sgt. Jason Clark, commenting on people who make crystal meth

Walter White isn't a rocket scientist; but as a respected research chemist who once contributed to a Nobel Prize–winning discovery, he's in a similar league. Then, as a high-school science teacher he resorts to manufacturing meth to pay for the expensive medical treatments related to his cancer and build up an inheritance to provide for his family after his death.

Trust Me, I've Got the Degrees to Prove It

For generations, the standard image of a scientist has been an authoritative figure in a white lab coat, usually a white male like Walt. Stereotypical scientist-types are still regularly featured in ads for products like health and beauty aids, and viewers may actually be persuaded, since surveys from the early 2000s show that scientists are among the most trusted professionals.

Scientists are expected to know everything about everything: the Professor on *Gilligan's Island* is a perfect example. As if in a salute to this kind of ingenuity, during the Season Two episode "4 Days Out," Walt uses his understanding of chemistry to improvise a battery for their stalled vehicle, after Jesse demands that he "think of something scientific" and Jesse's suggestion of building a robot was out of the question.

Jesse also assumes that Walt knows everything about the effects of chemicals on the human body ("you're supposed to be a scientist"), and is frustrated by Walt's uncertainty whether the drug dealer they exposed to phosphene gas will experience delayed effects. Likewise, drug kingpin, Tuco, expects Walt to know how to perform CPR on an unconscious henchman: "Do something! You're smart, right? Do that thing!" (season two, "Seven Thirty-Seven").

It seems ludicrous that a character like Tuco would suddenly be so trusting. Yet sometimes people do assume that someone with a PhD is essentially the same as a medical doctor. In the summer of 1988, a case of weather instruments en route to a research station in northern Ontario was mistakenly directed to the local hospital, because someone had assumed that anyone named "Dr." must be working there. A few years later—in a more serious situation—a researcher from the University of Guelph was abducted by rebels while he was working in Indonesia. Someone had overheard him being addressed as "Dr." and had believed that he would be able to treat an injured fighter. Fortunately, he was released unharmed.

Changing Expectations

Scientists themselves—as well as historians and philosophers who study how science is carried out—have been debating what is and isn't a science for more than three centuries. Just as perspectives on artwork, civil liberties, and many other aspects of human culture have shifted over time, science has also changed. Lewis Thomas notes that although alchemy and astrology are viewed as superstition rather than real sciences today, only a few hundred years ago someone like Walt would have identified himself as an alchemist. According to Sandra Harding, the word 'scientist' did not actually appear until the 1840s, when the Scientific Revolution was well under way. Up until then, the term used was 'natural philosopher'.

Authors like Thomas Kuhn, in *The Structure of Scientific Revolutions* (1962), attempted to describe what distinguishes modern science from earlier "pre-science" approaches to understanding the world. They were hoping to develop a universal set of rules for how to construct and test a scientific hypothesis. According to Imre Lakatos, proper scientific methodology includes a comprehensive program for guiding future research, and modern science is more organized about filling in these gaps than pre-scientific society was. Lakatos felt that within a research program there would be much less bickering over fundamental theories, or over what kinds of observations are relevant to solving problems.

Eccentricities like Jesse's insistence on adding chili powder to his crystal meth as his "signature" would be more consistent with the pre-scientific approach, where there was considerable variability between individual practitioners. In fact, it was to the advantage of alchemists to hang onto their trade secrets and make them so difficult to understand that outsiders (and even other alchemists) would be unable to figure them out.

With an organized, standardized scientific method that required co-operation and correction of mistakes, scientists had a strategy that could deliver results. By working together, scientists could develop generalized theories that were applicable in many different situations, and increased their chances of making accurate predictions of phenomena ranging from weather to where to find gold. Although we're no closer to manufacturing precious metals from lead than the medieval alchemists were, this is the next best thing, and Walt's creation of the ultra-pure crystal meth that so impresses Tuco is another example of these kinds of improved techniques.

Besides its practical results, science had a powerful appeal as a philosophical approach for making sense of the world. Its hypotheses were confirmable through empirical evidence, repeatable, and above all, it was accessible. At least on the surface, it appeared egalitarian—doing "good science" and getting results that made sense didn't depend on aristocratic birth, or some kind of divine grace. So, it was possible for relative novices like Jesse to improve their laboratory results, just by following instructions from someone like Walt—ultimately even Badger could learn how to become a competent chemist!

No matter who practices it, science itself is a human activity, and it can be influenced by human feelings and intentions. In the late twentieth century, the increasing recognition of diversity in Western societies affected scientific education and research. By then it was also becoming evident how destructive technology could be to societies and environments, while the displacement of ancient forms of knowledge by modern science was resulting in the irretrievable loss of potentially valuable information. It was as if researchers had suddenly discovered that, against all predictions, Jesse's chili powder *was* indeed a vital ingredient in the meth recipe.

Prominent scientists like Edward O. Wilson and Carl Sagan were saying that the world was a mess, and that some of this was due to the very scientific discoveries that had created modern societies. Some, like Jared Diamond, noted that instead of collaborating on problem solving, scientists themselves were busy arguing over whether "hard" physical or "soft" social sciences were more important.

Traditional Knowledge and the World of *Breaking Bad*

A combination of social and historical factors created the conditions for the emergence of the Traditional Knowledge movement. It raised the possibility that non-Western cultures, or groups within our society that have been excluded from the mainstream, have their own ways of understanding the world that were being overlooked by science. Paul Feyerabend argued that authors such as Lakatos were unfairly assuming that Western science was superior to other forms of knowledge, and using inadequate methods to judge that knowledge. Feyerabend's supporters didn't claim that Western science was irrelevant or that all types of information were equally effective; rather, they argued that it was difficult and probably not desirable to try to impose a single way to evaluate them, especially given that Western perspectives aren't immune from error or bias. Cultural context is often overlooked, especially when trying to transfer information and techniques among different societies, and this can often affect the adoption's chances of success.

Researchers like Nancy Turner in Canada and Helen Verran in Australia have lived and worked with aboriginal communities for years, learning not only their taxonomic systems for identifying plants and animals, but also how their cosmology and cultural beliefs shape their views about how knowledge is recognized and passed on. Jan Harold Brunvand, in *The Study of American Folklore* (1978), documented recipes and mechanical inventions devised by local people and still used in rural areas today. Even children developed innovations, including a (rather sinister) exploding toy crafted from machine nuts and bolts, and filled with the heads cut from wooden matches.

Ironically, in some of these non-mainstream or subsistence settings, intimate knowledge of how to survive in harsh conditions can be more valuable than scientific information, especially in a time when science is devalued to the extent that even highly-placed government officials boast about ignoring advice from experts. For *Breaking Bad*'s drug underworld, in some ways, scientific experience is more jealously valued than in mainstream society. Walt ends up using his knowledge of meth production as a bargaining chip to save his own life and Jesse's life, too.

Even if cookers do not require in-depth knowledge of organic chemistry to copy meth-making recipes, the person or persons who originally developed them had to have some idea of what chemicals were required, and which common household products contained them in sufficient quantities. Tom Kiesche portrays Badger's cousin, Clovis, in the show. Although his character has to write the chemical names on his hand in order to remember them, in real life Kiesche did an undergraduate biology degree with a chemistry minor, then worked for a pharmaceutical company before becoming an actor. Even he didn't report having encountered those particular chemicals during his course work.

The meth-cooking equivalent of Brunvand's homemade, labor saving devices is the "shake-and-bake" method of producing the drug, by mixing the chemicals in a two-liter pop bottle rather than in a glass flask over a heat source. Shake-and-bake is spreading rapidly across the continent. While it's extremely hazardous (the bottle can explode into a fireball if opened at the wrong time), it can also be done on the run, without cumbersome equipment of the type illustrated in Walt and Jesse's mobile RV cooking lab. Like Walt's brother-in-law, Hank, and his colleagues in the fictional DEA unit, some real-life officers are dismissive of these small-time cookers. Others point out that the development of this new technique required a considerable amount of ingenuity and experimentation—characteristics that aren't associated with unintelligent people.

Jesse Becomes a Scientist

The training of scientists often involves a student-supervisor relationship similar to those found in apprenticeships. It's a similar arrangement to the medieval trade guilds, and as Lewis Thomas describes, to the ancient alchemists. Walt and Jesse stumble into just such a relationship out of necessity. It begins as a delightful perversion of what occurs in mainstream academia: instead of having his pick of top-scoring applicants, like he would if he'd taught at a university, his protégé's poor school record and rebelliousness emphasize Walt's exile from the usual domain of the scientist. At first things don't go well: Jesse has contempt for Walt's formal scientific approach, expressing his resentment for how Walt had assigned him failing grades as a student. At once triumphant and defensive, Jesse claims that his own work is "art," deliberately distancing himself from his former teacher's perspective.

When Walt first sees a meth lab, ostensibly on a ride-along with his brother-in-law Hank's DEA team, as a professional chemist he's horrified by its makeshift, sloppy procedures, and appearance. He berates Jesse for using a volumetric flask rather than a more robust boiling flask.

Jesse in turn, is proud of his own expertise, producing a marketable product under primitive conditions. He resents Walt's advice and has contempt for the older man's scientific approach: indeed, we learn as the plot unfolds that Jesse once aspired to be a graphic artist when he was younger. One clue to Jesse's perspective on knowledge is during his conflict with his gifted, more academically inclined younger brother, where Jesse insists that "Not all learning comes out of books." Consistent with his character, Jesse prefers experiential learning. This is what he ends up going through, under Walt's tutelage.

In the show, there are signs that formal and "street" science can be reconciled. Both understand the dangers of working with toxic chemicals and reject the idea of setting up a lab at home. Despite earlier disagreements over methodology, Walt listens to Jesse's advice to obtain an RV to use as a mobile cooking lab. When Jesse sees the purity of Walt's finished product, he expresses grudging admiration, though it's expressed in his own terms by referring to Walt as "an artist." Walt, meanwhile, acknowledges Jesse's understanding of the complex web of relationships between local drug dealers and buyers, and entrusts distribution to him.

Upon successfully cooking meth together, for a moment both Walt and Jesse are united in their feelings of accomplishment. There are some lapses; notably, when they have to dispose of a dead drug dealer's body by dissolving it in hydrofluoric acid, and Jesse makes do with the bathtub rather than a nonreactive plastic container as advised by Walt. The acid eats through not only the bathtub, but also the underlying floor, depositing the remains in the room below ("Cancer Man"). But there are signs that Jesse is learning from Walt: he becomes exasperated with the hapless Badger for fooling around in the lab, and begins to scold him just as Walt would ("Down").

Students watching the series can relate to Jesse especially if they are working on independent research projects such as a graduate thesis. In the sciences in particular, introductory courses tend to focus on learning basic skills such as laboratory procedures. While it's important that students become familiar with these techniques, so they won't set fire to the lab the way I almost did, at this level the problems posed tend to have definite solutions and to be fairly predictable. By contrast, students involved in original lab or field research can come up against a complex series of obstacles, often unique to their situation. This can range from the correct way to ask elders in an aboriginal community for information, to attaching a radio transmitter to wild animals as small as a lemming or as large as a California gray whale. It may involve having to transport a hundred kilograms of equipment into an isolated forest in Thailand, a beach on Hudson Bay, a dunefield in Algeria, or an ice shelf in the Antarctic. Often there aren't any textbooks available for that kind of knowledge.

Walt and Western Science

Walt's personal philosophy, which he tries to instill in his students during classroom scenes throughout the series, is not surprisingly based on empirical science, and the goal of understanding and controlling a complex world. As the plot unfolds, Walt is shaken by a series of progressively more shocking events that destabilize his rational viewpoint: his cancer diagnosis, the rival drug dealers who threaten to kill him and Jesse,

Walt's deliberate error that gasses their assailants, and at last Walt's murder of the surviving dealer, Krazy-8. Walt becomes distracted and begins to falter in the classroom, mirroring our culture's growing uncertainty about science and technology in recent decades.

In a broader analogy, Walt's situation is quite different from efforts like the Green Revolution, which arguably saved lives although it had some unanticipated negative social and environmental impacts. Instead, his decision to get involved in drug trafficking more closely resembles scientists' involvement with weapons of mass destruction, where it was evident from the beginning how damaging the knowledge could be. A destroyer of worlds, indeed—and as the impacts of Walt's activities become more widespread, this is literally what happens with a horrendous accident.

Walt's world, like ours, is inundated by science. The opening credits for the first episode have barely finished rolling when we find out that Walt's wife has already made decisions based on what she perceives to be scientific information: urging her husband to take echinacea for his apparent cold symptoms, and serving her less-than-delighted family a low-cholesterol bacon substitute for breakfast. In terms of health benefits, echinacea hasn't done as well in rigorous medical trials as lowering cholesterol. Her uncritical acceptance of both of these ideas in close proximity suggests that, for non-specialists, making sense of the latest research findings can be confusing. Understanding may be tenuous and ever-shifting, patched together from a mix of infomercials, media reports, quotes from peer-reviewed journals, anecdotes gleaned from co-workers. Even health care providers may supply inconsistent advice. Scientists like Carl Sagan lamented this type of free-for-all where spurious claims may go untested, contributing to a decline in critical thinking.

No Way to Lessen Its Negative Impacts

Given how influential science is in many aspects of our lives, it seems to be contradictory that we are also seeing a trend towards the abandonment of science and rationality in terms of shaping domestic and international governance. Or perhaps this has always been the case—only it's more evident now that we know where to look. One reason why policymakers and institutions were given high levels of trust and respect was that they claimed to be making decisions based on objective facts. In retrospect, the first decade of the twenty-first century may be seen as a time when our beliefs were shaken. Scandals rocked numerous financial firms and governments; high-ranking authorities not only admitted to ignoring factual evidence but did so proudly.

The unfolding story of Walt's decision and all the changes it sets in motion is reminiscent of the model developed by sociologist Jacques Ellul, who predicted that technology ends up subverting human wishes and ideals. Ellul's view was grim, suggesting that, even with best of intentions, once we embrace technology there's no way to lessen its negative impacts or make it more humane. This view fits well with the relentless progression of consequences resulting from Walt's production of crystal meth.

A final irony is the plot development in the second season where Walt appears to be responding to cancer treatments, which may remove the life-or-death reason for selling drugs. True to his original belief in empirical science, advanced chemotherapy treatments appear to be working. But by then it's much too late to return to the way things used to be. He may as well try to un-invent a weapon of mass destruction.

17

Breaking Bonds

Denise Du Vernay

Although completely enthralling, cinematographically beautiful, and more engaging than most shows on television at the time, the first two seasons of *Breaking Bad* didn't seem to offer any new or improved attitudes from its contemporaries regarding sexual politics on TV.

With only two principle female characters who aren't particularly interesting (although Skyler does have her moments when she's pushed) feminist critics might be deceived by these first two seasons, assuming that the show isn't particularly pro-woman. Especially when network TV is letting us down (with few exceptions, such as *The Good Wife*) feminist critics, not to mention many television viewers, turn to cable yearning to see strong and effectual female characters who are not victims or mere eye candy. We don't often get what we want, and what we got from the first two seasons of *Breaking Bad* was a fantastic, albeit not very feminist, drama.

Except Walter (whose complexity is discovered in the pilot), in the first two seasons, all the principle characters follow the status quo and, with the focus on Walt, are even archetypal; Skyler White, the pregnant, kind, loving mother; Marie Schrader (Skyler's sister), dramatic, more than a little crazy; Hank Schrader, alpha male; Jesse Pinkman, twenty-something still annoyingly full of teen angst; Walter, Jr., moody teenager; Saul Goodman, lawyer, shifty to comedic levels à la Lionel Hutz; Gus Fring, heartless, intimidating drug dealer.

More Dimwitted Male Characters?

For feminist media scholars, a look at sexual politics in television isn't just taking a count of the female and male characters
(although, admittedly, we do like it as equal as possible). It's
not just noticing how scantily clad and attractive the women
are, or counting the gay characters, or judging a show by how
many of the conversations between female characters center
around men. We look at the aforementioned criteria, for sure,
but also conduct more nuanced analyses, such as the enforcement of heteronormative and traditional gender roles and the
systemized punishment for breaking those rules. We also consider the characterization of female characters: Are they complicated? Victimized? Realistic? A show that has only one lead
female main character for four male characters can still get
high marks for its single, compelling female character, even
while failing the numbers game.

Feminist culture critics pay attention to male characters as
well, and aren't the only viewers to notice the tired, unfair male
stereotypes littering the evening television lineups. How many
more dimwitted male characters does Hollywood have up its
sleeve? How many more simple, beer-drinking, football-watching dads are collected in piles of potential pilot scripts?

How does *Breaking Bad* do? Looking at Walter White, quite
well. He's not one of those beer-drinking, football-watching
dads, standard in many Hollywood TV scripts. Part of what
makes watching *Breaking Bad* satisfying is the evolution of its
characters. In the pilot episode, Walt is a high-school chemistry
teacher who's so afraid of conflict that he refuses to demand
respect from his indifferent, slacker students. He has followed
the rules in life: he got an education, bought a house, started a
family—his life should be gravy. But yet he struggles financially, even forced to work part-time at a car wash, has a son
with cerebral palsy, and has an unexpected daughter on the
way. Then he's diagnosed with lung cancer. When he finds out,
we watch as he changes from meek and impassive to aggressive and intrepid, while keeping his cancer to himself.

The viewer knows from Walt's teaching that he's not usually
one to throw his weight around, so the family is shocked when
Walt knocks down an obnoxious bully teasing his son at a clothing store in the pilot episode. The alter ego Walt has created for
his meth-cooking self (the not-yet-named Heisenberg) is seep-

ing into his real life. That night in bed, a sexually aggressive Walt pushes Skyler onto her side and Skyler, surprised at his intensity and erection, says, "Walt! Is that you?"

Although different, Walt hasn't completely changed. Also in the pilot when Walt speaks his video message, "Skyler, you are the love of my life; I hope you know that," we believe him. And when he addresses Walter Jr., "There are going to be some things that you'll come to remember about me in the next few days. I just want you to know; no matter how it may look, I only had you in my heart" his words are genuine.

Even at the start of the second season, Walt isn't yet consumed by power and still sees meth as a financial necessity. When Jesse and Walt see how crazy Tuco is and realize what they've gotten themselves into ("Seven Thirty-Seven"), Walt, nervously muttering like Rain Man, soothes himself by mentally adding up the money he seeks to earn for Skyler and the kids after he's gone. "Adjusting for inflation," he says, the cost of two kids in college at "good state schools," the remainder of mortgage, home equity line, and their living expenses, he arrives at $737,000. Eleven more deals "always in a public place from now on," he says more to himself than to Jesse, "that's doable."

In the Season One episode, "Cancer Man," the viewer understands why Walt had been hesitant to tell his family about his cancer: as soon as they know, they look at him with sadness and pity. He's seen as a victim and it disgusts him. After Skyler breaks down at a dinner with Hank and Marie, Hank says privately to Walt, "No matter what happens I want you to know I'll always take care of your family." Walt doesn't respond, but his resolve to provide for them intensifies. As a result, Walt takes his anger out on a caitiff who stole his parking space and irritated everyone at the bank—when Walt sees him later at a gas station he starts the man's expensive convertible on fire. While Walt's angry and frustrated at feeling helpless, his impending death makes him behave recklessly and he prefers feeling powerful like Heisenberg than ineffectual like poverty-stricken cancer victim Walter White.

Usurping Gus

Heisenberg's influence on Walt makes him prideful. He refuses to accept help and is angry with Skyler for telling people about his cancer (not understanding that it's not just his problem, but hers too). In the first season episode, "Gray Matter," Walt's previous business partner Elliott (apparently fabulously wealthy from a business that Walt left for the safety and predictability of teaching) learns of Walt's cancer and offers Walt a job. When Walt refuses, Elliott and his wife then offer to pay for his treatment. Skyler is relieved at the prospect; she wants Walt to see a high-demand specialist who has agreed to take him on thanks to Marie's connections.

In Walt's mind, not just breaking the law but creating a horribly nasty drug that ruins a lot of lives (plus the risks in doing so) are more acceptable than taking charity. Although Walt never tries his "Blue Sky" meth, he knows its purity and is strangely proud of his accomplishment, which is obviously more gratifying than teaching.

In Seasons Three and Four, Walt no longer simply wants to come up with money to provide for Skyler and his children. In fact, Walt's cancer is in remission. It isn't about financial security anymore; Walt simply now wants to become Gus. At the shocking end of the fourth season, when the camera closes in on a lily of the valley plant near Walt's pool, we realize that Walt was behind Brock's poisoning—not Gus as Walt had convinced Jesse. Walt risks killing a child in order to keep Jesse on his side and to motivate him to kill Gus.

This capability for evil is in stark contrast to the Season One episode, ". . . And the Bag's in the River," when Walt is forced to choke Krazy-8 to death. He struggles with the decision, even making a pro-con list. The "let him live" side is long and includes morals (Walt still has them, after all) but the single item on the con side of his list is compelling: "He'll kill you and your whole family if you do."

Even so, the viewer suspects that Walt won't be able to kill Krazy-8, despite the danger in letting him go. Walt makes him sandwiches and provides him with water and toilet paper. (Jesse isn't pleased every time he comes home to find Krazy-8 still alive in his basement because, according to a coin toss, it was Walt's job to kill him). Krazy-8 successfully gets Walt to bond with him while he's locked to a pipe in the basement.

Over a few beers, Walt discovers he'd actually shopped at Krazy-8's family's furniture store. Krazy-8 is the first person Walt tells about his cancer, telling him, "It's not a conversation

I'm not even remotely ready to have" with his family. Krazy-8 offers to write Walt check if he frees him, tells him that he just wants to go home. Walt cries and says, "I don't know what to do." "Yeah, you do," answers Krazy-8.

Walt goes upstairs for the key when it occurs to him that he might have a weapon. Walt removes the broken pieces of a plate from the trash and lays the pieces out like a puzzle. He cries when he realizes that there is one large, sharp shiv missing that Krazy-8 is most certainly planning to use to attack Walt as soon as he's freed.

Walt returns to the basement and walks toward Krazy-8, who thrusts toward him as if to stab him with the shiv. Walt is then forced to choke him with the U-bike lock that's held him to the pipe for several days. Walt cries while and after he takes Krazy-8's life and repeats, "I'm sorry" over and over. Walt doesn't take killing this man lightly.

This scene is in stark contrast to the cold, calculating plots Walt is later capable of. Not only does Walt poison a child, but he also kills two of Gus's dealers and he convinces Jesse to kill Gale (who, although he's a meth cook working for Gus, is largely a good and innocent person). And in the gripping fourth season (the most recent at the time of this writing), after failed attempts, Walt does succeed in killing Gus by creating an explosion that results also in Héctor Salamanca's death, with no regard for potential casualties. His motivation for being involved in this life in now a thirst for power, and has changed drastically from his original goal of acquiring $737,000.

Jane, Skyler, and Marie

Now that we've seen a bit of Walt's character development, what about the female characters on *Breaking Bad*? Would feminists see a sexual political shift in the show, from the first through the fourth seasons? The character of Jane Margolis (introduced in the second season) is problematic for a feminist reading. On the one hand, she's a recovering addict with daddy issues who allows her new relationship with Jesse to derail her sobriety, painting her as powerless to not only drugs but also to a *guy*. On the other hand, she's enterprising in her attempt at blackmailing Walt for more money. Unfortunately, though, Jane suffers for both her own and Jesse's sins. The role of Jane serves mostly as a means for developing Jesse as a character; his love and mourning for her makes him more compelling to the audience.

Although Skyler can stand up for herself when required, she's in many ways painted as an emotional victim. In one particular moment of weakness exposed to Hank, Skyler has a meltdown that starts with anger and finishes with tears. After she blubbers about Marie, money, and the old hot water heater that's ruining the utility closet, an uncomfortable Hank says "You want me to take a look at that utility closet?" while he, the guy that he is, hugs her awkwardly ("Seven Thirty-Seven").

Even though Skyler would like Walt to be open with her, she mostly allows him to take the lead and call the shots until early in Season Two when Walt seems to be on the verge of tears and then quickly shifts to aggressive and almost rapes Skyler in the kitchen. She makes him stop. Then he goes outside to cry. Skyler follows and tells him that she knows it's not fair that he has cancer and that Walt is scared, but says, "You cannot take it out on me." Skyler is misreading the situation; Walt isn't taking out his fear and frustration on her but is allowing his secret life to affect his overt life with his family. Still, we're proud that she stands up to Walt, and she doesn't allow what she believes to be his complicated feelings about inoperable lung cancer (and strange moods she attributes to marijuana use) to be used as an excuse to mistreat her.

In the episode, "Cat's in the Bag . . .," Skyler confronts Jesse about selling pot to her husband and demands he not sell to him or call their house again. She's clearly nervous and uncomfortable, thus picks up Jesse's "yo" as a means of deflecting her fear in an effort to seem like she's mocking him. Defending her family isn't something she's internalized quite yet as her role, but even so, we have an idea of how strong she can be to protect her family. This scene, along with her successful escape from a shoplifting charge by faking labor ("A No-Rough-Stuff-Type Deal"), serves as foreshadowing for the strength she exhibits later, while also serving as contrast for those future demonstrations of courage.

Marie, for reasons the viewer doesn't quite understand, suffers from kleptomania (resulting in Skyler being detained at a store and almost arrested when she attempts to return a stolen baby gift), coupled with selective denial. Skyler can't abide shoplifting and Marie's subsequent lies about it. Her anger at Marie's dishonesty indicates how she might react should she find out what Walt is doing. There's talk among the characters that some people enjoy the adrenaline rush of stealing, so Marie might be addicted to stealing the way that Jesse is addicted to meth (and later heroin) and Walt becomes addicted to the power of being Heisenberg.

Character Development

Happily, there's a shift in Season Three when both Marie's and Skyler's characters deepen, along with the male characters. The friendship between Jesse and Walter complicates further. Walter is no longer making meth to secure his family's future; he has turned meth into a career and now thinks like a mobster. It isn't until Season Three that Walter is truly breaking bad; he's no longer simply a law-breaker (and occasional killer out of necessity) but has become a monster, bent on power. He'll now kill to advance his position, not just out of self-preservation.

The complexity behind Gus's motivation starts to come to light, raising questions about his past, and in the Season Four episode, "Hermanos," during a flashback, Gus's back story is revealed. We learn the root of his animosity towards Héctor Salamanca, the murder of Max, Gus's former partner—the other 'brother' of Los Pollos Hermanos and possibly his romantic partner as well. This hint at Gus's possible homosexuality is perfect; it's subtle enough to show sexual orientation as a non-issue in most aspects of life, but also serves to rock heteronormative assumptions. A powerful man emulated and feared by all who know him is gay? Why not!

In the absence of the calm, moral center that had been Walter, Skyler takes over as head of the household. It's not only that she has kicked Walter out and is pursuing a divorce (and is, in essence, a single parent) but also that she has become stronger and is determined to care for her family. Ironically, especially in Season Four, Skyler has to clean up the mess created by Walt. Skyler now makes the family's financial decisions. She figures out the cover story (Walter Jr., Marie, and Hank believe that Walter has a gambling addiction) and even devises a plan to launder the money: the very car wash where Walt moonlighted after school until he quit in the pilot.

When her former boss, Ted, gets into trouble with the IRS, Skyler steps in, hoping to prevent an investigation that would almost certainly result in a probe into her personal finances. She arrives unexpectedly at Ted's meeting with the auditor (dressed like a floozy and acting like a ditz) taking responsibility for keeping the books but claiming she couldn't have done it wrong because when she used Quicken, it didn't flash warnings at her. Her ruse is successful; if Ted pays the IRS bill he'll be off the hook. Unfortunately, Ted doesn't have the money, so to make the problem go away, Skyler arranges for Ted to receive an inheritance from a relative in the old country, an inheritance that just happens to be in the exact amount he owes the IRS. When Ted doesn't pay his tax bill, Skyler confronts him. He attempts to blackmail her for more money. Skyler contacts Saul for help, who sends his goons to force Ted to write out a check to the IRS. Unfortunately Ted panics, tripping into some furniture. At the end of Season Four, it's not known whether Ted is dead. Skyler is now breaking bad, too.

The Sexual Political Shift

Along with Skyler, Hank and Marie are developed in Season Three. Until Hank loses control and puts Jesse in the hospital ("One Minute"), his character is testosterone-filled, even comical. Despite his position in the DEA, he smokes Cuban cigars, uses racial slurs with co-workers, and makes crude sexual remarks in front of his wife and Walter, Jr. (Hank has a special affection for Shania Twain, from whom he would like a "tuggy.") After the beating, though, when Hank is worried that his career in law enforcement is over, he cries with Marie, quickly recovering and demanding her silence about his situation. The DEA has also taken his gun away, which contributes to his feelings of impotence. Marie is forced to become the head of her household while managing the energy to stay positive about Hank's physical therapy and to somehow handle his verbal abuse. Because Hank is dependent on Marie, his regression brings him to start keeping secrets from her. Previously, Hank would have had no problem doing whatever he wanted, with or without Marie's approval. Hank's odd rock collection, an honest obsession at first, becomes the screen for investigative trips (for which he coerces Walt to drive).

Marie is not only concerned about her husband but also has to, presumably for the first time, worry about money and be in charge of paying bills. She's forced to be strong (although her kleptomania returns) and put up with Hank's moodiness. Marie is also upset that Hank can no longer keep a gun. Not only does she feel angry on his behalf, but the gun also holds symbolic meaning; she feels that without Hank at full power, they are in danger.

Skyler and Walt pay for Hank's physical therapy costs. Although Walt feels responsible for Hank's injury, he's invigorated by his position of helping the man who had been prepared to take care of his family not long before.

Who's Breaking Bad Now?

Skyler analyzes the dangerous and complicated situation her husband's career has created for the family, and puts her accounting and negotiating skills to work. She deals with the situation. She's not a part of it by choice, but takes action and refuses to be dominated by Walt or Saul. Her character in Season Four is a sharp contrast to the patient, caring wife lovingly transitioning the family to veggie bacon we were introduced to in the pilot episode. She learns to break bad. Skyler is now strength coupled with emotion, which makes for a quality female character.

Even with but two principle female characters, Skyler's depth makes *Breaking Bad* pass almost any analytical criteria a feminist scholar might employ. She has developed beyond the archetypical wife and mother ubiquitous on television to a venturesome, creative business partner. In the first two seasons, the title of the show clearly refers to Walt. In Seasons Three and Four, *Breaking Bad* applies to Skyler, too.

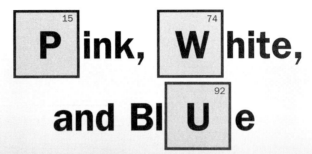

Pink, White, and BlUe

18

Walter White's American Vice

JEFFREY E. STEPHENSON

We are what we repeatedly do.

—ARISTOTLE

In *Breaking Bad*, the show's writers and directors have masterfully created a sympathetic, and occasionally darkly humorous, anti-hero, Walter White. Walt's troubles are the troubles of an ordinary person of today, and we sympathize with his situation.

His work leaves him uninspired and even somewhat depressed; he has family members who don't understand him and even belittle him; even his car breaks down at the worst possible moment! Diagnosed with cancer, he faces the prospect of insurmountable financial debt, which only adds to his economic misery, hounded as he is by creditors from very early on in the first season. This last fact about Walt's situation becomes crucial not only to understanding the popularity of the series— we all know someone who in recent years has fallen under crushing financial debt—but also the greater message behind *Breaking Bad* and the choices of Walter White, a thoroughly modern and thoroughly average man.

Of course, it's how Walt copes with his cancer diagnosis and what he chooses to do to deal with the financial burdens of his life that generate the pathos of the series, not to mention the growing interest in his plight. After all, it's not every day that a high-school chemistry teacher decides to break bad and transform himself into a meth cook and dealer. But we mustn't forget that Walt is doing things that are just plain wrong, as well as downright vicious, and that's also part of the show's appeal.

Absolute Right and Wrong

We all know it's not right to cook and sell meth, but why? There are a variety of moral theories out there that give us reasons why actions are moral or immoral. Probably the most popular moral theory by virtue of its apparent simplicity of application is *deontology*. Following in the footsteps of Immanuel Kant (1724–1804), deontologists hold that there are absolute right and wrong ways of thinking and behaving in the world, and that it's our duty as rational creatures to think and behave the right way. The most fundamental principle for deontologists is *universalizability*: you're supposed to act in such a way that you could will that *everyone* would act in the same way in the same circumstances.

Deontologists then show that certain kinds of activities are absolutely wrong, because they cannot be universalized. Lying, for instance, is strictly morally forbidden for deontologists, because you cannot will that everyone should lie. In fact, if all people lied, there would be no truth and consequently no basis for the liar to get away with lying since the liar depends upon there being truth for the lie to work in the first place! Murder is another immoral act because you can't universalize it: there'd be no one around for you to murder then! The same goes for stealing, as there'd be nothing left to steal.

For deontologists, consequences don't enter into the moral discussion. For example, it's immaterial that telling a lie might help someone feel better, say, about her hairstyle, or that telling the truth might result in someone's death. And it's not the fact that people are killed or harmed in some way when we murder, rape, or steal that's the reason we don't do these things. Consequences don't matter; what matters is that you the right intention of universalizability in mind when you act.

It's adhering to the rigid principle of universalizability and *not* considering consequences that gives so many people a headache over deontology, however. The idea that I'm obligated to tell Nazi inquirers the truth about the Jews hiding in my basement (in a classic counterargument to deontology) strikes reasonable people as problematic at best. If we consider Walt's situation with Krazy-8, we can see that from the deontological point of view it's immoral for Walt to kill Krazy-8; however, from Walt's vantage point we can see that, in a sense, he had an obligation to kill Krazy-8 because Krazy-8 would've killed him and his entire family if he were set free (pretty bad consequences for Walt and his family). It's a kind of madness to think that you can't consider the consequences of actions, and this leads to the criticism that deontology is a contradictory moral theory.

Consequences, Consequences, Consequences

A very different kind of moral theory is *utilitarianism*, made famous by John Stuart Mill (1806–1873). Utilitarianism focuses our attention solely on consequences of actions for the majority of people affected by a decision. If an action's outcome is going to benefit the majority in some way, then the action is the moral one and should be performed. For instance, Walt's chosen path of producing quality meth to create financial stability for his family seems wrong on the face of it, no doubt. However, from the utilitarian perspective, it could be argued that cooking and selling meth is an expedient means to securing his family's financial future after he's dead. A greater number of people are going to be happier if he cooks and sells meth than if he doesn't.

Having set out to make money from cooking meth, Walt finds himself murdering two people early in his drug production career, and murdering people is generally considered immoral. However, the utilitarian can say that the people Walt murdered—Krazy-8 and his cousin Emilio—were hardened drug dealers without any socially redeemable qualities. Walt has in fact done a greater number of people a favor by eliminating two people who are habitually creating greater harms to society.

For utilitarians, good outcomes = moral acts. But utilitarianism has some troubling conclusions. We generally think of murdering people as bad, but on the utilitarian calculus murdering some people, in some circumstances, is not only acceptable, *it is what we ought to do* in order to bring about good consequences or make people happy. And notice that Walt is doing the same thing that Krazy-8 and Emilio are, yet Krazy-8 and Emilio are condemned for it because they contribute to the misery of society, while Walt is encouraged to do so because he contributes to the greater good of his family members in addition to society by reducing his debt and removing unsavory characters. How can it be, we wonder, that the same act is morally wrong *and* morally right? Something must have gone wrong with any theory that would expect us to accept a straightforward contradiction like this.

The utilitarian approach is based solely on actions and consequences, and there's no consideration whatsoever of Walt's personality and psychological well-being. In fact, there's supposed to be no consideration of personality or psychological wellbeing for the deontologist either, since acting according to principles that can be universalized is the primary focus. A major problem, then, is that utilitarian and deontological theories essentially ignore individuals and their characters, and make us into mere conduits for right actions with good consequences. Walt's ambitions, thoughts, beliefs, desires, and intentions are, literally, immaterial to the moral judgment we would make about him.

Virtue Counts for Something

Virtue ethics—put forward by Aristotle (384–322 B.C.E.), among others—is a moral theory that not only looks at the consequences and intentions of a person's actions, but also at his beliefs, desires, and ambitions. The virtue ethicists' central idea is that if you have a virtuous personality, psychological disposition, or character (all meaning the same thing here), then not only will you likely perform morally right actions, but also these actions likely will have good consequences.

We want to not only perform right actions that have good consequences—we also want to be *virtuous persons* performing right actions that have good consequences. You can get a demon to do the right thing (deontology) yielding good consequences (utilitarianism); however, he's still a demon. Thus, virtue ethics can act as a kind of complement to the deontological and utilitarian positions, rounding out our moral lives.

Followers of Aristotle see virtue as a good habit where a balance is created in your character. The idea is to promote the "not too much" or "not too little," but the "just right" in our characters so that our actions and reactions to situations reflect this hitting of the mean between two extremes. The virtuous person has cultivated the kind of character whereby he or she knows how to act and react in the right way, at the right time, in the right manner, and for the right reasons in each and every moral dilemma encountered. However, the way in which you cultivates a virtuous character is through choosing actions that are conducive to building that virtuous character. So for example, if you want to cultivate the virtue of honesty so that you can actually be an honest person, then you need to act honestly time and time again so that the virtue can "sink in" to your character. The more Johnny actually tells the truth when asked whether he has done something wrong, the more Johnny cultivates the virtue of honesty. The more Suzy lies when asked whether she has done something wrong, the more she cultivates the vice of dishonesty.

Virtue ethicists have a general list of virtues, including honesty, prudence, generosity, integrity, affability, and respect, to name just a few. The simplest example is that of courage: courage is a moral virtue the vice of deficiency of which is cowardice (too much fear) and the vice of excess is rashness (insufficient fear). Human flourishing consists essentially in cultivating the virtues like courage and avoiding vices like cowardice and rashness.

Vicious Walter White

Even if it can be argued from the deontological or utilitarian perspectives that what he's doing is right or good, from the virtue ethics perspective Walt is clearly vicious. He's a man whose moral compass is inappropriately aligned. In fact, it's *outrageous* for anyone to think that he's to be praised for entering a world of violent drug lords and dealers. Why?

First and foremost, it's because Walt places his family directly in harm's way. He's not a noble man looking out for the best interests of his family; he willingly, deliberately continues to put the lives of his innocent family members in jeopardy, under the false premise of saving his family the financial hardship that will occur for them after he has died. Walt's judgment has been warped by years of poor decisions and the compounding consequences that attach to them. He claims to be focused solely on the financial situation at hand, instead of focusing, for instance, on his family in the way that a loving and caring man would do. He misses the birth of his daughter because he has to complete a lucrative drug deal. At the end of the second season we learn what Skyler thinks of Walter's constant evasions, lies, and inexplicable absences: she leaves him.

But before events get to this point, why didn't Walter know that his wife would be disgusted with his activities if she knew about them? Why can't he see that the legacy he would be leaving his family is actually a legacy of violence, lies, and deceit, of financial boon brought on only by sacrificing his very limited time with his loved ones to make drugs in a desert and sell them to repulsively violent drug thugs?

Walt also habituates himself to the vicious persona of Heisenberg, an alter ego that comes at the end of a series of vicious decisions. For example, after he witnesses Jesse's involvement in a meth-making operation, Walt blackmails Jesse into partnering with him to make and sell the drug in purer and ever larger quantities. Walt's mental abuse of Jesse only escalates as the series goes on, and his continued violent outbursts aimed at Jesse's incompetence begin to show Walt for the vicious man he has voluntarily and enthusiastically become. Walt also watches as Jesse's girlfriend, Jane, dies during a heroin induced vomiting fit. He has now actively murdered two men, engaged in the coercion of a much less capable underling, and has failed to intervene when a young woman was dying. Finally, how is it that Walter has the equipment to even commence this enterprise? It's because he's a chemistry teacher in a public school, with access to beakers, flasks, masks, and other material purchased with taxpayer money. So we can add defrauding the public and theft to his list of vices. These cannot be the actions, consequences, attitudes, beliefs, or intentions of a virtuous man.

Walt also contributes to, and perpetuates, a social evil. Consider the drug of choice involved in the series: crystal methamphetamine. Walt is producing massive quantities of crystal meth by the end of Season Two. This is not a drug like LSD that has interesting mystical or other hallucinogenic properties contributing to creative, artistic impulses. It's a dangerous drug in general, one that typically results in destruction of personal relationships, not to mention health (rotted teeth and blown out noses are just two); its addictive properties are well documented. The experience of crystal meth is one of high energy, frenetic, hyper-driven, and undisciplined activity. Indeed it's the drug of a society obsessed with activity, action, movement, getting places, doing things, succeeding. It's the drug of hysteria and capitalism, of the rampant fury of accomplishment.

The show's creator, Vince Gilligan, says in the commentary on the first DVD of the series that he wanted the show to be about "a good man who loves his family, and who decides to become a criminal." But *is* Walt a good man at the start of the show? Hardly. He clearly isn't virtuous. He's not surrounded by friends and family who think highly of him, he's not successful in his career, he's financially burdened, and so doesn't have the freedom that comes with fiscal responsibility. He blames others for his misfortunes; and he consistently creates justifications for his actions that aren't in keeping with reality, let alone with virtue. Walter is a confused man at best, and a vicious one at worst.

Virtue and Moral Responsibility

Many of us can easily relate to Walt. This is a man who lives in the same unsympathetic economic and political system we do, and he's had things happen to him that are beyond his control. Even his body, being overtaken by metastatic lung cancer, isn't under his control. We might think that Walt is largely an unwilling cog in a machine that seems to grind individuals into nothingness. He isn't responsible for what has happened to him, we believe. Or is he? This is one of the crucial elements involved in moral theory in general and virtue theory in particular: To what extent are we responsible for what happens to us in our lives?

Walt tasted outstanding professional success in the early part of his research career. In fact, some of the research on which he was a project manager contributed to a Nobel Prize. But he's now a chemistry teacher in a public high school, surrounded by disinterested, disrespectful, and disaffected students. He's dissatisfied with his life as a teacher, even though we're all probably familiar with the mantra of how important high-school teachers can be in the lives of their students. Walt's role as teacher leaves him feeling empty, lame, aggrieved, and insulted. We learn eventually that his former graduate student lover and another research partner with whom he had begun a scientific business venture eventually married and continued with the successful science company after Walt, in an apparent fit of jealousy and pride, walked away from the venture.

We begin to see a portrait of an ambitious young Walt who becomes embittered and clearly loses his way, who feels his life as a high-school chemistry teacher is not only disappointing but also futile by his own estimation. Walt is a man haunted by broken dreams, a once ambitious, proud, dynamic, and even charismatic man who is now a high-school teacher with little self-respect and no friends who are his intellectual equals.

Still, Walt has made his own choices in life—they weren't made for him. He chose to walk away from academia and from a life as a lucrative corporate researcher. He chose to marry Skyler, to become a high school chemistry teacher, to work a second humiliating job at a car wash to try and make ends meet, and to bring a second child into the world. He has, in fact, chosen every aspect of his life up to the point where he is diagnosed with lung cancer. And he has chosen, at a critical juncture, to create and later sell meth as a means of securing his family's financial future.

Taking responsibility for our actions is one of the central virtues that a rational adult with a free will can cultivate. If we don't take responsibility for what we do, we're no better than animals or machines, and we shouldn't want that!

Vice and the American Psyche

It should strike us as odd that *Breaking Bad* and other American television shows have elevated and glorified confused or outright vicious characters, and this perhaps says something important and disturbing about America as a society and about the character of the American people. Shows like *The Sopranos* and *Dexter*, where violent thugs and a pathological murderer are somehow transformed into heroes of a sort whose actions are often viewed as being morally ambiguous or complex, or even morally virtuous, are additional manifestations of this peculiarly American pathology. Walter White is simply its most recent example.

Walter White—whose last name, with its connotations of peace, faithfulness, innocence, and cleanliness, imbues the character with a positive sense of purity before we even meet him—is a frustrated high-school teacher whose life is representative of a very narrow understanding of what constitutes success: money, with professional respect a significant second.

The corrupting influence of the American capitalist ethos as currently manifest is pervasive in *Breaking Bad*. Walt is engaged in a system where he's pressured constantly (and for years) to think in terms of financial success, and the sense of empathy with which we approach Walt leads us blindly to embrace the fact that our economic system in its current form is acceptable. We all suffer under the delusion that success in terms of material gain is the appropriate measure of a good life; we *too* are obsessed with material wealth and the status that attaches to it, which leads us to a distorted sense of understanding of Walt's plight, and the consequent warped judgment that this vicious man is morally virtuous. But there are numerous reasons for thinking he's not virtuous, as we have shown. *Breaking Bad* provides the opportunity to critique the types of values we have as a nation, and virtue ethics helps us get clearer not only about the virtuousness of individual people, but also about the virtuousness of societies of which individuals are composed.

America suffers from a lack of considered judgment about its own values, especially in terms of the ethos of success by any means necessary. In the business sphere, people are praised for the extent to which they can make money for shareholders, even if the environment and populace suffer. This is a distorted value system. Walter White's economic plight is symbolic of a corrupting value system and of a society crumbling under the weight of its own unchecked commitments to the American dream of success and consumerism, which now comes at the terrible price of not only sacrificing virtue amongst its citizenry, but also of encouraging, if not out and out praising, viciousness.

19

Meth, Liberty, and the Pursuit of Happiness

Aaron C. Anderson and Justine Lopez

Breaking Bad's protagonist, Walter White, is a status quo-challenging, law-disregarding, meth-cooking, high-school teacher. He may also be a hero of American liberty! John Stuart Mill's essay, *On Liberty*, has been integral to understanding democratic republics like the US since its publication in 1859, and it can actually help us make sense of Walt (and his alter ego, Heisenberg) as a sort of hero—or is it anti-hero—of justice, liberty, and human progress.

Fundamental to Mill's argument is a critique of democracy and the enforced conformity that it brings. He's wholeheartedly against conformity and argues that if we perform an action merely because it's the socially accepted thing to do, then we're doing a disservice to the cause of human liberty. The heroes of liberty are the people who think for themselves and test *all* ideas and lifestyles, even if their ideas turn out to be wrong. Believe it or not, Mill thinks that someone who's wrong but thinks for himself or herself offers more to the cause of human progress than someone who's right but who doesn't think for him/herself! Pursuing thoughts and actions outside the norm of society has inherent value, as these challenge the status quo. Thinking and acting differently, in other words, benefits everyone, even those whose ideas are being challenged.

So, can we consider Walt's illegal activities to be an exercise of the liberty that Mill so eloquently champions? Can we consider laws against meth cooking as merely the legislated "tastes" and "preferences" of the majority?

To Cook or Not to Cook

When we first meet Walter White we would never expect him to become New Mexico's largest meth manufacturer. After all, Walt isn't your average cook. With his wire-rimmed glasses, plaid shirts, and khaki pants, he really is your quintessential high-school science teacher!

This changes when he finds out he has inoperable lung cancer, and by the end of Season One Walt has begun the drastic transformation into his alter ego—the bald-headed, pork-pie-hat-wearing drug lord, Heisenberg. While we might not agree with him, we can understand why Walt came to make the decisions that lead to this transformation. As Walt puts it in "Bit by a Dead Bee": "My wife is seven months pregnant with a baby we didn't intend. My fifteen-year-old son has cerebral palsy. I am an extremely overqualified high school chemistry teacher. . . . I make $43,700 per year. . . . And within eighteen months I'll be dead."

So, what would you do if you were in Walt's shoes? Okay, maybe cooking ultra-high-grade methamphetamine isn't the first thing to pop into your head! But, using Mill, it *might* be possible to justify Walt's extreme actions and perhaps find something noble and even good in his behavior. Viewed in this philosophical light, Walt's decision to make and sell meth can be viewed as an example of what Mill calls "the sovereignty of the individual over himself." According to Mill, one of the main goals of a liberal democratic society is to determine where this "sovereignty of the individual over himself" ends and "the authority of society" begins.

For Mill, the "authority of the society" is justified in interfering with the lives of individuals only when someone has harmed, is harming, or will be (likely) harming someone else. So, thinkers since Mill speak of his *harm principle*, which goes something like this: As free individuals having sovereignty over ourselves, we should be completely free to make decisions about our own lives. However, as soon as our actions harm others, society begins to have some say over our behavior.

Mill goes on to argue that, as a society, we are free to voice our disapproval of other people's actions, but we shouldn't be allowed to impose *legal* penalties on others just because we don't agree with their behavior. This is because individuals are the most interested in their personal well-being and are therefore the most fit to make decisions regarding it. For Mill, it's not the place of other individuals, the ruling class, or the government, to make decisions for you or me, or to limit our ability to make decisions for ourselves, so long as others are not harmed by those decisions.

Mill's ideas can be applied to many of *Breaking Bad*'s characters, from Walt and his decision to cook meth to Jesse and his decision to use it. For example, after his friend (and dealer) Combo is shot while slinging meth in the second season episode "Mandala," Jesse spirals into addiction. He starts by smoking crystal in order to cope with his problems, but rapidly graduates to shooting heroin and comes dangerously close to OD-ing. Although we might find Jesse's drug use to be disturbing and even "wrong," these are ultimately Jesse's individual decisions. And, according to Mill, we should be free to disapprove of his actions, but not to penalize them (as long as he isn't hurting anyone else).

Of course Mill's harm principle is made much more complex in light of Walt's decision to cook and sell meth. Should Walt be free to manufacture crystal meth? And if he is, what sorts of penalties can society *justly* impose on him and still call itself a "free" society?

The Pursuit of Happiness

Breaking Bad is chock full of characters who are less than what society deems "perfect" or "good." Skyler, a devoted wife and mother of two, instigates an illicit affair with her boss, Ted Beneke, and later buys a car wash to launder money for Walt's meth business. Marie, a picture-perfect wife and nurse by trade, is a closet kleptomaniac and steals a pricey diamond tiara for Walt and Skyler's baby. Gus, a seemingly model citizen and owner of Los Pollos Hermanos, is a ruthless killer and a major player in the meth trade. Even Hank, an upstanding DEA agent, has his issues, including an affinity for illegal Cuban cigars!

Believe it or not, Mill actually sees value in the "alternative" lifestyles of these characters because they represent what he calls *individuality*. For Mill, individuality—or the pursuit of individual and independent decision-making—is key to human progress and is directly related to the pursuit of truth and the perfection of humankind. The potential for the progress of humankind resides in every individual's unique thoughts and actions. And in order to encourage free thought and action, Mill argues that "there should be different experiments of living." That's not to say that Mill would approve of all the actions of *Breaking Bad*'s characters (especially Gus, the "ruthless killer!") but rather that "free scope should be given to varieties of character, short of injury to others."

Mill argues that there's always value in an individual's unique thoughts and life choices. Even if our choices end up being "wrong," new ideas and alternative lifestyles serve the valuable purpose of questioning the status quo and continuing the debate about what is right and most beneficial for humankind. Because Mill argues that the status quo should always be tested, it can also be argued that Walt's "alternative lifestyle" of cooking meth is beneficial for society, making Walt a sort-of hero!

You're probably wondering how Walt's decision to become a meth cook can possibly be construed as a good thing. Well, in this case, cooking crystal meth—along with lots of other "illegal" activities—can count as an example of what Mill calls *individual spontaneity*. Factoring in college tuition, mortgage, and cost of living, Walt figures that he needs $737,000 to provide for his wife and two kids after he dies. For a teacher who makes about $43,000 a year, those numbers don't really add up! Therefore, Walt is forced to think outside the box to come up with a creative solution to his money problems using the one thing he knows best: chemistry.

Despite risking jail time, losing his family, or even getting killed, Walt makes what he believes is the best decision for his family. Walt essentially tries out a new "plan of life" that *may* contain some nuggets of "truth," *despite* its illegality and *despite* society's disapproval of it. The result of Walt's new life plan, or of any alternative life plan, may be totally wrong, but because it challenges the status quo it can potentially help humankind's progress toward a more just and free society.

In this way, *Breaking Bad* explores the limits of liberty: At what point can a just society say what you or I choose to do is not permitted or illegal? Mill is always quick to remind us that even society's most widely accepted views may be wrong as often as they are right. And, even if society's views are right, if they aren't questioned then they run the risk of losing the force of truth. According to Mill, the majority and those in charge tend to not think highly of individuality. But, alternative lifestyles that are practiced by a minority of the population, such as those seen in *Breaking Bad*, can contain truths or partial truths, and should therefore be protected if we as a society are dedicated to liberty and the pursuit of truth and perfection.

No Harm, No Foul

While it can be argued that Walt's alternative lifestyle may benefit society, there's no doubt that he's done some dirty deeds along the way. (To jog your memory: Walt strangles Krazy-8 with a bike lock, allows Jesse's girlfriend, Jane, to asphyxiate on her own vomit, fashions the suicide bomb that kills Gus. . . . Need we go on?) But Walt also has a less direct impact on the people who surround him, especially in relation to the well-being of those who use his product. Those in favor of drug and alcohol prohibition often argue that because these substances *always* harm users their use should be limited (or even banned). Taking Mill's principle of harm into account, at what point is Walt harming others by cooking crystal? Should Walt be permitted to cook and sell meth knowing full well that it will hit the streets, be consumed, and therefore damage the health of those who use it?

On Liberty was written in the mid-1800s during a temperance movement, which promoted prohibition and anti-alcohol legislation. In his discussion of alcohol use, one of Mill's primary aims is to debunk the idea that intoxicating substances should be restricted because they physically hurt users. Mill voices a general opposition to the criminalization of vices and even specifically writes that alcohol intoxication "is not a fit subject for legislative interference." Mill keenly points out the oddity of trying to restrict the use of alcohol to protect the health of the user, noting that, "there are many acts which, being directly injurious only to the agents themselves, ought not to be legally interdicted."

By extending this idea to drugs, in this case meth, it can even be argued that educated cooks such as Walt and his short-lived lab assistant, Gale, actually benefit society because their blue meth is pure and therefore less harmful to users. Actually,

Gale who is a self-proclaimed libertarian, justifies his job as a meth manufacturer by saying, "There's crime and then there's *crime*. . . . Consenting adults want what they want. And if I am not supplying it they will get it somewhere else. At least with me they're getting exactly what they pay for—no added toxins or adulterants" (Season Three, "Sunset").

The notion of harm is crucial to Mill's arguments about the extent and limits of liberty. As mentioned earlier, Mill's harm principle demands that we be free to exercise our individuality provided we do not harm others. In fact, as long as an individual action doesn't harm anyone else, preventing someone from expressing their individuality by criminalizing their actions actually constitutes harm in and of itself. So perhaps it can be argued that inhibiting Walt from cooking and selling meth would do more damage to society than good.

While we're not allowed to harm others, Mill argues that we should be free to cause some injury to ourselves. So by Mill's logic, drug use is an individual decision. "Users," like Jesse, Badger and Skinny Pete, who use Walt's crystal are free to use drugs and potentially damage their health because in doing so they do not negatively impact anyone but themselves. Therefore it can be argued that Walt is not the one who should be punished for their individual decisions.

That's not to say that harm can't be inflicted indirectly. Regarding indirect damage caused by substance use, Mill accepts that harm is committed when an individual neglects obligations such as debts or financial responsibilities to his or her family. However, Mill argues that if an individual is to be punished, he or she should be punished specifically for neglecting his or her duties and *not* for using alcohol (or, by extension, drugs). Ultimately, Mill argues that our "choice of pleasures" and our way of spending our money, after we fulfill our "legal and moral obligations to the State and to individuals" are our "own concern" while allowing the government control over such chemicals is extremely likely to be abused and harm the cause of liberty.

Crime and Punishment

While Walt does smoke a joint, pop a few pills, and get rip-roaring drunk on more than one occasion, for the most part he's a pretty straight-laced guy. But while Walt doesn't really do drugs, he does make them. So can the same liberty that Mill argues should allow individuals to consume alcohol be extended to those who manufacture alcohol—or in this case meth?

Much of Mill's discussion of liberty and law relates to the *use* of alcohol during his time. However, Mill's argument can easily be extended to the consumption and manufacturing of illegal drugs today. What's important in Mill's discussion of alcohol use is the argument that consumers shouldn't be punished because punishment could actually damage the whole cause of human freedom and progress. While this seems like a bit of a slippery slope argument, Mill doesn't want society to take away any personal liberties, especially if those liberties only concern the individual making the choice.

The issue of punishment is a key one for Mill as well as for *Breaking Bad*. After all, throughout the show Walt does face some dire consequences for his actions. He's constantly trying to evade capture and the punishment that comes with it: For example, he's confronted with divorce if he's caught by Skyler, he's faced with prison if he's discovered by Hank, and he's threatened with death if he wrongs Gus. However, Mill argues that it shouldn't be up to society to dictate Walt's behavior. According to Mill, Walt should be free to manage his own life and make his own individual decisions. However, once Walt starts to harm someone else then, argues Mill, he deserves to be punished.

So, at what point does Walt deserve to be punished for his actions? Do manufacturers cause more or less harm to others than users do? As a manufacturer does Walt deserve to be punished? Mill, for his part, is not much concerned with manufacturers. He draws attention to the prohibition laws in his day and argues that these laws are much more concerned with stopping the use of alcohol than they are with preventing the production of it. So, by extension, it seems Mill would frown on the prohibition of manufacturing drugs and would argue that these laws are mostly concerned with prohibiting the *use* of drugs and are therefore imposing unjust limitations on individual liberty.

The Dangers of Democracy

According to Mill, republics and democracies, including those that pride themselves on being based in the "will of the people," can pose serious threats to justice and progress. Citizens who value liberty need to guard against the ways in which the majority can restrict progress and freedom. While in the US we have a tendency to speak grandly of the possibilities of democracy, Mill warns that democracy has a tendency to enforce a sort of "collective mediocrity" in which citizens replicate behaviors simply because they are the accepted norms of the majority or of the ruling class. In many ways, the characters found in *Breaking Bad* reflect how the majority can influence custom and legislation—as they relate to drugs and alcohol in the US—and hinder liberty in the process.

Mill's essay constantly draws attention to the dangers of legislated morality: While legislation may appear to prohibit things that could be damaging to society, in many instances it serves to reflect the opinions of a few that have acquired the status of "custom" and the force of law. These laws come to be accepted without question, and can deprive individuals of liberty and cause a regression of humankind. For example, in the first season Marie panics when she thinks Walt Jr. is "on pot." She even goes so far as to have Hank take Walt Jr. to a seedy motel to meet Wendy, a drug-addled prostitute, in order to teach Walt Jr. about the dangers of this gateway drug (". . . And the Bag's in the River"). While Marie acts overly concerned about the impact marijuana use could have on Walt Jr., we later learn that Marie was a big pot smoker in her youth!

Here, Marie serves as a prime example of someone who, for lack of good reason, is blindly following the custom of being anti-drug simply because it's the socially acceptable thing to do—and because her husband is a DEA agent! As Mill points out, replicating even the most correct ideas, simply because they are socially-accepted, stops human progress dead in its tracks. So customs come to replace reasons for behavior. Mill calls this the *magical influence of custom*. Ultimately this use of custom amounts to despotism in its effect on the thoughts and actions of individuals.

American society tends to accept the production and consumption of alcohol because it's more-or-less customary to do so while that same society looks down upon, stigmatizes, and prohibits the use of other drugs because that's the socially accepted thing to do.

Think about it: Hank loves to drink alcohol, but if Hank were to conform to an anti-alcohol mindset, which was customary in Mill's day, then it wouldn't be socially acceptable for him to imbibe. As a DEA agent his job would probably involve busting alcohol manufacturers. And because Hank bottles his own homebrew (called Schraderbrau) he would not only be breaking with custom he could even be breaking the law! Similar to Marie, Hank is blindly following custom by maintaining that alcohol is okay and meth isn't when, in fact, both are drugs that were at one time or another considered illegal in the US.

In Mill's view, majority opinion can ultimately be more dangerous and tyrannical than the laws and legal penalties of a repressive government. And this conformity to custom for custom's sake causes the degradation of human intellect and a "mechanization" of human beings. For this reason, the "individuality" which is expressed through the behavior of Walt (and his alter ego, Heisenberg) is crucial for progress and the liberty of society.

DARE . . . to Be Different

Before he was diagnosed with lung cancer, Walt spent his entire life playing by the rules. But through his transformation from straight-laced science teacher to bad-ass drug dealer Walt actually became an unlikely hero of justice, liberty and human progress! Through the story of a high-school teacher turned drug manufacturer, *Breaking Bad* provides a test-case of Mill's philosophical principles of liberty and harm. By applying *On Liberty* to *Breaking Bad* and its protagonist Walter White, we're constantly confronted with this question: Do Mill's principles hold up in the extreme case of a meth cook?

In order to answer this question, it's crucial to remember Mill's words: "In this age, the mere example of nonconformity, the mere refusal to bend the knee to custom, is itself a service." While Mill was writing in the 1850s, his words still ring true. We need to test *all* ideas in a society, including the most accepted and "correct" ones. So while it might be hard to justify with Walt's extreme actions, Mill actually allows us to find some value in the alternative lifestyle of a meth cook. And whether Walt's right or wrong, his "criminal" behavior is heroic simply because it tests out new ideas and lifestyles, challenges the status quo, and in the process aids the progress of humankind.

Spontaneous Reactions

High-School Teachers Who Have Broken Bad

- Something close to *Breaking Bad* was revealed at the end of 2011 when a seventy-four-year-old university mathematics professor and her twenty-nine-year-old son were charged with cooking meth in their Somerville, Massachusetts, home. The professor would use old Snapple bottles in the meth-making process, and one of her ex-students noted that, "She has never taught a class where she wasn't drinking from Snapple bottles."

- On April 19th, 1973, in Hillsdale, New Jersey, a seven-year-old Brownie Scout named Joan was sexually assaulted and murdered by a high-school chemistry teacher who lived three doors down from her. The teacher confessed to the murder. Her surviving family members pushed for Joan's Law, which denies the possibility of parole to offenders who murder while committing a sex crime. A federal version of Joan's Law was signed by US President Bill Clinton in 1998.

- On February 26th, 1995, a high-school chemistry teacher was accused of strangling his seventeen-month-old daughter with a drapery cord and beating his six-year-old son and wife to death with a pipe in Lake of the Ozarks, Missouri. Days before, he had shown the students in his chemistry class the pop-up book he had bought as a present for his daughter. In October of 1996, with the prosecution having no physical evidence, he was acquitted of the crime.

- On July 21st, 1925, high-school biology teacher John T. Scopes was found guilty in Tennessee of teaching evolution in class and fined $100.

- On August 4th, 2011, high-school biology teacher Beau Schaefer was reprimanded by a Libertyville, Ilinois, school board for teaching creationism in class. He still teaches biology—minus the creationism part—at Libertyville High School today.

- In the fall of 2011, possibly because she was married to the football coach, a high-school teacher in Antioch, Illinois, accessed the school's database and changed the grades of 240 students, many of whom were on the athletic ineligibility list. She was charged with misdemeanor computer tampering.

- "I know what I'm doing. I watch CSI" is what a Phoenix, Arizona, woman claimed to her husband on the phone in 2007 while she was being interrogated by police for having sex with one of her sixteen-year-old high school students. She's #16 on Zimbio's list, "The 50 Most Infamous Female Teacher Sex Scandals." Not surprisingly, Mary Kay Letourneau ranks #1 on this list.

- "Boston High School Teacher Fired For Starring In Gay Porn!" So reads the headline of a 2011 YouTube video featuring a story about a Boston-area high school English teacher who starred in the 2010 gay porn classics, "Fetish World," "Just Gone Gay #8," and, of course, "Ass Fucked by a DILF #2" as Hytch Cawke (pronounced like the famous movie director's name, "Hitchcock"). This may not really be a breaking bad moment for Hytch Cawke (maybe a breaking *naughty* moment?), especially if you think that people have a straightforward right to engage in this activity and then teach your kids how to dissect sentences, but it sure makes for great dinner conversation!

- On August 30th, 2010, a high-school English teacher in Denver, Colorado, used the N-word in his class. While reading the short story "Poison" by Roald Dahl, the teacher chose to insert the N-word in the intentionally left blank space in the line, "You dirty black BLANK." Proceeding to joke about the Ku Klux Klan and talking about his racist past in class immediately after reading the story probably didn't help his case, and he was fired a few weeks later.

● Some time in 2010, a high-school chemistry teacher "killed it freestyle" when he apparently performed a rap featuring the elements of the Periodic Table.

● In 2010, a high school student in San Mateo, California, broke bad and was charged with attempting to murder his former chemistry teacher. Frustrated with his Hillsdale High School experience, he wanted to destroy people and property at the school, but fortunately never got the chance to. He was also charged with attempting to explode a destructive device in an act of terrorism, possession of a destructive device in a public place, carrying a concealed dagger, carrying a concealed explosive, and attempting to explode a destructive device with the intent to kill.

Chemists Who Have Broken Bad

● On the evening of April 29th, 1844, French chemist Augustus Dalmas murdered Mrs. Sarah M'Farlane by slitting her throat in a London alley. He gave himself up to authorities soon afterward, "but being considered of unsound mind" he was "order to be confined as a criminal lunatic."

● In a December 1881 edition of *The Popular Science Monthly* (now *Popular Science* magazine), one of the authors claims that the chemist "murders to dissect," meaning that in order to understand the basic elements of some thing, that thing needs to be broken down into fundamental parts—apparently even killing it, if it's a living thing. Of course, it's mostly a figure of speech, but a chemist or any other scientist who thinks, "Since science can do it, science is justified in doing it, whatever it is" might be breaking bad by doing something ethically questionable. Consider a curious chemist "murdering to dissect" the neighbor's cat to further his biochemical research.

● Apparently fearing a military draft, in Sydney, Australia, a chemist named Harris Cocker murdered his wife and four children before killing himself on August 1st, 1918.

- Although not chemists per se, James Watson and Francis Crick were studying bio*chemistry* in the Cavendish Laboratory at the University of Cambridge in 1953 when they discovered the structure of DNA to be the double helix, twisty ladder thingy we all are now aware of. However, there will always remain the question as to whether the two broke bad by "borrowing" unpublished data produced by Rosalind Franklin. Franklin was a British biophysicist and X-ray crystallographer who took pictures of DNA, and an X-ray photograph of B-DNA taken by Franklin (known now infamously as *Photograph 51*) was shown to Watson and Crick by one of Franklin's lab colleagues—without Franklin's knowledge or permission—just before the duo published their famous work in 1953. BTW: it's widely rumored that Crick was on a wee bit of LSD when he helped figure out the double-helix structure of DNA. If so, then, dude, you can totally see things that other people can't like see when they're like not riding the dragon, man.

- On a rainy night in 1958 in Doylestown, PA a world-famous chemist named Earl Flosdorf—known for inventing a method of freeze-drying blood to extract plasma—blew his own head off with a 16-gauge shotgun, after having blown half of his wife's face off with the same shotgun in front of their young son minutes before. Flosdorf was known to be generally reserved... but could rage on occasion.

- "Fake Chemist Steals from Elderly Ladies" is the big news for January 14th, 2010, in West London, as it's discovered that a con man posing as a chemist had gone to the homes of two separate old ladies claiming that their paperwork related to their prescription drugs had gone missing. When the women left the kitchen to look for copies of the paperwork, the fake chemist stole their purses and buggered off.

- In early 2011, a chemist employed at Bristol-Myers-Squibb was charged with poisoning her husband to death with thallium, the main killing ingredient in rat poison. The husband thought he had the flu and checked himself into the hospital. By the time doctors figured out that it was thallium in his system, it was too late to treat him. Their toddler son is in foster care until the chemist's family can make more permanent arrangements to come to the US to take care of him.

- In 2011, a US Food and Drug Administration chemist and his son were charged with numerous counts of insider trading related to drug company stocks. The two had netted some $3.6 million dollars over a five-year period, based upon information from the US FDA databases that the chemist had access to.

- Consider this: A man's wife is dying of an illness, and needs a specific drug. The local chemist has the drug needed to cure his wife, but the man can't purchase the drug because he can't afford it. And the chemist won't give the man the drug.

  Now, a question: Is the chemist a total *asshole*, or what? Just kidding, that's not the question. . . .

  Actually, the scenario goes like this: The man breaks into the chemist's office, steals the drug, gives the drug to his wife, and his wife is cured.

  Now, the *real* question: Is the man breaking bad in his actions here?

Infamous Meth Users and Cases

- First, check out the following list containing some of the street names for meth:

  Chalk, Chicken Feed, Crank, Peanut Butter, Speed, Stove Top, Tick Tick, Working Man's Cocaine, Yellow Powder, and of course, Hillbilly Crack.

- Methamphetamine is a stimulant (obviously!) and was first synthesized in 1893, in Japan. Japanese, American, English, and German military personnel (as well as Japanese factory workers) used meth during World War II because it enables people to do an incredible amount of work for long periods of time without sleep. It also fries the shit out of your brain afterwards! After World War II, the Japanese military sold meth to people on the civilian market, precipitating one of the world's first epidemics of meth abuse in Japan during the 1950s.

- In 2010, the US DEA reported 11,239 meth lab busts. Although meth "super labs" exist today in California and northern Mexico, Missouri is the state consistently with the most incidents of meth lab busts. In 2004, for example, there were 2,786 busts in the Show-Me State, and only 120 in New Mexico, Walter White's home state. (In fact, as we were in the very act of writing this paragraph, the *Chicago Tribune* just reported the following on-line: "Addictive Meth is Scourge of Rural Missouri.") All of the ingredients for making meth can fit in a suitcase, so meth labs are found pretty much anywhere. Maybe the folks in Missouri need to be stoked so as to take in all of the sights in Branson, Missouri, non-stop, such as the Shoji Tabuchi violin show!

- Meth labs have blown up basements of houses, attics of houses, roofs of houses, wings of houses, rooms of houses, entire houses, apartments, condominiums, townhouses, duplexes, garages, back rooms of business establishments, trailers, hotel rooms, motel rooms, hostels, cars, vans, busses, RVs, tractors, doghouses, and chicken coops.

- Faces of Meth (an obvious play on the cult classic, "Faces of Death") is a drug prevention project that uses before and after mug shots of folks on meth to demonstrate the horrible effects of meth on the face and body. Check out some of the mug shots at: http://www.facesofmeth.us/main.htm. It's enough to scare you away from the drug, for sure!

- In 2006, a woman was arrested for soaking postcards with meth and sending them to her boyfriend and other inmates at the Washington State Penitentiary in Walla Walla, Washington. Throughout the years, others have sent "meth mail" in the forms of postage stamps, Christmas cards, Easter cards, thank-you notes, and even sympathy cards.

- In 2009, the US DEA busted an old dude at a retirement village in Live Oak, California, who was smuggling meth in three different hollowed-out canes that he used to get around the city with. When confronted by the DEA, he faked having a heart attack to avoid being busted, and in the process ten more bags full of meth fell out of his coat pocket!

- In 2011, police in Indonesia busted a woman who was trying to smuggle meth into the country from Malaysia. She had shoved the meth in a greased prophylactic so far up her ass, it apparently was in her stomach when they caught her.

- "Mexicans Smuggle Meth in Nacho Cheese" is one of the headlines on December 9th, 2011, in the on-line periodical, *the fix*, which is a "daily website about alcoholism, addiction, recovery, and the drug war."

- For three years, meth was able to keep a University of Richmond law student awake for days in order to attend classes, produce papers, and study for her exams. After getting her JD in 2011, her first day in court was actually as the defendant in a case where she and others were prosecuted for distributing more than five hundred grams of meth. She's now enrolled in the Lawyers Helping Lawyers program and plans to take the Virginia bar exam.

- In 2011, a former sheriff offered a man meth in exchange for sex, and was busted in a sting operation. He was charged with felony distribution and possession of meth, and one count of misdemeanor prostitution solicitation. He also was recipient of the US National Sheriff Award, and drove his cop car through a hailstorm of bullets to save a wounded officer in a shootout.

- Cooked meth gives off a distinctive smell akin to burned plastic and ammonia, so it was easy for police to trace the smell of meth being cooked in the toilet of an Ardmore, Alabama, motel room, just three days before Christmas in 2011. The suspects, husband and wife, had been cooking up "Christmas presents" for family members. They also had stashed several ounces of marijuana in a tin inside the toilet's tank. Ho, Ho, Ho! Meth-y Christmas!

- In 2009, it was reported that a Colorado minister named Ted Haggard—who met regularly with President George W. Bush to offer spiritual guidance—finally admitted to having sex and doing meth with a male escort for some three years in the early 2000s. Haggard was/is still married and regularly preached/preaches against the abomination of homosexuality and drug usage (go figure!). In a 2010 CNN interview, Haggard claimed that his feelings toward men had miraculously disappeared as a result of counseling, therapy, and, of course, prayer. In September of 2011, it was reported that Haggard was scheduled to appear on ABC's *Celebrity Wife Swap*, where he'd be swapping his wife with Gary Busey's (who lately seems as if *he's* on meth!). God, if you exist, help us!

The Bad Elements

AARON C. ANDERSON is a PhD candidate at the University of California, San Diego, finishing his dissertation, an analysis of aggression in the horror movie. He is currently on the job market and spends his free time contemplating the moral and ethical implications of cooking meth as the practice of freedom.

> *While working in Cancún during Spring Break, Aaron and his homie, Bronne, threw a fire extinguisher off a tenth-floor balcony of the hotel where they were staying. They didn't hit anyone, but did get kicked out of the hotel.*

ROBERT ARP is a philosopher and ontologist with interests in philosophy of biology, ontology in the information-science sense, and philosophy and popular culture. See his website at: <www.robertarp.webs .com>. Probably given his control issues, he's had caffeine (for sure!) and a wee bit of alcohol on a few occasions, but he's never tried any illegal or illicit drugs.

> *In grad school, Rob used to swing his cat around by her tail, over his head, and called it "catapult." Get it? CAT-a-pult. (She actually dug it, so no worries.)*

KIMBERLY BALTZER-JARAY is a moderately tattooed realist phenomenologist with interests in ontology, history of philosophy, and aesthetics. Philosophically, the evidence of her breaking bad are those moments when she declares out loud (many times in public!) that she likes Immanuel Kant, she curses worse than any sailor when she talks about Heidegger, and she likes to refer to Schopenhauer as "Ol' Artie—that furry cutie." As for the rest, she pleads the Fifth and quotes a Cagney line: You'll never take me alive, Copper!

At a party many years ago, Kimberly saran-wrapped a drunk friend (who had passed out) to a chair, as revenge for making her the designated driver too many times. She left that person wrapped to the chair, and went home. She heard that the next morning wasn't pretty, but she didn't care. After that incident, the two weren't really friends, but Kim wouldn't say that she suffered from that loss.

ADAM BARKMAN is Associate Professor of Philosophy at Redeemer University College. He's the author of *C.S. Lewis and Philosophy as a Way of Life* and *Through Common Things*, and is the co-editor of *Manga and Philosophy* and *The Philosophy of Ang Lee*.

Once during his pre-teen years, Adam opened a pack of baseball cards at Target and then thought to himself that since the cards were now "loose," he could take them. . . .

RAY BOSSERT is a Visiting Assistant Professor at Franklin and Marshall College, where he teaches courses on Renaissance Literature, Shakespeare, and "Geek Lit." His academic interests range from political slave discourse in seventeenth-century England to anti-modernism in J.R.R. Tolkien.

Ray broke bad by scribbling quotations from Augustine on a bathroom stall.

PAT BRACE is a Professor of Art at Southwest Minnesota State University, where she teaches courses in Art History and Humanities. She has a special interest in the aesthetic analysis of popular culture. For Pat, breaking bad means buying bad art (like Precious Moments figurines) at the Goodwill store and smashing them with a hammer. Try it. It's very therapeutic.

Pat broke bad early when at the age of four she was challenged to a race by the little girl down the street. Believing she could run faster with her eyes closed, Pat did so and proceeded to run head first into the extremely sharp chrome tail fin of a 1959 Cadillac. When her horrified parents saw the blood streaming down her face (scalp lacerations bleed badly) she knew she was in big trouble, so she said the other little girl hit her in the head with a brick. She would like to take this opportunity to publicly apologize to Pam Filiger, wherever she is today.

J.C. DONHAUSER is a PhD candidate and assistant instructor at the University at Buffalo and a lecturer at Buffalo State College. His interests fall at the intersection of the philosophy of science and metaphysics, and address problems regarding applications of scientific theories for purposes of environmental policy and intervention. His high-school nickname was "Badger."

As a child, Justin sent his little brother out onto a frozen pond to retrieve a ball Justin had accidentally kicked into the middle of the pond. It was the beginning of spring and the ice was thin. When his little brother fell in, Justin couldn't jump in to rescue him because he couldn't stop laughing. Luckily, a neighborhood friend had less of a sense of humor and the gumption to rescue Justin's little bro.

DENISE DU VERNAY is the co-author of *The Simpsons in the Classroom: Embiggening the Learning Experience with the Wisdom of Springfield*. She has contributed her work on media studies to several websites, such as *OC Weekly* and Splitsider.com, and anthologies, including *SpongeBob SquarePants and Philosophy: Soaking Up Secrets Under the Sea!* and *Homer Simpson and The Promise of Politics*. She has taught courses on *The Simpsons*, literature, composition, humanities, and speech for over ten years. When she cooks with her former students, it's sometimes inappropriate but never illegal.

Once, when Denise's flight was canceled, she pretended to be angrier than she really was so she'd be bumped to first class on the next flight, like she saw happen with the guy in front of her in line. That free, in-flight vodka tonic was the best of her life (so far).

STEPHEN GLASS is a graduate of the University of Warwick, where he wrote his dissertation on *Breaking Bad* and *Mad Men* as film-philosophy adaptations. His other interests, piqued at university, include film form, ideology, psychoanalytic film theory, and representations of body horror and sex in film. He was hooked on *Breaking Bad* from the moment Krazy-8 rose from the dead and it became a zombie drama.

When Steve's flatmate's phone went missing, for the next week Steve answered his friend's calls, spoke at length with his parents, signed up for several charity service and local theater auditions, and finally broke up with his girlfriend.

JEFFREY A. HINZMANN is a graduate student at the University of South Florida. He has been published in *30 Rock and Philosophy* and *The Walking Dead and Philosophy*. When he's not doing these articles, he's writing his dissertation and comparing his future with Walter White's. He occasionally wishes he had put a little more time into learning chemistry and the art of remorseless killing.

Given his keen ability to mismanage time, Jeff once arrived to give a conference talk mere moments before it was due to begin. He's very glad he didn't break worse.

LISA KADONAGA is a geographer who researches and teaches at the University of Victoria on Vancouver Island. Although her colleagues have expressed alarm about her increasingly-grim choice of specializations (global environmental change, endangered crop biodiversity and food security in Afghanistan, psychosocial hazards of toxic contamination, the Time of Thirty Tyrants in the Roman Empire during the third century C.E., and now *Breaking Bad*), she hastens to add that she's really quite perky and optimistic, and hopes that her penchant for disasters will not have an adverse effect on her social life, such as it is.

> *Lisa once 'borrowed' a neighbor's unsecured wireless signal while visiting her parents. (Her excuse: she needed to download the contributor's agreement related to this book!) If the neighbors got billed extra for exceeding bandwidth quotas this month, she hopes their kids didn't take the fall.*

DAVID KOEPSELL teaches ethics in the philosophy section of the department of Values and Technology at the Delft University of Technology. His spouse, VANESSA GONZALEZ, is a post-doctoral researcher at Leiden University. Vanessa likes to 'cook' too. With the proceeds of this book, they hope to buy a car wash and get a steady income to provide for their daughter.

> *David and Vanessa simultaneously broke bad when, due to lousy service at a restaurant where the chef insisted that frozen berries were fresh (although each had bitten into a miraculously frozen berry), they wrote a deservedly lousy review and stole a tiny, decorative chicken.*

GREGORY LITTMANN is a professor at Southern Illinois University, Edwardsville. He has published in metaphysics and the philosophy of logic and has written book chapters for volumes relating philosophy to *Breaking Bad, The Big Bang Theory, Doctor Who, Dune, Final Fantasy, Game of Thrones, The Onion, Sherlock Holmes, The Terminator,* and *The Walking Dead*. Don't smoke meth. That shit will fuck you up!

> *Greg Littmann has never broken bad. He's never even broken normal.*

JUSTINE LOPEZ recently graduated with an MA in Communications from Cal State Fullerton, where she researched the cultivation of gender-related stereotypes in television advertising. As a freelance writer and aspiring journalist in a tough economy, she often kicks herself for not majoring in chemistry, . . . at least then she could cook crystal to pay her ever-increasing bills.

> *Justine has been known to 'buy' books from Barnes and Noble, read them, and return them a month later for a full refund. She refers to Barnes and Noble as "the thirty-day library."*

DANIEL MIORI is a physician's assistant practicing palliative care in Buffalo, New York. He's also clinical adjunct faculty at the University of New York at Buffalo's medical school as well as a member of the ethics committee at Millard Fillmore Gates Circle Hospital where he works.

> *Between 1991 and 1995, Dan got fifteen moving violations, fourteen of which were for speeding (and one left turn on red). By New York law at the time, it was enough to have his license taken away 4.9 times. He was able to keep his driver's license because of a pretty good paycheck and a very good attorney. Maybe not Saul good, . . . but good enough.*

OLI MOULD is a geographer with interests in urban issues, sub cultures, philosophy, and the intersection of all three; he also blogs at taCity.co.uk. He often goes for days unaccounted for, disappears for hours in a lab, spins intricate lies and eats a lot of fried chicken. Rumors of involvement in "cooking" can be discounted though as these are just normal characteristics of the modern day academic.

> *Oli often strays into the underground systems and sewers of cities, figuring that a bit of urban exploration hurt no one, but the cops don't like it. He also once took a whizz on the back door of a Chicago Irish pub.*

DARRYL MURPHY is an instructor at Brock University with interests in ancient and medieval thought (Aristotle in particular), the history and philosophy of science, and technology. Darryl's street name is Professor D, but he hasn't appeared in any composite sketches or wanted posters.

> *Using one of his many aliases, Darryl signed up for a second Audible account just to get the free promotional audiobook.*

CRAIG SIMPSON is a PhD student at Trinity College, Dublin. His primary research interests include the relationship between contemporary Hollywood film, cultural theory, and philosophy (philosophy and film, film *as* philosophy). The *Breaking Bad* character that he can relate to most is Saul Goodman . . . and he finds this somewhat disturbing, as he would never decorate his office like that.

> *Craig and his buddies once hid a 'flatulence simulator' in an empty cinema seat just before the beginning of the movie* Maid in Manhattan, *which they had bought tickets to. Then, with a remote control in hand, let it off at the most inappropriate moments possible. Amazingly, it wasn't found until the end of the movie, and as you can imagine there were some rather irate people demanding their money back. It's not one of his prouder moments, in that he had the misfortune of seeing a film with Jennifer Lopez in it.*

JEFFREY E. STEPHENSON most recently held an appointment as Visiting Assistant Professor of Philosophy at Case Western Reserve University. He's an ethicist with interests in virtue theory, medical ethics, and puzzling about human behavior (including his own). He currently lives in Boise, Idaho, with his doctor wife, two dogs, and cat, none of which is interested in breaking bad, ever.

Under immense pressure from friends in middle school, Jeffrey lifted a box of snap-n-pops from a Kmart, and then promptly peppered his peer-pressuring friends with the ill-gotten gains in revenge.

SARA WALLER is an Associate Professor of Philosophy at Montana State University, where she does work in the philosophy of human consciousness and animal minds. Specifically, she has done work on social, co-operative serial killers such as dolphins and coyotes, as well as on asocial human criminals. This volume allowed her big break into research on the badness of social, co-operative, criminal human consciousness. This research has failed to reveal any mind-altering substances more effective than the printed word.

In junior high, Sara snuck into the chemistry lab of her school and stole the laughing gas. She shared the 'getting high and giggling' experience with her friends down by the river. So, there is a little Walt in Dr. Waller. She broke bad at age twelve and hasn't stopped.

MEGAN WRIGHT recently completed her MA in English literature. Her research interests include women's and gender studies as well as philosophy. The closest she's ever come to amphetamines is taking her allergy medicine.

On more than one occasion, Megan has had dessert before dinner, but not the hard stuff—just chocolate cake and ice cream, not peanut brittle or Jolly Ranchers.

Index

Lacan, Jacques
  on constructed reality, 175
  on the Real, 173, 177
Lady Macbeth, 67, 74, 75
Lakatos, Imre, 183, 184
Last Men, 91–92
Letourneau, Mary Kay, 224
lung cancer, treatment of, 30

Macbeth, 67–69, 74–76
Macduff, 72–74, 76
Machiavelli, Niccolò, 107
Mad Men (television show), 91,
  99
  "The Mountain King," 92
  "My Old Kentucky Home," 92
  "The New Girl," 98
  "Out of Town," 98
  "Shut the Door, Have a Seat,"
    97
  "The Suitcase," 98
  "Tomorrowland," 97
  "Wee Small Hours," 98
Margolis, Donald (character),
  13–14
Marie (character), 196–97, 220
  character development of,
    198–99
  and existentialism, 133–34
materialism, 16
  and soul, 17
medical coercion, 31–32
meth
  abuse and addiction issues,
    156–57
  as adult decision, 139–140,
    144
  consequences of, 141–43, 145
  dangers of, 208–09
  effects of, 126–27
  and government authority,
    144–46
  as immoral, 157
  and immoral inaction, 166
  and irrationality, 145

in Japan, 227
lab busts, 228
and morality, 120–21, 153,
  159–161
"shake and bake" method, 185
smuggling of, 228–29
versus legal drugs, 163–65
"meth mouth," 160
Mexican cartels, 107
M'Farlane, Sarah, 225
Mill, John Stuart, 31, 35, 116,
  126, 140, 205, 213–15
  on alcohol, 217, 219
  on custom, 220–21
  on democracy, 219–220
  on individuality, 215–16
  On Liberty, 145, 217, 221
  on prohibition, 219
  on punishment, 219
Milton, John
  Paradise Lost, ix
Mohammed, 151
moral culpability
  and self-defense, 6
  and proximity, 166–67
moral responsibility, 209–210
  active-passive distinction, 8–9
  elements of, 4–5, 13

Nietzsche, Friedrich, 97, 99
  Overman of, 91, 93, 94, 96
  Superman of, 85–86
  on will to power, 81

objective moral principles, 150
Overman, 91, 93, 94, 96
Oxford Committee for Famine
  Relief (OXFAM), 123

performative contradiction, 140
Paul, Saint, 155
Plato, 18
Prohibition, 126, 149